Business and Management Communication

A Guide Book

Ritch Sorenson

Texas Tech University

Grace DeBord

Texas Tech University

Ida Ramirez

Texas Tech University

Prentice Hall

Upper Saddle River, New Jersey 07458

Library of Congress Cataloging-in-Publication Data

Sorenson, Ritch.
 Business and management communication : a guide book / Ritch Sorenson, Grace
DeBord, Ida Ramirez.
   p.   cm.
 Includes index.
 ISBN 0-13-087053-6 (pbk.)
   1. Business communication.   2. Business writing.   3. Business presentations.
 I. DeBord, Grace.   II. Ramirez, Ida.   III. Title.
HF5718.B778 2001
658.4'5—dc21   00-060665

All interior visuals have been used with permission from the following sources
by C. B. Grafton (ed.), Dover Publications, Mineola, NY:

Old-fashioned illustrations of books, reading and writing (1992).
Old-fashioned mortised cuts (1987).
Pictorial archive of decorative and illustrative mortised cuts (1983).
Humorous Victorian spot illustrations (1985).
Trades and occupations (1990).

Vice President/Editorial Director: James Boyd
Senior Editor: Linda Schreiber
Editorial Assistant: Virginia Sheridan
Assistant Editor: Jennifer Surich
Media Project Manager: Michele Faranda
Senior Marketing Manager: Debbie Clare
Production/Manufacturing Manager: Gail Steier de Acevedo
Production Coordinator: Maureen Wilson
Senior Prepress/Manufacturing Manager: Vincent Scelta
Manufacturing Buyer: Natacha St. Hill Moore
Cover Design: Bruce Kenselaar
Composition: Impressions Book and Journal Services, Inc.

Prentice
Hall

10   9   8   7   6   5   4   3   2   1

ISBN 0-13-087053-6

Contents

Preface

everal years ago, our team of writing and speaking experts was assembled to teach a managerial communication course in our College of Business. The College was committed to providing students with preparation in both writing and speaking. We were given the challenge of accomplishing the task in a one-semester course.

Combined, our team has over 50 years of experience teaching communication. We have advanced degrees in both speaking and writing and have published research about both oral and written communication. In addition, we have experience in delivering writing and speaking seminars for managers. We have also professionally edited business documents.

Using our combined expertise, research, and trial and error, we determined the essentials for student success in writing and speaking. We called upon our combined experience to design a course that would cover essential writing and speaking knowledge and skills. However, we could not find a text that met our needs.

So, over several years, we developed our own set of readings that resulted in this text—one that addresses business communication concerns and that is "fat free." That is, we get to the point quickly and provide essential guidelines.

The text was written with the assumption that successful communication is vital in business. We provide guidelines for developing messages and making them clear and acceptable to your business audience. We suggest ways to analyze your audience, organize your message, and make your message concise. Then, we provide specific guidelines for memos, letters, reports, résumés, and letters of application.

We show how to prepare speeches and present them effectively. We conclude the book by demonstrating how to communicate effectively in employment interviews. The appendices in the book provide conventions for grammar, punctuation, mechanics, and style. One appendix also shows you how to critique your own speech so that, when you view a video of yourself giving a speech, you have a basis for improvement.

Our students like the text. It covers issues that are important to them. The explanations are straightforward for success in writing documents or delivering speeches. We are confident that you will also find the text immediately useful.

CHAPTER 1

The Communication Process

Your success in business will depend upon your ability to communicate. No matter how much knowledge you have, if you can't communicate that knowledge, you won't succeed because other people won't know what you have to contribute. Moreover, if you remain in a business career, you'll probably become a supervisor or manager and will spend about 60 percent of your time engaged in some form of oral or written communication. If you're a poor communicator, you'll be a poor manager.

On the other hand, if you're a good communicator, you increase the likelihood that you will be successful and rise to the top. Two very successful graduates of our university returned to campus recently and emphasized the value of communication skills. One had become the CEO of a large, well-known corporation. When asked what advice he would give to others who wanted to follow in his footsteps, he responded that management requires that you represent your organization both internally and externally, which, in turn, requires you to write and speak well. He had worked diligently to improve his writing and speaking skills throughout his career.

The second graduate developed a business software implementation firm into a multi-million dollar success. He said that when he graduated from our university, he unfortunately had not developed good writing skills. Since graduating, he has worked very hard to eliminate his writing deficiencies in order to present himself in a professional and credible manner. He strongly recommended that college students develop good writing skills before they enter the workforce.

The purpose of this book is to help you develop two of the most important communication skills—writing and speaking. This chapter discusses the communication process and how writing and speaking fit into that process. The remainder of the text provides guidelines for improving speaking and writing.

When you communicate, you engage in three basic processes:

- sending messages
- receiving messages
- establishing relationships

Although we will discuss each process separately, the processes overlap. Understanding these processes provides the foundation for making communication successful.

SENDING MESSAGES

An engineering manager in Albuquerque sent teams to survey plots of land and, too frequently, found that the teams misunderstood directions and surveyed the wrong site. The manager and the teams blamed one another. Ultimately, the manager realized that such errors could be avoided by changing his approach to communication. Instead of giving only oral directions, he accompanied these with written directions and a map. The written directions and maps provided a focus for discussion and a basis for common ground that helped the manager and the teams build understanding.

This example demonstrates how you might change your approach to communicating to improve mutual understanding. Communication is the process of sending and receiving messages to create similar meanings among people. For communication to occur, a message must be sent and accurately understood. Effective communication occurs when a speaker or writer, and a listener or reader agree about the meaning of a message. Misunderstandings occur when the message is sent in a form that the receiver cannot understand or when the receiver misinterprets the message.

As Figure 1.1 shows, the first step in the communication process is forming thoughts or feelings that you want others to understand. In the preceding example, when the engineering manager formed a mental map of the survey site, he had performed the first step. The next step in the process is translating the thoughts or feelings into symbols that may represent those thoughts and feelings. Think about the multitude of symbols that the manager might use to get his survey teams to the right location. He could write words on a piece of paper describing the location, speak additional words of description, and make a drawing showing the location. The writing, spoken words, and drawing are all symbols of his thoughts.

FIGURE 1.1 Sending and Receiving Messages

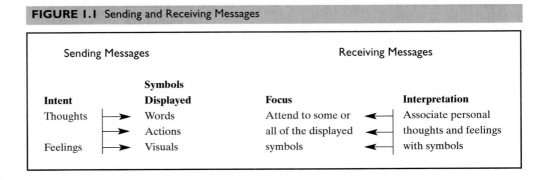

Every day, we use an endless variety of symbols to represent our thoughts and feelings: words, font styles, drawings, pictures, music, paintings, clothing, hairstyles, jewelry, facial expressions, gestures, and so on. We become so accustomed to using symbols that we don't often consciously notice them.

Additional symbols could be used to convey the manager's authority or his right to give directions. These symbols are available everywhere at work. The teams meet in the manager's office, where he sits behind a large desk. He writes directions on "official" company stationery, and his voice rings with authority, suggesting that the teams should listen. If he's angry, happy, or anxious, his facial expression, gestures, and tone of voice will express those feelings. All of these symbols convey the manager's authority and how the manager feels about his subordinates and their situation.

However, even with the multitude of symbols available, symbols cannot fully convey thoughts and feelings. Symbols may represent—literally, present again—how you think or feel, but your words and actions may not be adequate to convey your thoughts and feelings.

For instance, a handshake may not adequately express the friendly feeling you have for another person. Or you may not be able to think of words to completely describe an idea. Moreover, individuals vary in their abilities to articulate their thoughts and emotions in both words and actions. Some people are very expressive; some are not. Many times, individuals attempt to mask their behavior so others can't read their feelings. Thus, symbols can also be used to intentionally mislead and manipulate (Habermas, 1979).

In addition, symbols do not actually transfer meaning from one person to another. Instead, when you communicate, you choose to display symbols to which you attach meaning; you hope that people who observe the symbols attach the same meaning. Some people assume that "meaning is in words"—that everyone assigns the same meanings to words, guaranteeing complete understanding.

However, every individual assigns somewhat different thoughts and feelings to symbols. For example, even the common word *car* can have different meanings. Those who have a new, trouble-free car probably assign different meanings to the word *car* than those who have a "junker" that continually breaks down. To some, a car might mean a place of refuge and a source of entertainment. To others, it may mean only a source of transportation to and from work. To an owner of a restored "classic," a car is a work of art. To a parent with children, it's a bus.

You can't guarantee that the receiver of your message will interpret symbols the way you intend or that you can accurately interpret others' symbols. However, there are some things that you can do to enhance the likelihood of understanding.

Use symbols familiar to your audience. Every organization and profession tends to use technical terms and acronyms that can increase the accuracy or speed of communication. However, recognize that not everyone understands specialized language, so choose "layman's" language for those who may not understand.

Define symbols. Recognize that other people may not use symbols the same way you do. When you use unfamiliar symbols or common symbols that for you have special meaning, describe the meaning for the other person.

Use multiple kinds of symbols. The more different kinds of symbols you use to represent the message, the more likely it will be that the receiver will pay attention and understand your meaning. A formal written report won't have the same impact as the report combined with an oral summary. Typically, oral communication and visual aids are better at gaining attention and conveying feelings, and written communication is better at providing a permanent record of exact meaning. A combination of writing, speaking, and visuals provides a rich variety of symbols that enhances understanding. Thus, when a message is important and you want an audience to understand, use a combination of the following approaches.

- **Meet face-to-face.** Speaking face-to-face allows you to use multiple kinds of symbols including spoken words, facial expression, gestures, and tone of voice.

- **Be an expressive speaker.** Provide clear descriptions of your thoughts and open expressions of your feelings.

- **Use visual aids.** Visual aids focus attention, reinforce the message, and help people to remember.

- **Provide a hard copy.** A written summary or report provides a permanent and complete record for people to study and review.

Repeat your message. In a speech or written document, preview what you're going to discuss, present the material, and then summarize. Present your message more than once to your organization in different message formats. Repetition helps people to "get it."

Use concrete symbols. Concrete symbols specifically describe your meaning in ways the audience can visualize. Concrete is the opposite of abstract or vague. Specific and vivid symbols provide a word picture. Instead of referring to a car (abstract), refer to a 1999 black Lincoln Continental (specific), which helps the audience visualize the car. Instead of providing a verbal description of how to use a spell-checker on a computer, illustrate the process in drawings or on a computer screen.

RECEIVING MESSAGES

For communication to occur, another person must accurately interpret the messages you display. You know from experience that interpretations can be totally inaccurate. The symbolic nature of communication makes it almost impossible for someone else to completely understand your thoughts and feelings.

First, for a message to generate mutual understanding, the receiver must focus on your message. Our busy, information-rich world competes for our attention and limits our ability to focus on just one thing. Even when you want to focus on a message, your mind may wander. For example, when you study, your eyes may scan the page as if you're reading, but you may find that you've mentally tuned out the writing. You can't accurately interpret something that you've mentally tuned out.

Second, even when people focus on your message, they may elect to pay attention to only select parts. For example, if you present both a written and an oral message, your receiver may focus on the oral message and miss important written comments. Or, when you angrily present a message, the receiver may focus primarily on your anger and miss some important content.

Third, as mentioned previously, other people may assign different interpretations to symbols than you do. For example, many people have different interpretations for the word *school.* To a message sender, it may mean college or graduate work. To a message receiver, it may mean elementary or high school. To the sender, it may mean the best and most challenging element of life; to the receiver, it may mean the hardest and most unpleasant part of existence. To the sender, it means privilege; to the receiver, it means duty. Thus, when the sender uses the word *school,* the receiver doesn't accurately interpret his or her meaning.

People also attach unique meanings to behaviors and gestures. These meanings are often associated with the immediate context and a person's frame of mind. Sometimes people interpret our actions in a way we wouldn't have imagined. For instance, suppose you forget to acknowledge a colleague in the hall because you're distracted and troubled. However, your colleague, who feels neglected, interprets your action as a snub—an interpretation far from what you intended.

Because of the symbolic nature of communication, people will misinterpret one another. For that reason, we offer guidelines to help you minimize misinterpretation.

Limit distractions. You can't focus on a message when you're extremely rushed, emotional, or stressed. Therefore, when a message is important, eliminate distractions. Don't do two things at once. Close the door, put your work aside, and focus. Similarly, if you catch someone at a busy or emotional time, find another time to give your message when the person won't be distracted. To avoid missing information, don't carry on side conversations at important meetings. Arrange to be alone when you need to read and "digest" a report.

Seek specifics. When another person uses abstract terms, ask for concrete clarification. The more abstract the language, the more room there is for misinterpretation. For example, if someone says that the project has been delayed, you might ask for specifics—which project, and will the project be delayed a day, a week, or indefinitely?

Paraphrase. To paraphrase means to summarize in your own words your understanding of the other person's message. When you want to ensure correct interpretation, paraphrase the other person's comments, or ask another person to paraphrase your message. You might say something like, "Just to be sure I understand what you're saying, let me summarize . . . " or "To be sure I've communicated clearly, please summarize what you understand me to have said."

Familiarize yourself with others and their situations. Often, busy managers don't pay enough attention to correctly interpret the actions of employees. For example, in performance evaluations, the manager and employee may radically disagree on what an action like overuse of sick leave means. To the manager, it may mean a way to avoid work. To the employee, it may mean the job isn't challenging enough or doesn't fit his or her abilities. For accurate interpretation to occur, two parties must be closely connected; they must take the time to discuss perspectives and seek to understand the meaning of each other's words and actions.

Find ways to make the message meaningful. Sometimes, you might not pay attention to a message because it doesn't seem important. When you're listening to or reading a message that doesn't seem meaningful to you, think of others who might benefit from the message, such as subordinates, and listen or read with the goal of passing the message along to them. As a message sender, make your messages meaningful by pointing out their potential influence on the listener. For example, if you're proposing changes in the hiring process, point out how the process will make hiring easier for your audience.

ESTABLISHING RELATIONSHIPS

A number of years ago, two new female managers of grocery stores approached one of us at the end of a management seminar. One of the managers said in a high-pitched, timid voice, "I need some help. The guys on the dock just won't do what I ask them to." The other manager, overhearing the first, said in a deeper, more commanding voice, "I have no trouble with those guys. I just tell 'em what to do, and they do it." In these brief interactions, it quickly became apparent that these two managers created very different relationships with their subordinates. The first manager sounded like a pushover. The second manager commanded attention and response.

We establish relationships along two primary dimensions: dominant–subordinate and cold–warm (see Figure 1.2). Every time we communicate, we either dominate or subordinate. Dominating is an attempt to control communication; subordinating is yielding control. *When we dominate, we anticipate that others will subordinate; when we subordinate, we signal a willingness to have others dominate.*

Every relationship involves power and control, which we establish by dominating or subordinating. *We indicate the kind of relationship we want with others by the way we speak or write.* For example, to dominate, we might speak loudly and curtly, as did the gruff manager in the example above; or, we might speak enthusiastically or in an entertaining manner to draw attention to ourselves and maintain control of a conversation. We might also use nonverbal indicators of power, such as expensive clothing, a large desk, or a domineering stance or tone of voice.

To dominate when we write, we might use aggressive words or phrases to intimidate the reader, such as, "This business will not tolerate sloppy work areas!" We might

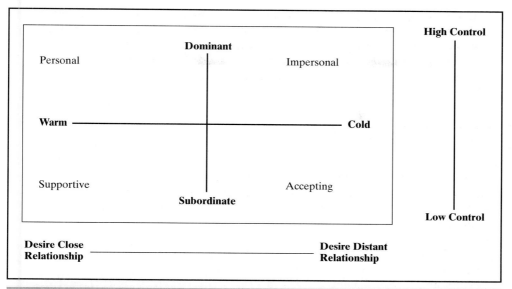

FIGURE 1.2 Dimensions of Relationship

also use a writing tone that makes us sound knowledgeable and certain, for example, "The answer to your dilemma is obvious. You need a strategic plan."

To subordinate, we might speak quietly and hesitantly, readily relinquishing the speaking floor, as did the timid manager in the previous example. In writing, we can subordinate by using an apologetic, meek tone: "I hesitate to ask this, but would you please keep your work areas clean?" Other nonverbal signs might be used to subordinate, including inexpensive or informal clothing, subdued facial expressions and gestures, weak postures or stances, and lack of status symbols, such as titles, large desks, or letterheads.

One form of dominance is the ability to control information flow—who sends and who receives messages. Normally, the person with greater authority controls who talks and who listens and is more frequently in the talking role. In one-on-one conversations, we use nonverbal behavior to signal whether we want to speak or listen. We show that we don't want to be interrupted by continuing to speak, speaking more quickly and loudly, breaking eye contact with someone who tries to interrupt, and holding up a hand signal that indicates we want to keep the floor. We demonstrate a desire to listen by falling silent and looking at the other person with a questioning look on our face.

In businesses, subordinates may look for superiors' nonverbal signals to know whether to speak or listen. Organizations use numerous signs of authority to indicate who is in charge, who should speak, and who should listen. Some organizations signal authority with expensive suits, penthouse offices, huge desks, receptionists, and organizational positions printed on company letterhead. Clearly, these organizations want communication to flow from the top downward. Other organizations use casual attire, similar furnishings throughout, and the use of first names to signal openness and two-way communication.

Along the cold–warm dimension, we invite the same behavior that we send. Smiling, warm word choice, and other positive behaviors are contagious, evoking warmth and support from others. Similarly, negative behaviors, such as a harsh tone, evoke cold responses from others. Typically, warmth signals a desire to maintain or strengthen a relationship, and coldness signals a distance or a desire to withdraw from the relationship.

The written tone and word choice also convey varying levels of coldness or warmth. For example, compare the following written comments. Even though the basic message is the same, the tone of the comments is very different.

> **Colder:** A general announcement: Effective immediately, all line personnel are laid-off. See the human resources department to obtain a copy of our severance policy and listings of potential positions with other companies.
>
> **Warmer:** A personal note: We regret having to let you go. We will do all we can to help you find new employment. Please see Mark in personnel for help with benefits and employment opportunities.

As Figure 1.2 shows, messages simultaneously include both dominant–subordinate and cold–warm dimensions. *A combination of warmth and dominance signals a desire to maintain or strengthen the relationship, while maintaining dominance or control.* In informal communication, friendly, talkative individuals often direct the flow and direction of communication. Such individuals often dictate choices made by groups as well. Thus, if you want to improve your interpersonal influence skills, develop your ability to be warm and talkative. In organizations, managers who are at ease in giving direction, but who also express warmth, tend to have subordinates who return the warm behavior and willingly follow the managers' directions. Thus, managers should most often demonstrate dominance and warmth in both oral and written interactions with subordinates.

The combination of dominant and cold communication signals both the desire to control and to limit, or even to withdraw from, a personal relationship. Often, written guidelines have a cold, dominating tone. Manuals and legal documents are frequently written in directive language that has no expression of warmth. Interpersonally, a good

example of cold, dominating behavior would be a Marine sergeant inspecting the troops or a prosecutor grilling a defendant. The nonverbal message is to sit up and listen—"I'm in control." It might be appropriate for a manager to exhibit cold, dominating behavior when reprimanding a subordinate. However, if the reprimand isn't followed up with warm communication, the subordinate may become distant and resentful, perceiving the manager as the enemy.

Subordinate actions combined with warm communication signal a desire to maintain or build the relationship while yielding to the other person. In most organizations that have a relatively positive organizational culture, lower-level employee behavior would fit into this quadrant. When subordinates write or speak to superiors, they should have a suggesting and tentative tone instead of a dictatorial tone. For example, an employee might express a subordinate and warm tone by writing, "I have examined the options and present my analysis. I would appreciate your guidance in making final recommendations." An inappropriate tone would be expressed by, "It's obvious to me what we need to do, and we need to get started immediately." Such a comment would signal a desire to both dominate and withdraw from a personal relationship.

Finally, subordinate behavior combined with cold nonverbal behavior signals a willingness to follow others, but no desire to build a relationship. For example, production line employees who don't see much of their manager may simply follow orders without an expression of warmth because they see little opportunity to build a relationship. Students who don't want any special relationship with a professor may simply do the assignments and be relatively impersonal in interactions.

A fairly neutral stance on both dimensions suggests a desire for neither dominance nor submission and neutrality about building a relationship. This stance might be appropriate when individuals are considered equals or members of a team. When team members become acquainted, they may desire closer relationships and begin to express increased warmth.

Relational communication is a very important part of communication. It is as important to clearly indicate your relational intent as it is to clearly communicate message content. Inappropriate relational messages, such as a subordinate nonverbally communicating that he or she wants to dominate a superior, will probably get an unfavorable response, no matter how good the content of the message. Use the following guidelines to examine and improve your relational communication.

> **Design messages with relationships in mind.** As you develop your message, whether oral or written, consider the kind of relationship you want with your audience. If you want a friendly, equal relationship, exhibit warmth combined with neither dominance nor subordinance. Use personal and friendly references in your writing, and consider sending handwritten notes. If you want to control and dominate, you should nonverbally signal dominance and control the conversation, varying levels of warmth as seems appropriate. Write messages that are directive and impersonal. If you want to go along and subordinate, signal your willingness to listen and submit. Write messages that are tentative.
>
> **Make relational signals consistent with desired relationships.** Often, we're unaware of our relational behavior and our tone when writing. The result is that we may send unintended relational messages. Like the timid manager who didn't understand why the guys on the dock didn't respond to her, we may

engage in self-defeating behavior. To overcome this tendency to send unintended relational messages, do the following:

- **Monitor both *how* you communicate and your *receivers' reactions.*** Ironically, most of the time *message senders focus on the content* and don't notice the relational message. However, *message receivers may pay more attention to the relational message* than to the content. If the receiver's response isn't what you expect, examine the way you present your message for hidden relational meanings.

- **Solicit feedback about relational messages.** Sometimes, we need assistance to understand how other people view the relational messages in our behavior and writing. Most people are hesitant to volunteer perceptions about relational messages. You may want to ask others, particularly subordinates, whether the way you present messages is consistent with your relational goals. For example, if your goal is to be positive and supportive, ask if the way you act and speak comes across in a positive and supportive manner.

- **Examine motivations behind your relational messages.** Relational signals are associated with attitudes. In order to change relational messages, especially your nonverbal behavior, you may need to clarify your attitudes, determine why you have the attitudes, and find ways to adapt or change. To illustrate, an engineer may believe that technicians have nothing to offer in a redesign of production facilities. The engineer may need to change that belief, or at least acknowledge the belief about technicians, before he can change his nonverbal behavior.

- **Adjust your relational messages.** Out of habit, you may use nonverbal behavior that is inconsistent with desired relationships. For example, a manager may espouse an open-door policy and seek input from subordinates, but may also exhibit curt behavior and avoid eye contact with subordinates, signaling that she really doesn't want interaction. Similarly, an individual may tire of being everyone's counselor, but continue to exhibit attentive, warm behavior that signals readiness to listen. If you genuinely want a different kind of relationship, learn to send new relational messages.

SUMMARY

The primary purpose of communication is to create common understanding between individuals. However, while symbols enable us to communicate, they can also get in the way of accurate communication. Our words and actions don't adequately represent our thoughts and feelings. Others' interpretations of our words and actions are colored by their thoughts and feelings. The communication process makes accurate understanding difficult. To aid you in creating effective two-way communication, we've provided guidelines to promote mutual understanding.

Communication also establishes relationships. By the way we communicate, we make a bid for dominant or subordinate and warm or cold relationships. We also control who sends and who receives messages. Design your messages to meet relational goals. We've provided guidelines for monitoring and adjusting relational messages to help achieve desired relationships.

CHAPTER 2

Designing Communication Strategies

After a long series of meetings, a management team selected a new insurance package for its employees—one that was clearly an improvement over the existing package. The team distributed a memo informing employees of the change and asking for a vote of approval.

Shortly thereafter, angry employees assembled to demand that the company retain the old package. The management team was shocked. After inquiring, the managers found that a climate of distrust had developed when the employees heard of the meetings without knowing exactly what was being discussed. The office was filled with rumors, and when the memo was released, too little information was provided for the employees to judge the new package on its own merits. Therefore, the employees read more into the changes than actually existed.

The management team then spent several days meeting with groups and individuals to explain the changes. After a considerable delay, and a tremendous amount of communication, the employees accepted the new plan.

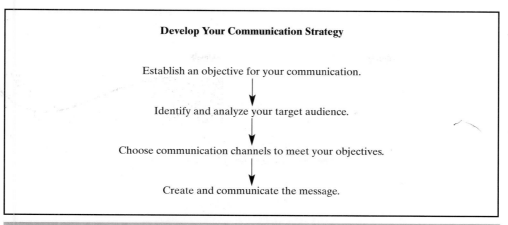

Develop Your Communication Strategy

Establish an objective for your communication.

Identify and analyze your target audience.

Choose communication channels to meet your objectives.

Create and communicate the message.

FIGURE 2.1 Steps in Developing a Communication Strategy

The management team learned that time devoted to developing a strategic communication plan to introduce the changes could have eliminated many of their problems. This chapter provides guidelines for developing a communication strategy. We suggest that, before you communicate, you should (1) establish your communication objectives, (2) identify and analyze your audience, (3) choose communication channels that best meet your objectives, and *finally,* (4) create and communicate your message (see Figure 2.1).

ESTABLISH COMMUNICATION OBJECTIVES

Communication objectives are designed to help managers achieve organizational goals. Organizational goals consist of general management objectives, such as expanding market share, and specific unit objectives, such as increasing the number of cutomer sales contacts. A communication objective clarifies what a manager hopes to accomplish through communicating. When the objective is clear, a manager is in the best position to choose the appropriate method of communication.

When forming a communication objective, you should pinpoint what you want the audience to know or do by forming a sentence similar to the following:

At the conclusion of our communication, my audience will know or be able to . . .
As a result of this communication, my audience will . . .

The following provides some examples of communication objectives that a manager might create in order to achieve management objectives.

As a result of this communication,
   my employees will agree to work overtime.
   upper management will agree to purchase new computing equipment for my
     field staff.
   my employees will better understand unit objectives.
   members of my unit will know specifically how to close a sale.

Notice that, in these examples, we *do not suggest a communication method.* We recommend that you *form the communication objective before you specify how you'll communicate.* Too often, managers focus on the method of communication instead of the desired outcome. In the example at the beginning of this chapter, the managers focused on the communication method—using a memo to distribute information—instead of the desired outcome—acceptance of the insurance package. Before you choose your communication method and design your message, you need to consider the needs of your audience.

IDENTIFY AND ANALYZE YOUR TARGET AUDIENCE

After you've defined your objectives, identify your target audience. Then, consider the characteristics and concerns of your audience. Finally, adapt your communication method to the audience.

Identify Your Target Audience

In an organization, choosing the right people with whom to communicate is extremely important. You may inadvertently overlook individuals who should receive your message and, as a result, create organizational or political problems. You may choose to communicate with the wrong person and limit the likelihood of achieving your objectives.

For example, one young supervisor felt that his employees deserved better work facilities. He sent a strongly worded memo to his employees, his manager, and the CEO. The CEO was perplexed when he got the memo and called the manager to ask what it was about. The manager said she had just received the memo and that it was news to her as well. The CEO was angry that the manager didn't know the concerns of her subordinates and that he was receiving memos about issues that she should handle. "You had better get your unit under control," he said. The manager was embarrassed and was very angry that her subordinate had sent this memo without consulting her first. The young supervisor was surprised to see the furor that a simple, well-intentioned memo could create.

The young supervisor in the previous example needed help in knowing how to go about communicating to achieve his objectives. Here are four ways you can learn *how to communicate* and *with whom to communicate* in your organization.

Consult with your manager. Because managers have more experience and a broader view than subordinates, they are in a position to know with whom you need to communicate in order to achieve your objectives. In the previous example, if the supervisor had consulted the manager, she could've helped him frame the request in an appropriate manner and could've advised him about how to guide requests through organizational channels.

Seek advice from a mentor. A mentor is someone with experience, preferably in your organization, who can guide you in forming communication strategies for achieving organizational goals.

Seek input from the organizational "grapevine." The "grapevine" consists of all the informal channels of communication in the organization. Most communication in organizations occurs informally. Sources who are connected in the organizational grapevine can help you to know about key players in the organization and how you might communicate with these people in order to accomplish your objectives. Seek to know the following:

- **Key decision-makers.** Besides the CEO, there are other influential people in the organization—usually in formal positions of authority. Find out who they are, the nature of their influence, and whether you'll need their approval to achieve your objectives.

- **Gatekeepers.** Formal and informal "gatekeepers" control the flow of communication. Managers are *formal gatekeepers* who control whether communication flows upward from subordinates or downward from upper management. If you want your formal message to make it to upper management, you need to make it acceptable to your manager. *Informal gatekeepers* are central individuals in the organizational grapevine. They can be good sources of information. You'll be better able to accomplish your goals when you can get informal information from these gatekeepers.

- **Informal Leaders.** Every group and organization has informal leaders. These are usually employees who are well liked, expert, and trustworthy. Informal leaders can provide insight into employee attitudes. To achieve some of your objectives, you may need to either get support from, or be prepared to rebut arguments presented by, informal leaders.

Use organizational norms and standard procedures. Organizations develop a set of norms or standard procedures that are used to handle repetitive organizational issues. Some standard procedures are written and include information on whom to contact about various organizational concerns. Many of these norms or standard procedures are not written, but they still guide organizational conduct. Sometimes, you may have to ask other employees for that type of information. In the previous example, the supervisor could've asked another supervisor about norms and procedures, for example, "How do I go about getting more facilities for my workers?"

After you have consulted your sources, you may find that you should send a memo to only one person. Or, you may find that you need to communicate with many people, using a variety of communication channels. For example, when promoting change in an organization, you may need to engage in a *communication campaign*—a promotional campaign similar to those used by political candidates. You may begin by discussing your proposal with your immediate manager and gathering information from informal gatekeepers. When you have a well-developed argument, you may then make an initial proposal to a key decision-maker, and finally make a formal presentation, accompanied with a hard copy summary, to a top management group. When the proposal is approved, you may need to make an oral presentation, with an accompanying written report, to all employees.

As you plan your communication strategy, consider that your communication may involve both *the initial audience* and *the ultimate audience.* Your initial communication may be to only one person. For example, your initial proposal may be to your manager in the form of a memo report. However, if your manager believes that your proposal has merit, he or she may pass the memo on to other upper-level managers. Upper-level management may, in turn, show it to the board of directors and other employees. Thus, as you plan your communication, keep in mind both the initial and ultimate audiences.

Analyze and Adapt to Your Target Audience

If you want your communication to be successful, you need to understand the knowledge, interests, and attitudes of your audience. The relatively little effort you spend analyzing your audience can be returned to you many times over as you find that your communication succeeds. The following provides some guidelines for analyzing and adapting to your audience.

Appropriate communication adapts to the audience's interests and concerns and adjusts to its background and level of knowledge. In addition, for business communicators, appropriate communication should normally get quickly to the point and clearly communicate the message. The purpose of appropriateness is to communicate so that your target audience understands and responds favorably to your message.

Sources of Information

Depending on your target audience, you can gather information on its interests and backgrounds from different sources.

Groups external to your business. Businesses communicate externally for a variety of reasons. They provide reports to stockholders, advertisements to prospective customers, contracts to suppliers, and product information to customers. Sometimes, organizations use surveys and individual, or focus group, interviews to gather information. Your goal is to identify the predominant values, interests, and knowledge level of the target audience.

You may be able to infer the characteristics of an external group by reviewing demographics. For example, if your audience is college students, you can probably assume that saving money and time is a big priority for them and that they place a premium on their leisure-time activities. If you're writing a sales letter to college students, you could focus on how your product or service saves time and money, and thus frees up more of both for outside activities.

Your business and groups within your business. Your business will have overall goals and objectives. It will also have an organizational culture that includes norms, values, and ways of doing things. In addition, subgroups within your business will have their own goals and subcultures. For example, production departments tend to have structured and pragmatic cultures designed to meet production goals, while research departments tend to have professional cultures that allow for independent analysis and discovery. Thus, you may infer some characteristics of your audience from departmental tasks and organizational roles.

Information obtained from the organizational grapevine, gatekeepers, and informal leaders can help you further define the goals and cultures of your business and groups within the business. In some cases, you may be able to conduct surveys of organizational members. Use these sources to identify the values, interests, knowledge, and concerns of the larger organization and relevant subgroups. **Individuals.** Identify values, biases, and attitudes of key individuals within your audience. You can gather information about individuals from the grapevine, information gatekeepers, and by interviews with the individuals themselves. Is the individual a computer whiz or a technophobe? Does he or she value relationships, or is the bottom-line the main focus? Is he or she a straightforward, tell-it-like-it-is type, or one who prefers a more roundabout approach?

Identify the individual's characteristics and opinions so that you can present your message in a way that he or she will understand and view positively. For example, words have different *implied* meanings to different people. To some people, *organizational control* means a positive move to accomplish goals, while to others, it means the stripping away of individuality and choice.

Types of Information to Gather

When you have identified your source or sources, you can begin gathering information. Whether you're analyzing individuals or groups, inside or outside your organization, you should find the answers to several questions.

1. How much does your target audience know about the topic? Determine the levels of knowledge of your audience. Sometimes you can assess knowledge based on job title or organizational position. Once you've determined the knowledge level, you can decide how to communicate.

When your audience knows very little, provide basic information and wording. Move from the familiar to the unfamiliar, use analogies, and use visual aids to clarify.

When your audience knows a lot, include advanced information and relevant technical language.

When some know a lot and some know a little, quickly review relevant background information to inform those who know little. Then, move on to your topic of concern. Define technical terms for those who may not understand.

2. What is your target audience's attitude toward you? Does it have a positive attitude toward you? Are you viewed as being a credible source of information on your topic?

If the audience has a positive attitude toward you, it will tend to be uncritical and respond favorably to your message.

If the audience has a negative attitude toward you, it will be relatively critical and evaluative. You should begin your communication by building rapport. In addition, you should identify and overcome possible objections by showing your audience potential gains based on argument, logic, and evidence.

If you're an acknowledged expert, you need to briefly remind your audience of your expertise. Your communication will likely gain the attention and support of your audience.

If you're not viewed as an expert, you can establish your credibility by referring to experience, studies, experts, celebrities, or other background that impresses your audience. In addition, you can establish your credibility by showing "you know what you're talking about" in your writing and speaking. Being organized, using language expected by an expert, and being logical and coherent will enhance your credibility.

3. What kind of relationship would best help you achieve your objective? As we suggested in chapter 1, you develop relationships with your audience based on the tone and style of communication. As you consider your desired relationship, ask yourself several questions. What kind of relationship do you currently have with your target audience? What kind of relationship do you need to accomplish your objectives? What relational message should you send to establish the desired relationship? Choosing the right relationship message requires that you balance the following issues.

Follow general business relationship norms. Your communication with higher-level managers would normally be formal, demonstrating respect for their position. The tone for most business communication would likely be professional and friendly, suggesting a desire to establish and maintain good relationships. The tone should be formal and neutral for documents that establish relationships, such as contracts and warrantees, indicating a legal or binding relationship.

Follow the relationship norms of your business. The nature of your communication should fit the norms of your business. Some businesses require a formal tone in meetings and memos. Some businesses are casual and allow a more friendly and informal style of communication. Within every business, the expected tone and style will vary depending on the context. Reports to managers will generally be relatively formal, suggesting a willingness to accede to authority. Communication among team members will generally be casual and informal, suggesting a friendly and equal relationship.

Follow relationship norms established in individual relationships. For example, you would choose an informal approach with friends (e.g., "Hank, let's talk after the meeting on Friday.") instead of the neutral and formal approach that would be used for people you don't know well (e. g., "The meeting is scheduled for Friday.").

Initiate relationships that will help you achieve your objectives. Any communication enables you to make a bid for the relationship you desire. For example, you can use a warm greeting in hopes of initiating a friendly relationship. Your choice of tone and style will be quite different depending on whether you want to be casual, informal, entertaining, serious, intimidating, or unconcerned. The other party may or may not reciprocate. Nevertheless, you can initiate the desired relationship and then adjust, based on the response you get.

Consider all of the previous issues as you choose how you will communicate. You should also consider the kind of relationship that's most likely to help you achieve your objective. If your objective is to get employees to meet their contractual obligations, you may want to use a formal style and tone in your communications. If your objective is to make subordinates feel like they're part of a team, you may want to communicate in a friendly and respectful manner. If your long-term goal is to build a friendly relationship with higher-level managers, in the appropriate informal contexts, you may find ways to initiate a friendly conversation.

4. How interested is your audience in your topic? Your audience needs a reason to listen to or read your ideas. Unless you know that your audience members are intrinsically interested in your topic, you'll need to find a way to entice them.

If your audience is interested in your topic, briefly remind them of those things that interest them, and then communicate your message.

If your audience has little interest in the topic, find ways to motivate them to pay attention. How can the document or presentation help the audience or the organization? The more specifically you can identify how your topic can help your audience, the more success you'll have. Will it solve problems, increase the likelihood of a promotion, result in increased salary, or answer questions? What's in it for him or her?

5. What is your audience's attitude toward your topic? How will your audience receive your message? Happily? Angrily? Neutrally? Anticipate how your audience will respond, and adapt your message accordingly.

If you must convey bad news, you can anticipate an angry or disappointed response. In this case, a buffer, which introduces the topic but says neither yes nor no, helps to soften the refusal. You could then add a factual explanation, before the actual refusal, that will neutralize your refusal. For example, if you're refusing a contract with a software vendor, a buffer might be to say that you like the company and enjoyed the sales presentation. Then, you could report that several employees tried the software and found that another company's software had more features useful to your specific work applications.

If your message conveys neutral or positive news, you can assume that your audience will receive it well, and you can get straight to the point.

If the audience has a negative or neutral attitude toward your topic or proposal, you will have to argue in your favor and present your proposal after your argument. You may have to settle for a small change in attitude or an acceptance of only part of your proposal. One approach that works well is to provide the audience with options. You could present three different forms of a proposal—modest, moderate, and full-blown—and allow the audience to choose.

If the audience has a positive attitude toward your topic or proposal, you'll need to spend little time arguing for your proposal. You can spend most of the time describing your topic or proposal.

6. What form of communication does your audience expect or prefer? Busy business people expect communications to follow established norms. Your messages are most likely to be accepted when you use the form of communication with which the audience is familiar. If you know the audience's preferences, follow them.

Consider audience expectations for written communication. Organizations develop their own conventions for internal communication. For example, some organizations want certain messages, such as updates on orders, put into e-mail for immediate distribution. However, they may expect other messages, such as policies and procedures, to be given in a formal presentation and distributed in hard-copy handouts. For memos, businesses may specify color-coded paper. For example, they may use red to call attention to highly important news. In addition, supervisors may have personal preferences, such as providing a very specific subject line on memos.

Many organizations also specify desired formats for incoming documents. If businesses specify guidelines, as many do for proposals and orders, follow them. Proposals and orders may be rejected, or at least delayed, when they don't follow prescribed guidelines.

In external documents for which organizations do not provide specific guidelines, follow widely accepted formatting conventions, such as those described in this book.

As you format your documents, consider the following:

Include all expected elements. For example, in a letter, include letterhead or heading, date, inside address, salutation, letter text, and signature block. In a memo, fill in the "To," "From," "Date," "Subject," and sign off on the memo.

Provide desired content. For example, on a resume, include your education and work history. In the first paragraph of a letter of application, include how you learned about the position, mention the specific position desired, and state that you'd like to be considered for the position.

Make the document appear readable. Use white space, headings, and graphics to make the document look professional, attractive, and easily scannable.

Consider audience expectations for presentations. Organizations develop norms for presentations. Some expect presenters to use projected visuals; others do not. Some expect extended time for questions at the end of presentations. Some expect all vendors to make proposals before extended discussions of the proposals occur. We've known businesses that have rejected proposals because conventions for presentations weren't followed. The more you can adapt your presentation to organizational conventions, the more likely you'll be to succeed.

Find out what the audience will expect before your presentation. To make the audience feel comfortable, adapt to all the conventions if possible. If you think you need an exception to conventions to accomplish your objective (for example, you need to use more multi-media than is normally used), get permission from the organization before your presentation.

Here are some conventions you should follow.

Time allotted for the presentation. Meetings for presentations are planned to accommodate time constraints. Violating the time limits provided for your presentation creates scheduling problems for others and probably won't be tolerated.

Nature of content. Many businesses expect a specific kind of content presented because they have developed norms for making decisions based on that content. For example, they may expect certain kinds of financial figures in quarterly reports or in sales presentations. Ask about those expectations, and adapt to them.

Visuals. Some organizations expect certain kinds of visuals, such as overhead transparencies. Others don't like the darkened rooms that are required for some projection equipment. Try to meet expectations. Check to make sure the equipment necessary for your presentation is available.

Questions. Businesses handle questions differently. Some expect an extended question period at the end of presentations. Others expect questions during the presentation.

Summary

In the example at the beginning of this chapter, the target audience was employees. The goal was to have the employees vote in favor of the insurance package. However, management did not initially assess and adapt to employee concerns. As the next section will show, the management team also failed to choose the most appropriate channels of communication.

CHOOSE APPROPRIATE COMMUNICATION CHANNELS TO ACHIEVE OBJECTIVES

After you've identified your objective and analyzed your audience, you're in a position to choose the appropriate communication channels. Businesses now have many communication channels from which to choose, as electronic communication has drastically changed the way businesses interact. More than ever, people can stay in immediate and constant contact. Many of those communication methods or channels are listed in Figure 2.2. As is illustrated, the communication methods or channels have different characteristics. Some allow for immediate, private, and personal communication, whereas others enable public and formal communication.

Channels of Communication

The illustration in Figure 2.2 was designed to help you think about potential advantages and disadvantages of each communication channel. For example, face-to-face communication tends to be with one person, private, unstructured, and informal. Because you can use gestures and facial expressions, face-to-face communication has rich nonverbal information.

On the other end of the continuum, manuals tend to be public and written for many people. They provide specific information in a permanent record. This type of communication is one-way and has limited nonverbal information.

The Internet can encompass all these forms of communication. On the Internet, you can communicate by e-mail, by voice, in chat rooms or electronic meetings, by video and audio, by displaying reports or letters, and by sending documents. With the use of portable computers and cell phones connected to the Internet, you have access to a highly versatile form of communication from almost anywhere.

Communication Channels

Characteristic		Face-to-Face	Telephone	Personal Note	E-mail	Small Group Meetings	Electronic/Video Conference	Voice-Mail/Page	Facsimile	Business Letter	Bulletin Board	Extemporaneous Presentation	Video/Audio Tape	Memo (defined group)	Report	Manuscript Presentation	Manual	
							Internet											
Audience	One Person																	Many People
Intimacy	Private																	Public
Input/Participation	Two-way																	One-way
Message	Temporary																	Low Impact
Attention Gaining	High																	Low
Nonverbal	Rich																	Limited
Precision	General																	Specific
Record	Temporary																	Permanent
Transmission	Fast																	Slow
Relationship	Informal																	Formal
Organization	Unstructured																	Structured

FIGURE 2.2 Characteristics of Communication Channels

In the following list, we summarize the strengths of each channel of communication.

INTERNET
- disperses information to a broad audience
- multimedia capability
- rich source of variety of information, including audio and video
- interaction between sender and receiver
- convenience, speed, and ease of use

FACE-TO-FACE, TELEPHONE, CELL PHONE
- two-way, interactive, and immediate communication
- rich nonverbal communication of attitudes and feelings
- personal attention that can build relationships and establish trust
- networks can be a reliable source of information and influence

E-MAIL, FACSIMILE, VOICE-MAIL, PAGE
- fast transmission to a dispersed audience
- control over sending and reading/hearing messages
- adapt messages to individuals
- permanent written record for e-mail, facsimile

SMALL GROUP MEETINGS, VIDEO CONFERENCE
- rich nonverbal communication of attitudes and feelings
- immediate interaction, participation, and response
- communication that creates understanding, identity, and commitment

ELECTRONIC CONFERENCE (CHAT ROOM)
- interaction among a dispersed audience
- frank (sometimes inflammatory) communication
- permanent written record possible

MEMO, BUSINESS LETTER, REPORT, AND MANUAL
- permanent record that can be dispersed
- carefully prepared, logical, and detailed
- personal control over when message is read

PRESENTATIONS
- prepared message that many hear simultaneously
- potential for rich nonverbal, multimedia presentation
- opportunity to adapt and interact with audience (extemporaneous presentations)
- permanent record (manuscript presentations)

You will undoubtedly use all these forms of communication and combinations of them in your business. For each message, be creative, and design a mix that best accomplishes your goals. Inventive business people have combined traditional forms of communication with electronic media in ways that improve and transform communication.

For example, traditionally, manuals were formal printed documents. Today, manuals can be integrated into computer programs for easy and ready reference. For businesses that provide loans over the telephone, on-line manuals can be integrated into loan application software that is readily accessible by agents. Previously, bulletin boards were relatively slow methods of transferring messages. Now, electronic bulletin boards can be one of the fastest ways to distribute or obtain information.

Communication Channels That Achieve
General Management Objectives

The primary functions of management are planning, organizing, leading, and controlling. These functions are used to help an organization accomplish general management objectives. All managers perform these functions to a certain degree, and the variety of communication media can enhance ability to perform management functions. In the following list, we describe how managers might use channels of communication to accomplish management functions.

Planning. Planning comprises managers participating in *small group meetings,* developing plans, and presenting them in the form of *formal reports* and *presentations.*

Organizing. Organizing involves delegating responsibilities, assigning roles, and coordinating work responsibilities. *Face-to-face* and *group meetings,* as well as *memos* and *electronic* and *telephone communications,* are used to coordinate. *Written manuals* describe roles and responsibilities. *Formal reports* summarize fulfillment of responsibilities.

Leading. Leading includes visualizing goals, motivating others, providing feedback, keeping employees informed, providing recognition, and using interpersonal influence to accomplish work. *Face-to-face* is the primary communication channel for leading. In addition, leaders also use *memos, electronic* and *telephone communications,* and *group meetings.*

Controlling. Controlling establishes standards for performance and determines whether standards are met. Standards, budgets, and goals are presented in formal *memos, reports,* and *presentations.* These kinds of communication are also used to determine whether standards or goals are met. Evaluations are often reported in *quarterly* or *annual reports* and *presentations.*

Effective managers must capably use all forms of communication. Lower-level managers spend most of their time leading, while higher-level managers devote more time to planning, organizing, and controlling.

Communication Channels That Achieve
Specific Management Objectives

In addition to fulfilling general management functions, employees must organize activities to accomplish specific organizational goals. Much of this form of day-to-day communication is informal. Three primary purposes for communication at this level are to coordinate, to inform, and to persuade.

Communicate to Coordinate   Coordination requires that you understand the overall picture and how employees fit into that picture. You must understand employees and their activities, and you must coordinate those activities to accomplish overall goals. You need to exchange information quickly and accurately. The following communication channels are important for the exchange of information necessary to coordinate.

Internet. The Internet is currently the most efficient method for gathering and sending information. Its potential for enabling people to stay informed seems almost endless. With the use of hand-held computers, electronic transmissions, and small video cameras, managers may be able to exchange audio, video, and printed information with any dispersed work site.

Face-to-Face. When it's possible, the best way to exchange information is to visit people in their work environment and see first-hand what's going on. Studies indicate that managers with the most effective work groups spend more time "managing by walking around," visiting employees, and seeing for themselves what's happening (Luthans, Hodgetts & Rosenkrantz, 1988). Chit-chat and non-verbal communication are rich sources for understanding another's perspective.

Small Group Meetings and Electronic or Video Conferences. Meetings can provide the means for exchanging information. Video and electronic channels increase the flexibility of location and time.

Communicate To Inform   Effective communication depends on everyone having a common understanding of organizational terms, practices, and norms. Good managers promote common understanding. We provide guidelines for informing in chapters 4, 8, and 15. Informing includes training and day-to-day updates. The most effective communication channels for informing include the following:

When people have very little understanding, use

Face-to-Face Communication. When people are learning new information, most tend to pay attention and learn faster when they can receive individual instruction and can ask questions.
Multimedia Presentations. Individuals differ in their preferences for learning. Some learn faster by reading, others by listening, and many by visualizing or by a combination of all these. Multimedia presentations include more forms of information, making it easier to learn quickly. Such presentations can include live presentations, videos, outline and picture visuals, role-plays, and written instructions.

When people have much understanding and require updates only, use

E-mail, Voice-Mail, or Memos. When possible, use e-mail to save time. If the message is highly important, use more than one kind of media.
Small Group Meetings and Electronic or Video Conferences. Regular employee meetings provide an efficient way to inform and discuss.

Communicate To Persuade   Persuasion changes attitudes or motivates others to action. It requires that you understand the knowledge, attitudes, and interests of the persons you hope to persuade. We provide extensive guidelines for preparing persuasive messages in chapters 4, 8, and 15. When you have your persuasive message prepared, the best channels of communication are the following:

Face-to-Face. Persuasion is most effective when appeals are adapted to individuals. Face-to-face communication allows the persuader to better adapt to individual desires and to understand and overcome objections.

Internet. On one hand, the Internet provides individuals the convenience of "window shopping," obtaining information, and easily purchasing desired products and services. On the other hand, the Internet provides persuaders with numerous ways of gaining potential customer attention, including links among Internet sites. Moreover, persuaders on the Internet have the ability to use audio and video communication.

Presentations and Video. Presentations and videos provide a powerful means for persuasion. Presenters can invest time and resources into identifying audience concerns and designing appealing messages. They can create enticing visuals, develop strong arguments, and prepare means for overcoming objections. When presentations are delivered repetitively, improvements can be made through trial and error.

Telephone, E-Mail, and Letters. Telephone, e-mail, and letters allow communication with dispersed individuals. When relationships already exist among the individuals contacted, interaction can be highly persuasive. When relationships don't exist, these forms of communication are less successful.

After you've completed the steps of strategically planning your communication—(1) established your communication objective, (2) defined your audience and its concerns, and (3) chosen your communication channel(s)—you're ready to develop your message and to communicate. The focus of the remainder of this text is to help you further define your communication objective and to create your message.

To illustrate a strategic communication plan in action, we return to the example at the beginning of this chapter. First, team members created a communication objective: to influence employees to vote in favor of the new insurance package. Second, they identified the audience as the employees. However, they did not identify the employees' concerns that the new insurance package may not be better than the old package. The management team didn't discover, until it was too late, that their employees needed more information to make a judgment.

Third, the team members' choice of a memo was not the best channel of communication. The employees needed information, answers to questions, and persuasion to convince them that the new plan was the best option.

To accomplish the information and persuasion goals, the management team could have prepared a visual presentation comparing each plan's benefits and costs. In addition, when the plan was first introduced, employees could've been given hard-copy handouts explaining the plan. To help the employees feel comfortable asking questions, managers might have arranged for the employees to meet in small groups with insurance representatives to discuss the plan.

DEVELOP YOUR COMMUNICATION SKILLS

This chapter suggests that managers must develop the ability to use a broad range of interpersonal, technical, group, presentation, and writing skills. Most people are familiar with the more informal skills associated with face-to-face, e-mail, voice-mail, and

Internet communications. Comparatively, more training and practice is needed for the more formal communication skills required for delivering presentations and writing memos, letters, and reports. Skills in these forms of communication are very important because they have high visibility in the organization. Judgments about individual competence are based on effectiveness in using such communication skills.

For example, documents that are difficult to read, sloppily written and full of grammatical errors will reflect negatively upon the author and the organization, especially when they're widely distributed. Such documents, at best, may confuse audiences and hinder communication. At worst, they may cause errors, low credibility, and loss of business. Similarly, poorly delivered presentations may result in negative reactions and loss of business. Several years ago, the dean of our college had several experiences that influenced him to improve communication education. Two of those experiences are described below:

> A vice-president of a large oil company showed me [the dean] a memo and asked me what I thought of it. The memo was full of grammatical errors and made no sense. I told him that it was almost unreadable. He said that an accountant, one of our former students, had written the memo. He indicated that the business relied on clear and accurate communication. Such writing would not be tolerated. Either that employee would have to overcome the deficiency or leave.

> An upper-level manager reported hiring one of our marketing students who apparently had very high grades. However, her first formal presentation was a disaster. She was unprepared and unorganized. She was so nervous she could hardly speak and made the audience feel uncomfortable. The manager said that such presentations would cost his area credibility. He could not comfortably put her in front of upper-level managers or customers. Her career was in jeopardy.

Because formal communications are so widely dispersed within and outside businesses, employees must develop writing and speaking skills that enable accurate, effective, and error-free communication. The form of communication must be impressive, so as to reflect positively on the organization.

The purpose of this book is to help you develop your communication skills so that you can achieve your communication objectives. The remaining chapters can help you design messages to achieve your communication objectives.

CHAPTER 3

Organizing and Developing the Message

Nothing is more annoying than having to read a document or listen to a presentation that is unclear and poorly organized. Making your audience search for your main point is something you want to avoid in both presentations and written documents. A good writing and speaking style is the key to helping guide your audience to the main point you want to convey.

Most documents and speeches for business audiences must get to the point quickly; all documents and speeches should be organized so that they are easy to follow. Generally, if you place your topic sentences strategically, connect your ideas logically, and eliminate unnecessary words and phrases, you will aid the audience in understanding your message. In the following pages, we provide guidelines for making your writing and speaking logical, coherent, and concise.

COHERENT ORGANIZATION

Coherently organized documents and presentations display principal ideas prominently. They are logical and easy to comprehend. Sentences and paragraphs are short. Most often, paragraphs in a document or points and sub-points in a presentation begin with the principal idea and follow with additional sentences that provide explanations, definitions, and illustrations.

Sentences

Effective business documents and speeches make principal ideas prominent. Begin by creating fast-starting sentences. The beginning of the sentence should tell "who did what" (subject and verb) or provide a key transition word. For example, examine the following sentences:

Slow start: Without a doubt and without consulting with authorities about the issue, we know that *employees must abide* by professional standards.

Fast start (subject and verb): *Employees must abide* by professional standards; this we know without a doubt and without consulting authorities about the issue.

Fast start (transition word): *Without exception, employees must abide* by professional standards. We will not rely on authorities to govern our actions.

Coherent organization also means sentences and paragraphs that make sense. The flow must be logical. Sentences should **include related ideas.** If ideas within sentences are unrelated, show relationships by creating more sentences or adding words of explanation. Here is an example:

Unrelated ideas: We will miss the completion deadline on the Johnson Project, and we will focus on internal reorganization.

Improved: We will miss the completion deadline on the Johnson Project. *To avoid future problems with projects,* we will focus on internal reorganization.

Paragraphs, Main Points, and Sub-Points

Effective paragraphs are logical groupings of sentences. Logical and coherent paragraphs are built around topic sentences (the main point), include related sentences, and are connected by transition words. Business paragraphs, and main points and sub-points, should be short. Long paragraphs and complex explanations are difficult for the audience to quickly grasp.

Topic sentences state the main idea presented in your paragraph or presentation point. Most of the time, the topic sentence should be the first sentence in a paragraph or spoken in a presentation point. State your idea up front, and then support it. Occasionally, you may prefer to make the point in the middle or at the end of a paragraph or presentation point for special emphasis. However, most writing and speaking is clearer and simpler when the topic sentence appears first since it signals the subsequent content for your audience. Whatever its placement, however, written paragraphs and main points in speeches should contain one topic sentence, not two or three.

Related sentences expand the meaning of the topic sentence. They provide explanations, examples, and conclusions. The sentences should all be related to the topic sentence. Here is an example:

Topic Sentence: The first responsibility of a speaker is to be heard.

Explanation: If the audience cannot hear you, its time and your efforts are wasted. Every audience member should hear every word of your speech.

Example: Notice that comedians and other entertainers speak loudly. They never reduce the volume of their speech below understandable levels.

Conclusion: Concentrate on making the person in the last row easily understand you.

The sentences should be linked to one another so that a reader or listener can follow your logic. Sometimes, the logic is clarified by placing sentences so that one idea leads into another. However, you can make relationships clearer by using **transitional words.** Here are some transitional words that signal relationships:

RELATIONSHIP	TRANSITIONS THAT SIGNAL THE RELATIONSHIP
Additionally	Further, furthermore, besides, too, moreover, and, also, in addition, next, then, equally important, finally
Example	For instance, thus, specifically, namely, as an illustration, for example
Contrast	But, yet, however, nevertheless, conversely, on the other hand, on the contrary, still, at the same time, nonetheless
Comparison	Similarly, likewise, in the same way, in comparison, in like manner
Concession	Of course, to be sure, certainly, naturally, granted
Result	Therefore, thus, consequently, so accordingly, due to this
Summary	As a result, hence, in short, in brief, in summary, in conclusion, finally, on the whole, therefore
Time Sequence	First, next, then, finally, afterward, before, soon, later, during, meanwhile, subsequently, immediately, eventually, in the future, currently
Place	In the front, foremost, in the background, at the side, adjacent, nearby, in the distance, here, there

Source: Troyka, L.Q. (1990). *Simon & Schuster Handbook for Writers.* (2nd ed.). Englewood Cliffs, NJ: Prentice Hall, p. 96.

Compare how adding a few transition words clarifies the relationships among sentences in the earlier paragraph.

Topic Sentence: The first responsibility of a speaker is to be heard.

Explanation: If the audience cannot hear you, its time and your efforts are wasted. Every audience member should hear every word of your speech.

Example: **For example,** notice that comedians and other entertainers speak loudly. They never reduce the volume of their speech below understandable levels.

Conclusion: **Therefore,** in future presentations, concentrate on making the person in the last row easily understand you.

You can also achieve organizational coherence by repeating key words and ideas throughout. Notice how similar words and ideas are repeated:

Topic Sentence: The first responsibility of a **speaker** is to **be heard.**

Explanation: If the audience cannot **hear** you, its time and your efforts are wasted. Every audience member should **hear** every word of your **speech.**

Example: For example, notice that comedians and other entertainers **speak loudly.** They never reduce **volume** below understandable levels.

Conclusion: Therefore, in future **presentations,** concentrate on making the person in the last row **easily understand** you.

Finally, you can enhance coherence by ensuring that pronouns clearly refer to their antecedents and tags identify sources so that readers and listeners don't get confused. Note how the relationships are shown in the following example.

> **Covey indicates** that **we** all carry maps in **our** heads. **He notes** that **we** have a variety of maps including **our** views of reality and values. **Covey suggests we** interpret everything through these maps. **We also note** that half of communication is using personal maps to interpret messages from others.

In summary, as you create your document or speech, ask yourself the following questions:

- Is the topic sentence clearly evident (usually the first sentence)?
- Do other sentences relate to the topic sentence?
- Do transition words show relationships among sentences?
- Are key ideas and words repeated to add coherence?
- Do pronouns refer to their antecedents, and do tags identify sources?

Long Documents and Presentations

Design long business documents and speeches to be easily understood. Appropriate use of descriptive headings and main and sub-points increases comprehension in these longer documents and speeches. Headings in a report, for example, help busy readers scan the document to find relevant content. Also, headings and point labels can be designed to communicate a coherent and logical message.

According to Dr. William Baker (1994), professor of business communication, the best way to maintain coherent organization is to create an outline and apply several tests to it. To demonstrate how the tests work, write the heading and subheadings that might appear in a document or speech that gives advice about improving communication. For the purposes of this exercise, you will need at least three subheadings. Make your headings and subheadings as descriptive as possible. An example is provided in the following.

Main Heading: Improve Your Listening Skills
Subheading: Nod Your Head
Subheading: Face the Other Person
Subheading: Eye Contact Maintained

Test #1. Is the sum of the subheadings equal to the heading?   To meet this test, you may have to add subheadings, drop subheadings, or change the wording for the heading or subheadings. To meet the test for our example, we'll change the main heading and add a sub-heading.

Main Heading: Show by Your Behavior That You Are Listening
Subheading: Nod Your Head

Subheading: Face the Other Person
Subheading: Give Short Verbal Comments
Subheading: Eye Contact Maintained

Test #2. Are the subheadings mutually exclusive? No overlap should exist among the subheadings. In our example, "eye contact" and "facing the other person" overlap, so we'll drop "facing the other person."

Main Heading: Show by Your Behavior That You Are Listening
Subheading: Nod Your Head
Subheading: Give Short Verbal Comments
Subheading: Eye Contact Maintained

Test #3. Are the subheadings organized in a logical order? For example, the subheadings could be arranged in a sequence that is alphabetical, chronological, spatial, or in order of importance. In our example, order of importance seems to be the most appropriate organizational sequence. Of the subheadings listed in our example, eye contact is the most important element, so we'll list it first.

Main Heading: Show by Your Behavior That You Are Listening
Subheading: Eye Contact Maintained
Subheading: Nod Your Head
Subheading: Give Short Verbal Comments

Test #4. Are all subheadings (headings at the same level) arranged so that they are grammatically parallel? In our example, "Eye Contact Maintained" isn't grammatically parallel with the other subheadings, so we'll change it.

Main Heading: Show by Your Behavior That You Are Listening
Subheading: Maintain Eye Contact
Subheading: Nod Your Head
Subheading: Give Short Verbal Comments

If you follow the tips we've provided, you will be able to create outlines for documents and presentations that are logical and easy to comprehend. Now you must add support material to prove your points and maintain interest in your topic.

SUPPORT MATERIAL

Once you've settled on an organizational structure for your document, you must think about what information you will use to support your points. Adequate support depends upon finding or creating a variety of related material. Support material is what you use to prove your thesis. Without it, your speech or your document will fail to convince your audience. For example, if you're trying to persuade your supervisor to implement sales incentives to increase motivation among your staff, you will be more successful if you provide statistical data to prove that sales have been lagging, anecdotal support to show positive employee response to the idea, and perhaps testimonials from other companies that have had success with such incentives.

Sources of Support

There are many sources to choose from for finding convincing support material. Some are easier to locate in university libraries, although others may be easier to find in bookstores. Where you will look for support often depends on your research topic. The following are some examples.

Textbooks

University textbooks are excellent sources of support material for businesses. Usually, authors of textbooks take care to include well-researched and commonly accepted content in their text. They often provide excellent examples, stories, statistics, explanations, and other information useful for support material. References are also included, which you might examine for more in-depth coverage of a topic.

Other Books

A large variety of special topic books about business are available. Often, you can find many books about the topic you have selected in library and computer databases. University libraries tend to have more academic books than public libraries, which may have more how-to books. Both types of libraries are good resources. Most bookstores also carry a variety of popular books relevant to many business subjects.

Newspapers, Journals, and Magazines

Students should become aware of publications in their major before they leave college. These resources will provide excellent support material for presentations and documents now and in the future. Become familiar with publications like *The Wall Street Journal* (a newspaper); *Business Week* and *Forbes* (magazines); and the *Harvard Business Review, California Management Review, Journal of Marketing,* or *Journal of Accounting* (journals). A broad understanding of business today will strengthen any business presentation or document. Popular magazine and journal articles are also available at most libraries. Look for articles in the *Reader's Guide to Periodical Literature, The Public Affairs Information Service Bulletin*, or *Business Periodicals Index*, as well as other indexes suggested by your librarian. Computerized literature searches are also available in most university libraries.

Experts and Professionals

If you think about it, you can probably identify people who, by virtue of their profession, can provide valuable information on many business-related topics. A bank officer can provide guidance about financial management. A restaurant owner may have excellent suggestions about management or motivation. A college professor can give insight about her or his area of expertise. Many of these people will respond favorably to a request for a short interview. When interviewing these experts, ask for permission to use their names as references in your document or presentation.

Personal Experience

Examples from your own experience are also a very good source of support material. Your work or leadership experience may be relevant to your message. For example, even an unsuccessful employment interview might provide useful support for a speech about job seeking. If you have experience being treated well or poorly as a customer, this might be an excellent resource for a presentation or proposal about sales. In many cases, however, you are not a recognized authority on a subject. Therefore, make limited use of personal experience, and combine this experience with other forms of support.

Service and Interest Groups

A major purpose of many organizations is to provide information to the public. Career planning and placement centers on most campuses provide brochures, libraries, and presentations on many topics relevant to careers. Civic and professional organizations also offer materials and presentations. In addition, some of the best support material may come from officer training or management workshops.

Internet

The Internet is becoming *the* major source of information. The speed and ease of the Internet makes it a valuable resource. We encourage use of the Internet with two cautions. First, be aware that information on the Internet varies in accuracy and credibility. You can find information from well-respected experts as well as from biased crackpots. You need to seek out credible sources. Sources that are credible in public, such as research institutions and mainstream publishers, are also credible sources on the Internet. Sources that lack credibility in public also lack credibility on the Internet, so you would be wise to look at Internet sources with a somewhat skeptical eye.

Second, don't plagiarize Internet documents. It's easy to download documents and pictures from the Internet and copy them into a document. This may seem harmless. However, this practice is the same as copying written material from someone else's publication and claiming it as your own. This practice is unethical, as well as illegal. In academia, such practices can result in failing a course or expulsion from school. In the business world, plagiarizing can result in legal action against the individuals and company that distribute plagiarized material. When you copy material from the Internet, you should clearly identify it with quotation marks or indented text and note the source. Also, when you paraphrase the content, you must give credit to the source as well. Correctly citing your sources not only helps you avoid ethical and legal problems, but it enhances the credibility of your document because it shows you are relying on respected sources for your information.

Types of Support Material

Good communication requires that you provide support material and information that clarifies, explains, and persuades, so your audience can visualize and define your main points.

Novice speakers and writers often provide too much or too little support material. Some bury the main point in irrelevant details and confuse or bore their audience. Others merely state main points without any support. From the audience's perspective, this approach is somewhat like reading the chapter headings of a book—you know what it's about, but you have no in-depth understanding.

When adequately supported, each main point should include the following:

1. Statement of the main point
2. Explanation
3. Support material

The statement of the main point identifies and labels the main point. It helps your listener or reader follow you through your speech or document. Use the labels already identified in the introduction. For example, for the first point in a speech about interviewing, the speaker might say the following:

My first point is that successful interviewees initiate friendly relationships.

This brief statement provides a label for the point. The speaker should then explain the main point by providing definitions, assumptions, or justification. For example, the speaker could add the following explanation:

You can initiate friendly relationships by smiling, extending a warm handshake, and being expressive. Friendliness during the interview enhances the likelihood of your being offered a job. Prepare yourself to be friendly and outgoing even when the employer is reserved.

This explanation defines and justifies the main point. It helps the audience understand the point and the assumptions related to it.

Support material clarifies the main point and provides convincing evidence. For variety and interest, include more than one kind of support in your speech or document. You might choose from statistics, examples, illustrations, testimony, quotations, definitions, and analogies.

Statistics

Statistics, numerical facts or data, are used frequently in business presentations and documents. They should be presented in such a way as to have meaning and impact. If the statistic is important, visualize it. If you do nothing else, list figures in a visual aid. But to help the audience immediately understand, convert the figures into charts or graphs (see chapter 5). For greater impact, add illustrations. For example, you could describe a 10 percent company turnover rate by citing actual numbers of employees lost and referring to individuals who have recently left. Here is a form of statistical support used to augment the previous main point about being friendly in interviews:

Forbes and Jackson's (1980) research showed that acceptable interviewees smiled almost three times more than unacceptable interviewees did.

Examples

To help your audience clearly visualize your message, use examples—instances or stories that show what you mean. The more concrete the example, the better. For example, if you wanted to clarify participative management, you could list the characteristics—willingness to involve subordinates in decision-making and to share decision-making responsibility with them. Or you could provide more concrete support by telling a story about participative decision-making. The story would be easy to visualize and believe. For example, for the main point about being friendly in employment interviews, you might say the following:

Our organization recently hired a secretary. We interviewed three individuals who were qualified for the position. One stood out head and shoulders above the others because of her friendliness and ability to establish rapport almost immediately.

Illustrations

To fully clarify an idea or process, you sometimes need an illustration—a demonstration or comparison. For example, you might best explain how to complete time sheets by including a visual aid of a completed time sheet in your document or presentation. You might show the ease of using a computer program by providing visuals that will come up on the computer screen, accompanied by directions about using screens. For the main point introduced earlier, you could illustrate a friendly greeting by including a picture of a smiling applicant greeting an employer with an outstretched hand or, in a speech, by demonstrating a friendly greeting and an effective handshake. You could also illustrate a friendly greeting with a word picture.

Come to the door with a smile on your face. Look the interviewer directly in the eye, extend your hand, and firmly shake her hand. Engage in brief, friendly chit-chat, preferably a short, enjoyable story that you can share with the interviewer. Thank the interviewer for the opportunity to interview.

Testimony

A good way to convince an audience is to provide testimony—the statement or declaration of a witness or expert. These statements can be your own or someone else's. For example, if you have failed in several job interviews, in a perverse way, you might be considered an expert and might share a negative interviewing experience to show how it shouldn't be done. Or, you might share some comments from a professional interviewer. Both kinds of evidence add clarity and credibility to your presentation or document. The following testimony supports the main point of our example.

According to Sydisha (1961), who has studied employment interviews, favorable decisions are more likely to occur when interviewees engage in positive social-emotional acts.

Quotations

Using statements from credible sources can not only clarify your point, but also add credibility to your message. Often, a quotation, a word-for-word repetition of a phrase from printed or spoken material, is memorable and emphasizes the point you want to make. The quotation has the most impact if it comes from someone respected in your organization, such as the CEO or prominent authors. For example, business speakers frequently quote both Lee Iaccoca and Tom Peters.

Definitions

An important part of education is learning new vocabulary. A definition, the meaning of a word or phrase, is often a good beginning to clarifying main points. Organizations develop their own unique definitions for many terms. New members of organizations need to know these words and what they mean. For example, at Walt Disney World, employees are called "cast members." When they are at work, they are "on stage," suggesting that they must play a certain role, and customers are called the "guests." By learning these definitions, employees also learn that they should entertain customers and make them happy. A definition that might be used to support our previous example might be:

According to Webster, "positive" means indicating acceptance, approval, and affirmation. Positive, friendly acts during an interview indicate your acceptance, approval, and affirmation of the interviewer.

Analogies

An analogy is a comparison. You may create a literal analogy and compare two things that are similar, such as two kinds of software, two events, or two kinds of operations. For example, you might say that word-processing is like typing with a memory in the machine. A figurative analogy, often a simile or a metaphor, compares two things that seem to have little in common. To illustrate, when describing how to secure a job, you might say that effective job seeking is like fishing: applicants aren't successful unless they present bait (qualifications) that fish (employers) are interested in. For the previous main point, you might say

An applicant in a job interview ought to be like a hostess at a party. She should be friendly, outgoing, and gracious in a manner that makes the interviewer feel good about participating in the interview.

In summary, adequate support of a point should include the statement of the point, explanation of the point, and support material to further clarify the point. For example, all three elements of the point we have been describing might look like this:

Statement of the Point: My first point is that successful interviewees initiate friendly relationships.
Explanation: You can initiate friendly relationships by smiling, extending a warm handshake, and being expressive. Friendliness during the interview

enhances the likelihood of your being offered a job. Prepare yourself to be friendly and outgoing even when the employer is reserved.

Support Material: Being friendly means being positive. According to Webster, "positive" means indicating acceptance, approval, and affirmation. Positive, friendly acts during an interview indicate your acceptance, approval, and affirmation of the interviewer. According to Sydisha (1961), who has studied employment interviews, favorable decisions are more likely to occur when interviewees engage in positive social–emotional acts.

Don't underestimate the importance of support material in your documents and presentations. While adding support does involve work—locating credible sources, finding relevant support material, and determining the most appropriate places to put the support material—it is essential that you do so if you want your speech or document to carry the weight it should.

CLEAR AND ACCEPTABLE BUSINESS MESSAGES

The crucial requirement of business messages is that the audience understands your message. Writers and speakers can do this by choosing words that are clear, descriptive, and accurate, as well as by using language their audience understands. Don't make your reader or listener guess at your meaning because you've failed to provide enough specific detail or because you've used unfamiliar words and phrases.

Clarity

You increase clarity when you use concrete words that are easy for others to visualize and simple words that are easy to understand. Your goal is to make your document or speech understandable for your audience. You increase and maintain understanding when you choose words that are simple, clear, and familiar.

Concreteness

Concrete words such as "textbook," "card table," or "Chevrolet" are specific, clear, and easily visualized. Abstract words such as "faith," "authorization," and "paradigm" are vague and difficult to conceptualize. Try to be as concrete as possible so that your audience can interpret your meaning as closely as possible. For example, stating "You may proceed" is much more abstract than stating more specifically, "You may take the van for your personal business as long as it is returned by 5:00 P.M. today with a full tank of gas." Saying, "Go ahead and apply for the position" is much less helpful than "Send your résumé to Kent Jackson, and indicate that I told you to apply for the job as my assistant." Here is another example:

Abstract: Let's meet soon.
Concrete: Let's meet at 1:00 P.M. on Friday, January 19th in the boardroom.

When abstract words are necessary, you can increase clarity by adding modifiers. Consider the following sentences:

Abstract: We will begin when Jack is ready.
Concrete: We will begin when Jack is ready with a complete set of plans.

Abstract: Our company makes a real contribution.

Concrete: Our company makes a real contribution by donating more than
$1,000,000 per year to the United Way.

Simplicity

In an attempt to impress others, some business people use jargon, technical language, acronyms, or euphemisms when simpler, more familiar terms would communicate their message more effectively. Compare the following example from a general, written in simple terms, with that of an accountant, written with technical and complex words.

> My guidelines are simple. Be selective. Be concise. Don't tell someone what you know; tell them what they need to know, what it means, and why it matters.
>
> GENERAL DAVID C. JONES
> CHAIRMAN, JOINT CHIEFS OF STAFF, 1978

> Except as otherwise provided in this section, all of the provisions of this article applicable to the tax imposed by section five hundred three of this article shall apply with respect to the supplemental tax imposed by this section to the same extent as if it were imposed by such section five hundred three, insofar as such provisions can be made applicable to the supplemental tax imposed by this section, with such modification as may be necessary to adapt such provisions to the supplemental tax imposed by this section.
>
> ACCOUNTANT

One way to make writing clear is to replace formal words designed to impress with simple words designed to communicate. Here are some simpler replacements for their longer, less-familiar counterparts.

STUFFY	SIMPLE
ameliorate	improve
commence	begin
execute	sign
remittance	payment
reside	live
paradigm	model
remunerate	pay

Readability Formulas

One of the best ways to assess readability of a document is to compute the Fog Index (Gunning, 1952) for your writing. The Fog Index estimates the grade-level at which you write. A Fog Index of 13 means the 13th grade level (freshman in college). For ease, many word processing programs automatically calculate the Fog Index or another similar formula as part of a writing analysis. We've provided instructions for computing your Fog Index score below.

1. Select representative text and count to the end of the sentence in which the 100th word appears (100 words plus additional words needed to complete to the end of the sentence).
2. Count the number of sentences included in step one.
3. Calculate the average sentence length (total words divided by number of sentences).
4. Count the number of words that have three syllables or more (usually long words—dictionaries break words into parts which appear as syl•la•ble).
5. Add the average sentence length (step three) to the total of three syllable words (step four).
6. Multiply the total from step five by 0.4 to determine the Fog Index or grade level.

As you can see, the Fog Index is based on the assumption that longer sentences and multiple syllable words are difficult to understand. The shorter the sentence and the word, the easier the text is to read. In general, this assumption is true.

The Fog Index works best with longer documents, such as reports. Because the Fog Index requires you to count out at least 100 words, shorter documents, such as letters, are difficult to assess. For those documents, use the Motor-to-Weight ratio described below. To assess the level at which you write using the Fog Index, take two or three representative samples of your writing and compute the formula using the guidelines provided. *Most business writing should be at about the 8th-grade level.* Most university students write at a higher grade level. If your writing level is above the 8th grade, shorten your sentences, and use fewer difficult words to make your writing easy to read. Because so much of business writing is scanned rather than read word-for-word, long words, sentences, and paragraphs tend to slow down your reader, thus wasting his or her valuable time.

As a rule of thumb, use the 8th-grade level as your guide. However, some knowledgeable readers may expect technical words that would raise the index. Other readers who are less knowledgeable may require simpler language that lowers the index. The key is to be sensitive and adjust your writing level to your reader.

Another readability assessment is the Motor-to-Weight ratio. Writing consultants for Arthur Andersen & Co. developed this test to assess how fast a sentence reads. The "motors" in a sentence are active verbs. The "weight" is all the other words. The ratio is based on the assumption that active verbs provide movement in sentences. "Be" verbs categorize (e.g., June *is* competent.), but do not convey action. Passive verbs are wordy and create inactive subjects (e.g., She *will be assigned* by June.). Active verbs show movement and action (e.g., June *assigned* the work.).

The ideal Motor-to-Weight ratio is 1:10. The ratio is the number of active verbs in a sentence to the number of total words. Pick a few representative sentences from your writing and compute the ratio for each one. If your ratio is higher than 1:10, consider shortening your sentences and adding more active verbs. Here are some sample sentences, highlighting active verbs and showing the Motor-to-Weight ratio.

RATIO	SENTENCE WITH ACTIVE VERBS IN BOLD
1:7	Jack **organized** the work to flow smoothly.
1:13	We **started** at 8:00 A.M. sharp because customers expected us to be there.

0:13	This insurance policy is the best for the money in the current marketplace. ("Be" verb.)
0:13	The position was established to lighten the workload of Doris and her staff. (Passive verb.)
0:17	The implementation of the new program and related activities is designed to save taxpayers time and effort. (Passive verb.)

You can use the Motor-to-Weight ratio for shorter writing, such as letters and short memos. If you get in the habit of regularly using readability formulas to check your writing, you will learn to reduce wordiness and increase clarity in both your writing and your presentations.

Style and Tone

Business communicators should be professional and courteous. The style and tone of your message is determined by the language you choose. Good communicators avoid being too formal or informal. They also use positive word choice, the "you" attitude, and unbiased language.

Positive Word Choice

Avoid choosing words that make readers defensive. Negative words directed at the reader or listener, such as *blame, poor, unreasonable, shortsighted,* and *slow,* will invite considerable ill will and lack of cooperation. Avoid criticizing and telling what you *cannot* do. Instead, choose wording that is positive and conveys what you *can* do.

Negative: We cannot send your shipment until we receive proof that you paid.

Positive: We're pleased you chose us for your business and will promptly send your shipment when we receive your payment.

Negative: We regret to inform you that it will be impossible to fill your order by the 24th of September because of production problems. We cannot fill it until October 15.

Positive: We will be filling your order by October 15 because of a delay in production until mid-October.

The "You" Attitude

A "you" attitude emphasizes the reader's interests. It avoids communicating a self-centered or "what's in it for me" attitude. It focuses on the reader's needs, feelings, and position. Such an attitude builds good will and elicits positive responses. The following examples show the contrast between "I" and "you" language:

I: *We* have received your order of June 20.

You: Thank *you* for your order of June 20.

I: *We* have shipped your order of office desks.

You: *Your* order of office desks should reach you within two business days.

I: *I* bring several years of business experience, which makes *me* highly
         qualified for the position.

You: *Your* company will immediately benefit from my experience and
         qualifications.

Conversational Language

Business language should avoid being too formal or too informal. A casual, conversational tone is right for most business letters and memos. Reading or writing conversational language is like talking to the person next to you. It uses familiar pronouns such as *I* and *you*. However, it does not become too informal, using slang and colloquialisms such as "y'all." The following are examples of conversational language:

Formal: It is most imperative that every sales associate proffer the utmost
                    courtesy to our clientele.

Conversational: Sales associates should be courteous to clients.

Formal: Pertaining to company reports, all figures must be verified for
                    accuracy before final printing, collation, and distribution.

Conversational: Please verify figures for accuracy before final printing and
                    distribution.

Unbiased Language

For business correspondence, choose words that are unbiased. While the reader might understand your message, you might offend him or her with language that contains cultural, gender, racial or ethnic, disability, or age biases. Offended readers could refuse to respond positively to you or your requests. Here are some examples of biased words and more neutral replacements:

BIASED	UNBIASED
domestic imports	U.S. imports
Asian salesman	salesperson
black lady	woman
elderly CEO	CEO
crippled	disabled
deaf	hearing impaired
businessman	businessperson
chairman	chairperson, head
foreman	supervisor
salesman	salesperson, associate
stewardess	flight attendant

As well as avoiding these biases, eliminate idiomatic phrases such as *give me the lowdown,* which can confuse non-local audiences. Another rule of thumb is to avoid mentioning age, race, ethnicity, disability, or gender unless it is relevant.

CONCISE BUSINESS MESSAGES

Well-constructed business writing is concise. It makes the point quickly with a minimum number of words. You can make sentences concise by using the active voice, shortening sentences, using simple words, and eliminating unnecessary words.

Strategies to Shorten Sentences

Short sentences have "punch" and are easy to understand. Long, complex sentences are difficult to follow and can be lifeless. In general, strive for sentences of about 10 to 20 words—shorter tends to be better. Shorten sentences by dividing long complex sentences into shorter sentences and by eliminating unnecessary words.

Often, writers create long sentences to show relationships. These long sentences can be subdivided and relationships explained with the use of transitional words such as *then, because,* or *however.* For example, compare the following sentences:

Long: Managers must not only find ways to get their own work accomplished, but they must plan and organize work for subordinates, motivate them, and follow up to ensure work is accomplished.

Divided: Managers must find ways to get their own work accomplished. *In addition,* they must plan and organize work for subordinates. *Then* they must follow up to ensure work is accomplished.

Sentences are often inflated by words that are unnecessary. When nominalizations, expletives, deadwood, and unnecessary prepositions are eliminated, sentences become shorter and clearer.

One way to shorten sentences is to **eliminate nominalizations.** Nominalizations are nouns made from verbs. To shorten sentences, change nominalizations into corresponding verbs. Here are some examples:

NOMINALIZATION	VERB
action	act
creation	create
detraction	detract
execution	execute
implementation	implement
nomination	nominate
service	serve
cancellation	cancel
come to an agreement	agree
make an observation	observe
make a decision	decide

Here is an example of a sentence with and without nominalization:

Nominalization: Johnson will provide representation for us.

Verb: Johnson will represent us.

A second way to shorten sentences is to **eliminate deadwood** or redundant words that add no meaning. The following are examples:

DEADWOOD	ESSENTIAL
absolutely essential	essential
at the present time	now
due to the fact that	because
in many cases	often
needless to say	(omit)
in the year of 2004	in 2004
whether or not	whether
serious crisis	crisis

A third way to shorten sentences is to **remove expletives** or dummy subjects in sentences. Below, notice how sentences are shortened when expletives are removed from sentences (expletives are italicized):

With: *It is* our expectation that this plan will be successful.
Without: We expect the plan to succeed.

With: *There have been* many times when we suspected theft.
Without: We often suspected theft.

With: *There is* seldom a case in which the ends justify the means.
Without: The ends seldom justify the means.

A fourth way to shorten sentences is to **eliminate unnecessary prepositional phrases.** Here are some examples of sentences with prepositions removed (prepositions are italicized).

Wordy: We are *in* discussions *about* your proposal.
Concise: We discussed your proposal.

Wordy: Your attention is requested *to* review the content *of* the enclosed contract.
Concise: Please review the enclosed contract.

Wordy: We are not *in* touch frequently enough *to* justify the added expense *of* a mobile phone.
Concise: We cannot justify a mobile phone.

When nominalizations, expletives, deadwood, and unnecessary prepositions are removed, you can replace many words with a few. Even seemingly short phrases can sometimes be simplified and shortened. Edit the following phrases to eliminate unnecessary wordiness:

PHRASE   **EDITED VERSION**

1. on a monthly basis _____

2. if conditions are such that _____

3. repeat it again _____

4. large in size _____

5. streamlined in appearance _____

6. in the final analysis _____

7. on the grounds that _____

8. with reference to _____

9. without further delay _____

10. subsequent to _____

Active Voice, Passive Voice, and "Be" Sentences

In terms of verbs, there are basically three kinds of sentences: active voice, passive voice, and "be" sentences. For most of your business writing, use the active voice. Using the active voice shortens sentences. It also makes the actor and the action clear to the reader. In addition, the active voice makes your writing action-oriented.

Sentences written in the **active voice** place the actor in the subject position followed by action verbs (run, act, organize, manage, blame, start, allow, etc.).

Active Pattern: Noun + action verb (+ noun or adjective)
Active voice: Billy refereed the ballgame.
Active voice: The store manager authorized those purchases.

In the active voice, the subject performs the action. In **passive voice,** the subject receives the action. Passive sentences always include "be" verbs. Here is a list of all eight "be" verb conjugations:

am
is
was
be
are
being
were
been

Note that the verb "have," and all its forms, are helping verbs as well. However, these verbs are not forms of "be;" the only forms of "be" are the eight listed above.

In addition to "be" verbs, passive sentences also include a past participle of an action verb:

Passive Pattern: Noun + "be" verb + past participle (+ noun or adjective)
Passive voice: The goal was reached.
Passive voice: A union strike was organized by Rob.

Notice that in passive sentences, the subject is not doing the acting, but rather, is being acted upon. In the first sentence above, the subject "the goal" does nothing; someone (we don't know who) is doing something to it—reaching it. In the second sentence, the subject "the union strike" does nothing, but is having something done to it: It is being organized by Rob. Overusing passive sentences will weaken your writing because most of your subjects aren't doing anything but, instead, are having things done to them: They are literally passive.

"Be" sentences classify. They always include "be" verbs, but no action verb follows. The "be" verb(s) is the main verb in the sentence. "Be" sentences can be concise and emphatic, but if you overuse them, your writing will become static because there is no action in these sentences. Here are a few examples of "be" sentences:

"Be" Pattern: Noun + Be Verb (+ Noun/Adjective)
"Be" sentence: Pirate is a lively German Shepherd.
"Be" sentence: Wendell was early.

As a general rule, use the active voice for most writing. However, you will find instances when passive or "be" sentences are preferable. Here are some guidelines:

1. **Use active sentences to tell who did what and to emphasize the doer of the action.**

   Michael participates in the program each spring.

   Dylan studied hard for the test.

   Rachel ate all of the ice cream.

   Most of the voters decided to choose the opponent.

2. **Use passive sentences to de-emphasize the performer of an action or when the performer is unimportant or unknown.**

   The dance recital was canceled.

   Cars were wrecked.

   Mistakes were made.

   Taxes were raised.

3. **Use "be" sentences to describe and classify. However, use these sentences sparingly.**

   The concept is difficult.

   We are in last place.

   The brochures are colorful.

   Our lawyers will be at the hearing.

Several sentences are provided below. Identify each sentence as active, passive, or "be," and rewrite passive sentences into active forms.

ACTIVE, PASSIVE, OR "BE"?

1. The invoice was itemized by Holden.

2. A letter of transmittal is enclosed with the report.

3. We are delighted with the weather forecast.

4. Sam has given his two-week notice.

5. All résumés will be carefully read.

6. Your business is important to us.

7. An application would be greatly appreciated.

8. Nancy's workload has been too light.

9. A proposal was written by our accounting group.

10. This computer system is too complicated.

SUMMARY

Many factors contribute to effective business communication, such as organization, concise language, the "you" attitude, and attention to style. While keeping all these factors in mind may seem overwhelming, at least initially, remember that many of the elements overlap, and others rely on everyday common sense. Learning to incorporate these elements into your business communication will result in effective messages.

CHAPTER 4

Instructing and Persuading

A study examining what "real managers do" indicates that effective managers spend most of their time communicating. They engage in exchanging information, paperwork, socializing, politicking, and interacting with outsiders (Luthans, Hodgetts, & Rosenkrantz, 1988). To be successful in these activities, managers must know how to instruct and persuade. The purpose of instructing is to provide information without necessarily attempting to influence attitudes or change minds. The purpose of persuading is to change attitudes or motivate to action. In this chapter, we first outline strategies for instructing, and then we provide guidelines for persuading. These chapters provide the foundation for developing written documents and speeches.

INSTRUCTION

Business organizations constantly exchange informative messages. These messages instruct others in procedures, guidelines, and directions. They also explain and provide general knowledge. Here are a few examples of instructional messages.

- Reviewing quarterly production figures
- Describing work techniques
- Illustrating how to use new software
- Describing marketing concepts
- Introducing new policies
- Briefing upper management on your unit's performance

When you consider all the instructional messages sent in organizations, clearly one of the primary jobs of managers is informing. The study cited at the beginning of this chapter indicates that effective managers, those who have the highest levels of production and the most satisfied employees, spend 44 percent of their time in routine communication. In the following example, one manager describes routine communication.

> I'll have to admit that the secret to getting things done in my department and keeping my people happy is simply to keep them informed. I constantly get on the phone to them or stop by their desks to tell them or ask them what's going on. I also keep up with my paperwork and meet all my report deadlines. (Luthans, Hodgetts, & Rosenkrantz, 1988, p. 68)

Of the time spent exchanging information, 45 percent is spent with subordinates; the remainder of it is spent with superiors (15%), others outside of the organization (23%), and others inside the organization (17%). Thus, effective managers must become experts in instructing a variety of people over a wide range of topics.

You have undoubtedly had some managers who were either effective or ineffective at instructing. Some provide no information. Others write or talk over your head. The most helpful understand your needs and present information in ways you can easily comprehend.

When instructing as a manager, you should first determine the information's usefulness and relevance to your audience. As is suggested in chapter 2, consider the knowledge level and interests of members of your target audience. Present information at a level that is understandable, but not boring. For example, if you are discussing a new benefits program for your organization, consider which parts will be relevant to your audience members and how much they want to know. As you plan your message, think of ways to most meaningfully convey information. For example, depicting the typical benefits for a family of four or for a single employee would help employees visualize a benefits program.

How Tos and Whats

There are two classes of instructional messages—how to do something and what something is. "How To" instructional messages provide specific procedures, techniques, or tactics for doing something in a *nuts and bolts* fashion. For the previous example about benefits, describing application procedures would be a "How To" message. Breaking the process down into step-by-step procedures and illustrating how to complete an application would clarify the process. Often, when you are providing "How To" messages, visuals are very helpful. You might consider using depictions, illustrations, and, for presentations, hands-on demonstrations.

"Whats" provide listeners with an opportunity to gain new knowledge or general understanding. Begin with the information that the typical listener knows and add to that knowledge. Here, you might use analogies to *connect the familiar to the unfamiliar.* For example, compare accounting with balancing a checkbook. Discuss how deposits and withdrawals in a checking account are similar to credits and debits. *Move from simple to complex or from basic to higher-level knowledge.*

Organizational Patterns

You may organize an instructional message in several different ways. After you've gathered information and analyzed your audience, choose the organizational pattern that makes it easiest for the audience to understand your message. Consider the following organizational patterns.

Big Point First

Managers like to get to the point. In many cases, when writing letters and reports, make the big point or state the purpose and conclusions early. Similarly, when delivering a presentation, get to the big point early. What do you expect audience members to know as a result of your message? If you expect them to know elements of a new benefits plan, tell them up front. Stating such expectations will help them prepare their minds to receive your message. Stating the big point first clarifies your purpose and makes the best use of your audience's valuable time.

Chronological

The chronological pattern presents events in the order in which they occur. A narrative of events is perhaps the most interesting chronological pattern. For example, to show how a person moves from interviewee to employee, you could tell your own story of interviewing, entering, and being socialized into the organization. Or you might discuss a production process from beginning to end. In another example, you might demonstrate how to use a computer from beginning to end: turn the computer on, boot and run the program, and shut the computer down. In another instance, you might identify current conditions and then show how chronological events led to these conditions.

Spatial

A spatial pattern organizes main points by proximity or location. Sometimes your audience will understand your subject more clearly if you organize subtopics by physical proximity. You can organize an instructional presentation spatially in many ways. One option is to categorize those geographical regions with which people identify. For example, analysis of market differences might be presented by breaking the United States down into northern, southern, eastern, western, and mid-western regions. A second way is to identify by specific location. The offices in a corporation, for instance, might be represented by the city in which they are located. A third option is to define topics by physical location. For example, you could give a tour of your facilities or provide a map that locates the names of offices and buildings in your corporation.

Categorical

Topics and categories divide information into subgroupings. Categories organize subtopics and make it easier for the audience to remember; three points are easier to remember than 15 separate sub-points. When possible, use topics and categories that are familiar to your audience. When introducing the budget, for example, discuss the allocations by departments, operations, and other categories already used by the organization. When discussing personnel in the organization, use traditional job classifications. If you use categories or topics that are unfamiliar to your audience, define them and justify their use.

Cause–Effect

A cause–effect pattern helps explain how one thing or action produces something else. When making cause–effect claims, justify the relationship with observations, statistics, or other reliable support. Remember that you can attribute many different causes to one effect. For example, suppose you claimed that turnover was caused by high stress within the organization. How will you substantiate your claim? Is it just a conjecture on your part? Do you have the opinion of an expert who has thoroughly examined the organization? Have you gathered information from a variety of sources? What if someone else in your audience has evidence that the cause is low pay instead? Be prepared to justify your claims with acceptable evidence.

Comparison/Contrast

One method you may use to promote learning is to compare or contrast something new to something with which the audience is already familiar. First, summarize characteristics and then compare or contrast. For example, a natural way of instructing about new software is to compare and contrast it with old software.

PERSUASION

A colleague of ours was hired by General Motors to help engineers improve presentations. The company had occasionally failed to get contracts with the United States government, not because of a poor product, but because engineers didn't adapt persuasive arguments to government administrators. The engineers had presented their proposals from an engineer's perspective. Our colleague helped engineers to identify the concerns of government administrators, to design arguments that addressed concerns, and to use "layman's" language. The result was more government contracts for General Motors.

As the above example illustrates, your success in business will depend upon your ability to persuade. Persuasion enables you to influence others to have a desired attitude toward you, your proposal, and your product or service.

This chapter discusses the basic elements of persuasion: (1) gain attention, (2) build rapport, (3) establish your credibility, (4) simplify your message, (5) appeal to emotion, (6) appeal to logic, (7) use action verbs and concrete nouns, (8) overcome objections, and (9) adapt your message to audience attitude.

Gain Attention

The most important element of any persuasive message is attention. If a reader or listener does not pay attention to your message, your persuasive attempt has failed. Individuals will not act on a message until they notice it.

Commercial advertisers understand the importance of gaining attention and therefore create advertisements that shock, amuse, or entertain to make consumers focus on a product or service. You should similarly design messages to gain the attention of your audience. The following guidelines can help you get the audience to "tune in" and "stay tuned."

Make the Attention-Getter Prominent

Advertisers on the Internet grab users' attention with color, movement, or flashing symbols. Similarly, you need to put your attention-getter in a place your reader or listener will notice—at the beginning of the document or speech.

Some communicators begin persuasive appeals prior to a document or speech. For example, direct mail advertisements put enticing messages on the envelope that promise "savings," "peace of mind," and "free vacations." Once the reader opens the envelope, other attention-getters are provided to motivate the individual to read on.

Use an Attention-Gaining Device

There is no limit to attention-gaining devices. In addition to using interesting words, writers attract attention with colors, unique fonts, figures, and pictures. Speakers catch the eye of the audience with movement and visuals. For example, one speaker started a speech by burning a $1,000,000 check and remarked that his company had just lost that much money. Another speaker, addressing motorcycle workers, had a friend drive him into the seminar room on a motorcycle.

Both writers and speakers can grab attention by finding creative and original ways of saying things. Here are some common means used to attract attention.

ATTENTION-GAINING DEVICE	EXAMPLE
Startling Statement	You'll be among the 10 percent of the people in this company who will die in the next two years . . . unless we change our safety procedures.
Analogy	One prominent author indicates that to be successful in business, you need to learn to "Swim with the Sharks."
Proposal or Solution	This company needs to immediately eliminate 15 percent of its employees.
Quotation	"The woods are lovely, dark and deep, but I have promises to keep . . ." This quotation from Robert Frost applies to our company. We have a commitment to our employees.
Bargain	You may now receive accounting software at half price with *free* service and training.
Story or Anecdote	Last week, a manager angrily yelled at one of our bank tellers in front of customers and employees. Everyone was shocked. The teller was humiliated.
Free Sample	When you volunteer, you'll receive one month's supply of allergy medicine free.
Rhetorical Question	How would you like to make at least $60,000 your first year after graduation?

Tell the Audience What It Will Gain

To gain and retain audience attention, you must answer one major question posed by the audience: "What's in it for me?" Sometimes your opening statement answers this question. For example, the first line in a letter might offer a free month's subscription to your e-mail service.

If the first statement does not tell what the audience will gain, one of the next sentences should. Persuasion requires a "you attitude." Think of how your audience will respond to your message. Explain how your audience will benefit from your message by gaining more money, an easier life, more comfort, an increased ability to perform, and more.

Build Rapport

Members of your audience will respond more positively to your message when they hold you in positive regard. You can initiate positive feelings by expressing positive regard for the audience and by emphasizing similarities between you and your audience.

Express Positive Regard

You can express positive regard in what you say and how you say it. Find ways to compliment or affirm your audience. You might congratulate audience members on accomplishments, acknowledge contributions, or express satisfaction with your association with the audience. Your tone and style should be warm.

Don't Say: I've been assigned to speak about possible investments for the firm.
Do Say: Congratulations to all of you for making investment decisions that have benefitted this firm, and therefore, all of us. This message will help you to learn about more potentially beneficial investment opportunities.

Emphasize Similarities

You can build a sense of "oneness" with your audience by talking about things you have in common and by expressing yourself in terms familiar to your audience. *Find those aspects of life experience that you have in common with the audience, and refer to*

them in your introductory remarks and throughout your message. You might identify common interests, attitudes, acquaintances, experiences, aspirations, or even limitations. For example, you could refer to a common interest in a popular sports team, a united desire for company success, your friendship with a popular member of the community, your desire to make contributions to a cause valued by audience members, or your difficulties in managing time—a concern shared by the audience.

"Talk the talk" of your audience. Use language that the audience uses and talk the way the audience talks. For example, with engineers, you might use logical, analytical, and technical language and present the information in a formal manner. With farmers, you might use more "folksy" lingo, incorporating agricultural terms and adopting an informal style.

Establish Your Credibility

When you present your message, your audience will wonder, "Why should I listen to you?" In other words, what makes you a credible source to discuss this subject? If your audience members don't believe you are credible, they'll lose interest. Enhance your credibility by referring to sources, organizing your message, and eliminating errors in word choice and grammar.

Refer to Credible or Well-Known Sources

If your audience recognizes you as an expert, you probably won't have to establish your credibility. However, even well-known experts can enhance their credibility by outlining credentials and accomplishments. When you need to establish credibility, do so by making reference to the following.

SOURCE OF CREDIBILITY	EXAMPLE
Studies	A study of 457 managers demonstrates that managers who have the most satisfied and productive employees spend more time communicating with them (Luthans, Hodgetts, & Rosenkrantz, 1988)
Success	We have increased productivity for hundreds of companies by as much as 110 percent.
Experts/Competent Professionals	Our engineers, who have won national awards for product design, have designed another winner.
Successful Personalities	The type of visionary leadership that we advocate was used by General Schwartzkopf in Desert Storm and by Lee Iaccoca in revitalizing Chrysler.
Your Expertise	For several years, I've helped many companies like yours improve sales performance.
Your Company's Strengths	Our company is *the* major supplier of network equipment, software, and integration services for broadband, multiservice networks.
Testimonials	Here's what one customer, who pays us over $50,000 a year, has to say about our service—"This service has saved our company tens of thousands of dollars."

Also, the *way* your message is presented can either lose or establish credibility. You'll lose credibility if your message is unorganized, full of grammatical errors, inappropriately worded, and illogical.

Organize Your Message

Alternately, a well-crafted message can enhance your credibility. Research on persuasion shows that, even when you are unknown to your audience, your ability to influence is enhanced when you're organized. Highlight and draw attention to your main points by bolding, underlining, or using a visual that summarizes main points. Structure the message in a logical order.

Eliminate Errors in Word Choice and Grammar

You lose credibility when you make errors in word choice and grammar. If, for example, your audience consists of computer experts and you incorrectly use a computer term such as RAM (random-access memory), your audience will question your expertise. Effective persuasion requires familiarity with and correct use of the language of the profession.

Glaring grammatical and mechanical mistakes suggest lack of expertise and education. For example, some of the most important persuasive documents are letters of application and résumés. You quickly lose your ability to impress an employer when those documents have grammatical or spelling errors. In fact, most employers won't seriously consider applicants who have grammatical and spelling errors in letters of application and résumés. Similarly, other persuasive documents and speeches shouldn't contain these errors.

Simplify Your Message

The audience should understand your message quickly. Major government contracts have been lost by companies such as General Motors, not because of product quality, but because the audience could not understand the writing and presentations of engineers. These engineers failed to write and speak in language that government employees would understand.

Your message should be simple and quickly grasped. Avoid complex sentences that are difficult to follow. Keep your paragraphs short—usually no more than eight lines. Provide transitions to make your text flow smoothly.

As a speaker, practice the presentation to make it flow smoothly without pauses and nonfluencies such as "ah" or "uhm." Speakers who speak fluently are much more persuasive than hesitant or slow speakers.

Appeal to Emotion

At times, particularly when sympathetic to your message, the audience can be moved by a message designed to elicit emotion. Emotional messages consist of vivid examples and language that creates either positive or negative feelings in your audience.

Use Vivid Examples

Vivid examples use concrete language to describe an emotion-arousing scene. For an emotional appeal to work, your audience must be able to visualize your description—the more specific, the better. For example, a safety supervisor in a manufacturing company distributed the following account to his subordinates to convince them to follow safety procedures.

> A maintenance technician servicing a plastics extrusion press failed to turn on the safety mechanism. He crawled into the cylinder used to press plastics into molds. Unexpectedly, the piston was activated. Within two seconds, the technician's body was smashed by the piston into the bottom of the cylinder, and his body fluids pumped into plastic molds. He didn't know what hit him.

This example evokes vivid visualization and strong emotions and will undoubtedly influence audience members to follow safety procedures. Similar concrete examples can be used to create positive emotions.

Use Emotion-Arousing Language

You can make your arguments appeal to emotions with the use of selected words or phrases. For example, to help your audience feel positively toward your proposal, use words or phrases that elicit positive feelings such as "winner," "highly profitable," and "a home run!" Similarly, promote negative emotions by using words such as "scheme," "risky," "dog," and "loser." Selected words can be used to generate a multitude of emotions including "pride," "hope," "fear," and "disgust"—all of which can move the audience in a desired direction.

Appeal to Logic

Most business audiences are convinced by logic. Logic relies on reasoning and evidence to convince. For business audiences, you need to know how to develop sound reasoning and solid proof to support arguments.

Novice writers and speakers often draw conclusions or make assertions without providing support in the form of either reasoning or evidence and, at the same time, expect the audience to accept the conclusion. For example, one manager wrote that a company needed overtime to meet production quotas. However, he didn't back his claim with any evidence to show that production quotas couldn't be met within normal work hours. The reader was left to wonder how the manager arrived at the conclusion, and the request was denied.

Adequate and sound logic requires the presentation of both clear reasoning and solid evidence. The following presents two types of logical reasoning: evidence-based reasoning and causal reasoning.

Evidence-Based Reasoning

Evidence-based reasoning arrives at a general conclusion based on specific examples, facts, or statistics. To be convincing, there must be (1) acceptable evidence, (2) a conclusion or argument, and (3) a relationship (often assumed and unstated) between the evidence and the conclusion. The following example shows the basic structure of evidence-based reasoning.

Evidence: A survey shows that "taking care of children" was the reason given for 40 percent of employee absenteeism.

A Conclusion: Establishing an on-site daycare center will reduce absenteeism.
Relationship Between Evidence and Conclusion: Parents desire an on-site day-care center; they will put their children in the center; and, when they do, they will miss work less often.

For the reasoning to be convincing, an audience must accept the entire argument, including the relationship (either stated or implied) between the evidence and the conclusion. Two basic questions could be raised about the reasoning.

First, is there adequate evidence to support the conclusion? In the previous example, a critical audience might question the meaning of the survey. When employees indicated that their reason for absenteeism was "taking care of children," what did that mean? Does children refer to pre-school, grade-school, or high-school children? Do parents miss work to find child care, to take children to the doctor, or to attend school activities?

Second, are the (implied) relationships between the evidence and the conclusion justified? In the previous example, there was no evidence provided to show that parents actually desire an on-site daycare center, that they would put their children in such a center, or that the daycare center would lead to less absenteeism. Skeptical managers may require more evidence from additional surveys, and from other companies that have daycare centers, before they believe the conclusion is justified.

Use Causal Reasoning

Causal reasoning asserts that one event occurs because of another event. You might predict a future event based upon a current event. For example, you could argue that because interest rates increased, stock prices will decrease. Such a statement is based upon the history of the relationship between interest rates and stock prices. Or you might explain a current event by a previous event. For example, you might say that increased turnover in your company is the result of better occupational opportunities, increased competition, and higher wages.

To be believable, causal reasoning must be based on commonly accepted knowledge or acceptable evidence. For example, claiming that stock price declines are the result of civil wars in Turkey would probably not be believed without considerable reasoning and evidence. However, commonly accepted explanations for stock declines, such as a decline in consumer confidence, would be more acceptable, especially when accompanied by results of surveys that show such a decline in consumer confidence.

Both persuaders and audiences should view cause–effect claims with care. Simply because one event follows another does not necessarily mean that one is the cause of the other. For example, Jill Bard, a car salesperson, might see a sales increase just after the company had a company party and conclude that the sales increased because of the party. Such an occurrence might be considered **anecdotal**—a single event that may or may not indicate a causal relationship. Other factors could have contributed to the sales increase, such as a major local event attracting more people to the area. Jill might be in a better position to claim causation if a review of sales records showed that after each company social there was a consistent increase in sales. Even then, she might examine other contributing factors, such as the time of year.

Use Evidence

Logic is based on both reasoning and evidence. To be sound, reasoning must be accompanied by believable evidence. The most concrete form of evidence is a fact. A **fact** is something that is directly observed. For example, an eyewitness might say, "I saw Mike in the office the day the money was taken." A fact is most acceptable when it is confirmed, and not contested, by more than one witness.

Statistics summarize facts, usually in a numerical form. Statistics can be a highly credible source of evidence. However, statistics can easily be misused, and both persuaders and receivers of persuasions should examine statistics to determine their validity. You should determine whether the data was gathered in an unbiased way by a credible source and whether there's sufficient data from which to draw an inference. For example, to either support or contest that Mike took the money from the office, hourly time sheets and financial records could be summarized in a statistical form to show a pattern of work activities and monetary losses. To be believable, such statistics should be accurate and supplied by an unbiased source.

An **inference** is a general conclusion drawn from evidence, usually in the form of facts or statistics. The more facts available to support the inference, the more likely the inference is to be true. For example, because Mike was in the office the day that the money was taken, you might infer that Mike took the money. If more eyewitnesses indicate that Mike was the only person in the office that day, the inference that Mike took the money is strengthened. If contrary evidence is presented to show that others, in addition to Mike, were in the office, then the inference that Mike took the money is weakened. Sometimes experts are asked to render an opinion about the validity of an inference. To be credible, experts should be authoritative, accurate, fair, and unbiased. For example, an expert on theft might comment on the likelihood that Mike took the money.

Avoid Fallacious Reasoning

Many persuaders use counterfeit reasoning. Upon first appearance, the counterfeit arguments may seem logical. However, an examination will reveal that the arguments are fallacious; they provide inadequate evidence, poor reasoning, or irrelevant facts. Being aware of common types of fallacies can help you to avoid using them and to critically evaluate others' reasoning. The following are common types of reasoning fallacies.

Straw Man The opposition is depicted as having a weak argument (the straw man) that can easily be attacked and defeated. Politicians often use this form of reasoning. For example, Republicans characterize Democrats as believing that "big government can run your life better than you can," and Democrats depict Republicans as "caring only about the rich." Both straw man arguments are oversimplifications that don't adequately represent the other party's position. However, such arguments are used frequently and effectively. When audiences accept the characterizations, it's easy to argue against either party. Pointing out the inadequacy of the straw-man argument—that it distorts or inadequately represents the position—can defeat such an argument.

Unwarranted Generalization You make an unwarranted generalization when you draw a conclusion from little or no evidence. For example, you might argue that, because you were ill after being in class, air-borne bacteria caused the illness. You would need more evidence of other student illnesses to justify your conclusion.

Bandwagon   You encourage your audience to jump on the bandwagon because everyone else has. For example, a vendor might argue that a company should buy a certain brand of accounting software because "all the other companies are buying it." There are two ways to critique this argument. The first is to find out whom the persuader means by "everyone." The second is to show that even though an idea might be good for others, it may not be good for you. Examine the idea based on its effect on you.

Diverted Attention   There are numerous ways for a persuader to divert attention from the issue at hand. One way is to launch a personal attack on the person who presents the idea, rather than the idea itself. For example, a manager might propose new management practices for improving relationships with employees. However, instead of examining the merits of the proposal, critics might focus the discussion around the manager's inexperience in dealing with employees. Another way to divert attention away from the issue is to get the audience to focus on an irrelevant issue. For example, a business leader who is accused of misappropriating company funds might refuse to answers questions about wrongdoing and instead discuss the future of the company.

Limited Options   Available choices may be over-simplified. For example, a manager might argue that there are only two approaches to managing overtime: the one she proposes and the one currently used. With some investigation, thought, or brainstorming, more options could certainly be generated.

Misplaced Authority   Non-expert celebrities are often used to endorse products. For example, drug companies might use an actor who plays the character of a doctor on television to promote a drug to relieve pain. While the actor may be popular, he or she is not an expert on drugs. A critical listener would realize that the actor's testimony is no more valid than that of any other non-expert person.

Action Verbs and Concrete Nouns

Action verbs create a sense of dynamism, excitement, and movement. Incorporate action verbs like act, join, buy, organize, stimulate, jump, expand, and acquire. Avoid "be" verbs that simply classify, such as am, are, were, and was.

One common shortcoming of novice speakers and writers is that they tend to communicate in abstract rather than in concrete terms. They make a general point but fail to support the point with a specific example. Audiences are quickly bored by abstract words because such words do not call forth visualizations. Concrete nouns, such as mansion or Ferrari, create more vivid pictures than do more abstract nouns, such as house or car. Compare the mental pictures created by the following descriptions.

Abstract: Employment interviews make people nervous.
Concrete: Your cold, clammy hand reaches out to nervously shake the interviewer's hand. Dry vocal cords can hardly utter your name. Sweat glistens on your forehead.

The abstract example above is difficult to visualize. The concrete example is easily visualized because it includes descriptive concrete nouns and action verbs.

Overcome Objections

Some people negatively view objections to their arguments. However, the success of your persuasive message may depend upon your ability to identify and overcome objections.

A common sales technique is to attempt to close the deal and, when the customer is not ready to commit, to identify and overcome objections. For example, an automobile salesperson might ask a customer if he or she is ready to sign a contract. When the customer says no, the salesperson asks for objections, such as price or color. This information is what the salesperson needs to pave the way to closing the deal. He might respond, "If I can lower the payments, get the car in the right color, and include air conditioning, can we do business today?" If the salesperson gets a favorable response to his question, he could then proceed to use concessions, persuasion, or negotiations to overcome objections.

Ideally, the objections to a proposal should be identified early, and the persuasive strategies to overcome them should be included in the persuasive message. This requires some advance research and strategic planning. The information about potential objections might come from consumer research, questionnaires, interviews, or customer focus groups. The basic question that is asked is "What would prevent my audience from accepting my proposal?" Once objections are identified, you can develop persuasive strategies to overcome objections and make the proposal appealing to the audience.

Adapt Your Message to Audience Attitude

Members of your audience will have different attitudes toward your proposal. Prior to designing your message, analyze your audience using the guidelines in chapter 2. Some audience members may be in favor of your proposal. Others may have mixed feelings or may be opposed to it. Approach your persuasive strategy differently based on audience attitude.

The audience that is in favor of your proposal   When your audience favors your proposal, (1) show how you are similar to your audience, (2) appeal to both emotion and logic (3) present only your perspective, and (4) get to your point quickly and ask for commitment. For example, when selling accounting software to an interested organization, you might refer to accounting experiences you have in common (similarity), tell a vivid story about problems your software addresses (emotional appeal), and ask a manager to sign the contract.

The audience that will have neutral or a mixture of attitudes   You should not expect to get a highly favorable response from a neutral audience. You may change some attitudes, but the audience isn't likely to immediately accept your proposal. For this type of audience, (1) gain attention and establish credibility, (2) identify similarities, (3) use primarily logical appeals, and (4) present both sides of the argument, overcoming potential objections.

For example, if you're selling accounting software to a neutral audience, you might begin by talking about the strength of your company and other companies that have adopted the software (credibility). Then discuss accounting experiences you might share (similarity). Outline the kinds of accounting problems encountered by the organization, and describe how your product handles those problems compared to other software from competing companies (logic). Summarize the strengths and weaknesses of your software, answering concerns about weaknesses (overcome objections). Then encourage the audience to raise additional objections, which you overcome before asking the audience to sign a contract.

The audience that will view your proposal unfavorably   You should probably expect relatively minor changes in the attitudes of an audience that reviews your proposal unfavorably. Follow the guidelines for the neutral or mixed audience. In addition, (1) summarize the audience's perspective and (2) ask for change or commitment, only after presenting reasoning and evidence. For example, when selling the accounting software to a skeptical audience, you might summarize the audience's criticisms of the software early in your message. Then, after presenting reasoning and evidence in favor of your accounting software, you might ask the audience to try the software free of charge for 30 days.

SUMMARY

Effective instruction requires planning and organization. The more simply and clearly you can present the message, the more easily your audience will understand. *Choose the organizational pattern that best fits the information. Avoid using more than one organizational pattern.* Starting with a topical pattern and switching to a cause–effect pattern might make it difficult for the audience to follow your logic.

The most successful persuasion attempts occur when you adapt to audience characteristics and perspectives. If you can see yourself through the eyes of the audience, you'll know its stance toward your proposal and can adapt your message to address its concerns. Some audiences will require you to establish your credibility, some will prefer logical appeals, and others will prefer emotional appeals. Spend time gathering information on your audience, and make your persuasive message fit the issues most important to the audience.

CHAPTER 5

Visual Aids

Visual aids can dramatically improve both presentations and documents by focusing an audience's attention. When speakers and writers use visuals effectively, they increase the likelihood that the audience will pay attention, be persuaded, and remember the material. However, when too many visuals are used, or they're used ineffectively, they could actually hinder the communication. In this chapter, we discuss how to design visuals and their use in business documents and oral presentations.

DESIGNING VISUAL AIDS

To be most effective, the visual should support your main points, enhance visual understanding, and present information clearly and effectively. To help you design visuals, we discuss the following guidelines: (1) keep visuals simple, (2) make visuals legible, and (3) convince with brief visual information.

Keep Visuals Simple

The first key to making effective visuals is **simplicity.** Visuals should get the point across quickly and concisely so that an audience's attention is quickly shifted back to the speaker or the document. To keep visuals simple, follow the guidelines listed below, and note how they are applied in the example.

- Present only the essential information necessary to make sense.
- Write descriptive phrases or words instead of sentences.
- Try to use only four to five words per line.
- Condense information to present it efficiently.
- Limit each visual to one topic and a limited number of subtopics.

Don't do this: long, detailed, and wordy

Gain the Attention and Interest of the Audience

1. Make the first statement interesting by using quotes, startling statistics, stories, or humor.
2. Build movement into your introduction by coming out in front of the lectern for the introduction and by moving when displaying the visual aid.
3. Use visuals to focus attention by showing an overhead transparency or object.

Do this: short, simple, and condensed

Gain Attention

1. Make an interesting statement.
2. Move around the lectern.
3. Use visuals.

Don't do this: too much detail, unnecessary legend, and labels outside figure

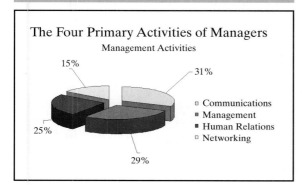

The Four Primary Activities of Managers
Management Activities

Do this: present only necessary information with labels inside figure

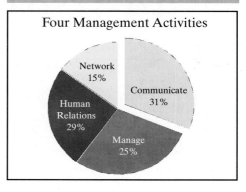

Four Management Activities

Make Visuals Visible and Legible

A legible, or easily read, visual helps quickly focus attention on desired concepts. A sloppy visual may not only be distracting, but also makes you look unprofessional. As you choose visuals, keep in mind the principles of legibility and ease of comprehension described below.

1. **Use size to communicate.** In presentations, every listener should easily see the visual. Use the following guidelines.

   - **Use different sizes of fonts for emphasis.** Larger, **bolder,** or *italicized* fonts indicate key information.

   - **Use large print on charts.** Print should be at least two inches high, and larger if the viewing distance is greater than 64 feet or if you want the statement to have special impact.

   - **For projections, use large fonts and big pictures.** Have typewritten print enlarged at a copy service. Ensure that all pictures, slides, and objects are large enough to be seen from the back of the room. Use at least a size 18 font on a computer-generated document; most of the time, you should use a 24 to 44 font so that the audience can easily see your visual. Use even larger fonts for emphasis.

This is how font sizes appear on a printed page.	This is how the projected font size appears from the back of the room.
18 font 24 font **36 font** **44 font**	18 font 24 font 36 font 44 font

2. **Use color for added interest and emphasis.** Use bright colors that are bold enough to be seen. Avoid too many colors (more than four) on any single visual aid. Templates in computer graphics programs, such as PowerPoint, provide excellent color combinations. Safe colors are darker-colored print on a light background. The following are good color combinations.

   FOR PROJECTIONS
   - black on white
   - dark red, dark green, or dark blue on white
   - black on yellow or orange

FOR CHARTS
- black, blue, and red on a white background

3. **Use neatness and a professional appearance to clarify and enhance your credibility.**

    Except for special effects, do **not** hand-print visual aids.

    Avoid using too many typefaces at once. For example, unless you have a good reason, avoid using **bold** and *italics* and <u>underlining</u> and <u>*shadow*</u> together.

4. **Print in easily read type.** Upper-case letters slow down your audience. Don't print too much material in upper case because capital letters are hard to read. Compare the following.

    Few capitalized words make text fast and easy to read.

    More Capitalized Words Tend To Slow A Reader Down.

    ALL CAPS ARE MOST DIFFICULT TO READ AND SHOULD BE USED SPARINGLY, PRIMARILY FOR TITLES.

Convince with Graphs and Visuals

Design your visuals to convey information quickly and convincingly. The variety of aids is limited only by your imagination. In oral presentations, you can use objects, people, pictures, posters, slides, movies, videotapes, charts, graphs, demonstrations, or clothing as visual aids. In documents, you can use tables, graphs, drawings, photographs, and charts.

In business communications, managers often present summary statistics and concepts in graphs and charts because they organize and quickly communicate much information. Computer graphics programs create these visuals quickly and easily. When possible, use graphs to summarize information because they convey it much more quickly and meaningfully than do raw numbers. We show how graphs might best be used for summarizing different kinds of data. First, compare the following raw data with a line graph.

Avoid this: raw data that is hard to visualize

Do this: this line graph quickly visualizes data. Use **line graphs** to display trends over time.

Comparison of Sales in
Eastern and Western U. S.
(millions)

Years	East	West
1995	2.10	3.62
1996	2.25	3.85
1997	2.52	3.25
1998	2.33	3.45
1999	3.52	2.70
2000	3.75	2.82

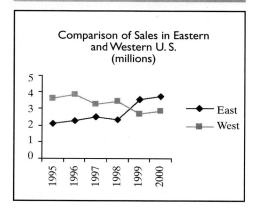

Comparison of Sales in Eastern
and Western U. S.
(millions)

Use **pie graphs** to show percentages of the total.

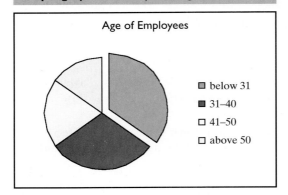

Use **bar graphs** to compare values.

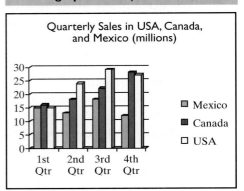

Use **graphs or pictures** to demonstrate relationships and processes.

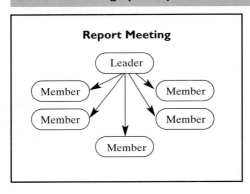

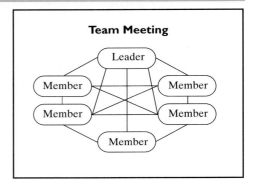

Visuals in Business Documents

Within business documents, use visual aids to help readers understand concepts and detailed analytical information. The following techniques will help ensure that the visuals will be effective.

Include only relevant information. Information added as padding may confuse readers and influence them to question the reliability of the report.

Use visuals to emphasize important points. Readers may miss important points made in the written text. A visual summary of points draws attention to them.

Refer to the visual at the beginning of the discussion. Your readers will refer to your visual as they read your text.

Summarize key points from the visual within your text. Don't assume that the readers will arrive at the same conclusions you want them to; you must point out *why* the visual's information supports your point. Discuss the visual in greater detail if the information or visual is complex or if the reader doesn't have the background to easily grasp the concepts.

When a graphic is one page or less, do not divide it between pages. Sometimes necessary explanation of your visual takes so much room that there is not enough space left on the page to fit your graphic. In this case, continue with your text, and place the graphic at a logical paragraph break on the next page or in an appendix.

Include graphics only within the middle sections of the document, not in the introduction or conclusion.

Label tables with Roman numerals; label figures with Arabic numbers. Follow with a period and a descriptive title. The label and title can appear either double-spaced above the graphic or double-spaced below it. If the report contains only one graphic, the label and title are optional. Note that *in this chapter* since we use graphics to illustrate and provide accompanying descriptive text, we don't label the graphics as you would in a business document.

This is how Roman numeral headings appear for table headings.

Table III. Monthly Sales Goals **Table IV.** Monthly Sales Volume

This is how Arabic headings appear for figure headings.

Figure 1. Summary of Sales Strategy **Figure 2.** The Sales Process

Make sure headings accurately describe the content of the visual. While headings should be as brief as possible, they should also give the audience a clear idea of the content in the table.

Provide enough information for the reader to identify all the content in the visuals. Label all information, and provide explanatory footnotes to clarify.

Using the following table adapted from Luthans and Larsen (1986, p. 169), we illustrate the important elements of a graphic in written text.

Roman numerals followed by a period

Double-space between heading and table

Heading describes table content

Labels describe column content

Table III. Directly Observed Activities of Managers in the Natural Setting

Activity	Mean frequency[a]	Relative percentage
Exchanging routine information	32	20
Processing paperwork	26	16
Decision making/problem solving	19	11
Planning/coordinating	17	10
Socializing/politicking	16	10
Interacting with outsiders	15	9
Monitoring/controlling performance	12	7
Motivating/reinforcing	8	5
Training/developing	6	4
Staffing	6	4
Managing conflict	4	2
Disciplining/punishing	3	2

Rounded to whole numbers to limit detail

Footnote adds description of table content

[a] Trained participant observers often checked more than one category.

VISUALS IN ORAL PRESENTATIONS

Visuals not only help you present information effectively in presentations, but they can help you organize your presentation as well. The visuals for the following presentation were developed in PowerPoint. They demonstrate how you might organize each part of the presentation. Note that each slide has the same *appearance, logo,* and *font* to give the slides a sense of coherence.

1. Give the presentation a title and, if desired, a subtitle that describes content and entices interest.

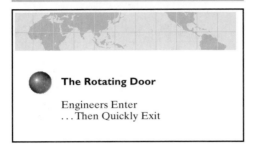

2. Provide a purpose statement and an outline of the main points.

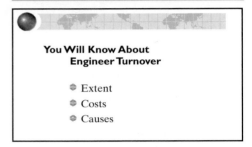

3. Provide information that establishes your credibility.

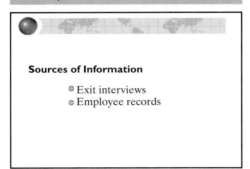

4. State your main point and provide support material.

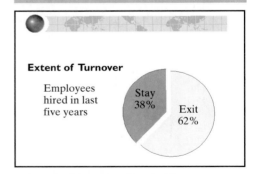

State and support main point.

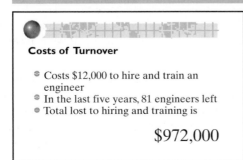

State and support main point.

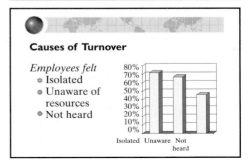

5. Provide reminder of your purpose and a summary of main points, including key support material.

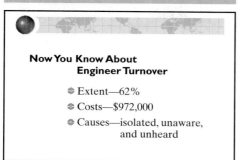

6. Provide a memorable closing statement that summarizes your message.

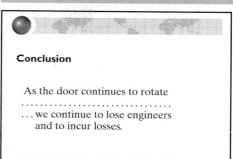

As you progress through the presentation, you want the audience to focus on what you discuss as you discuss it. One method of showing transition is an "add-on" aid; simply add each subpoint to the visual as you discuss it. Presentation software provides animation that allows you to add-on using a variety of features including "appear," "fly-in," and "dissolve." You can also add sound to announce transitions. The following are two methods for signaling transitions.

Make bold or change the color of text to show transition.

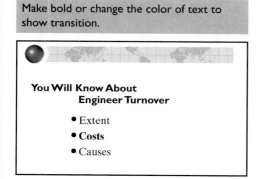

Progressively reveal text to show transition.

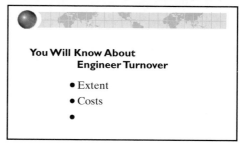

Present Visuals Effectively

Speakers often devote considerable effort to preparing visuals only to find that they don't have the desired impact. Like any other part of the presentation, effective use of visuals requires planning and practice. The following suggestions will help you present visuals effectively.

The purpose and main points should guide the presentation. Speakers should first outline their presentations and then design visuals to support main points. **The speaker should take center stage, not the visuals.** A living, moving, and expressing human being, on balance, has more ability to communicate and influence than visuals. Don't allow the visuals to be the primary focus of the presentation.

When possible, choose projection equipment that allows a lighted room. The brighter the room, the more likely the audience will be to stay alert and keep its focus primarily on you. Overhead projectors and modern multimedia projectors allow projection in lighted rooms.

Limit visuals to the most important information. Too many visuals may result in a **loss of control** over the presentation. You want to avoid reading a pile of overhead transparencies. When you are focused on reading visuals, audiences will focus on the screen or on handouts instead of you. As a result, your ability to express yourself is limited—you are held captive by visual aids!

Use visuals to reinforce what you want the audience to remember. Audiences focus their attention on, and remember best, what they see.

Reveal the aid only when it is used in the presentation. Put your visual away when you're finished. Displaying the aid before and after you use it in your speech will distract the audience.

Speak loudly when you use a visual aid. The visual competes for the audience's attention and adds background noise. Raising your voice helps the audience hear you over the machines and focus on what you have to say.

Face the audience when using the visual. Addressing a screen or a chart not only looks absurd, but it also reduces your contact with the audience and makes it harder for you to be heard.

Avoid passing visuals around during your presentation. Passing around examples or pictures draws the audience's attention away from the presentation. Either make the visual large enough to show to the audience as a whole, or pass it around after your presentation.

Practice using visual aids before the presentation. Prior practice will help you smoothly integrate displaying the visuals while you talk. Make sure that you know how to operate overhead projectors, video recorders, and other electronic equipment that you plan to use.

Arrive early to check out the equipment and set it up correctly. Avoid the embarrassment of fumbling with equipment in front of the audience.

Take the time to place and arrange visual aids before starting the presentation. The audience will allow you the time to get settled.

If you use a pointer or magic marker, put it down when you are finished using it. Don't distract the audience by unwittingly using a pointer as a baton or a marker as a juggling ball.

SUMMARY

If you follow the suggestions we've discussed, visual aids will work *for* you rather than *against* you. Remember to use visual aids as support, to keep them simple, and to present them effectively. Visuals can make the difference between a good and an excellent presentation or report. They can enliven a boring topic, help others understand complex processes and ideas, and convert fleeting ideas into memorable messages.

CHAPTER 6

The Writing Process

In writing, the final product is what counts. You may find that you are not satisfied with the final product but might not know how to improve it. This dilemma is like the golfer who consistently slices or hooks the ball but does not know why. Often, the solution is found by reviewing and practicing the basics. In this chapter, we review the basic elements of the writing process that can help you generate a better-written product. The elements of the writing process are planning, writing, revising, and proofreading (see Figure 6.1).

PLANNING

The planning step of the writing process includes forming ideas, analyzing the audience, specifying the purpose, and selecting style and tone.

Form Ideas
Begin writing by forming the ideas that you wish to write about. These ideas may be dictated by the situation, such as a request for information, or they may be created by

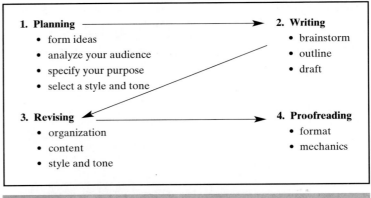

FIGURE 6.1 The Writing Process

you for, say, an internal proposal. Some ideas will not be born without time given to stimulation and incubation. Learn how others in similar circumstances approached the topic. Opening yourself to ideas through reading and discussions, as well as pondering or "sleeping on it," can help you develop ideas.

Analyze Your Audience

Who will be in the audience, and how do you want to influence them? Will you address a large, general audience, just a few individuals within your organization, or a single customer? What are their interests? How much information will they need? What are their attitudes toward you and the topic? What kind of relationship do you now have, and what kind of relationship do you desire? Answers to these questions will help you form appropriate ideas and shape them to address the concerns developed by your analysis.

Specify Your Purpose

When your ideas are formed and your audience defined, you are ready to specify your purpose. Your purpose is what you want the audience to know or do upon reading your document. One way to specify the purpose is to complete this formula: "Upon reading this document, my readers will know or will be inclined to do. . . . " Once defined, the purpose should influence every other decision you make about the document.

Think about your reason for communicating. Doing so will help you narrow your purpose so you're not simply throwing information at your reader. If you don't take the time to narrow your focus, then your reader must cull through the document to determine a purpose and separate the important information from the superfluous. Your reader may not only give up in frustration, but the interpretive nature of communication means that your reader may not receive the information that you deem most important.

Select a Style and Tone

Selecting a style and tone means planning how you will express yourself in writing. In general, business writing should be simple, direct, and conversational. However, in light of your audience and purpose, you should consider a number of issues. First, you want your writing to establish or maintain an appropriate relationship with your reader. If you are writing to your superiors, you might acknowledge the relationship by saying, "We suggest a new policy." For subordinates, you may want to be more directive: "All employees will comply with the new policy." When the relationship is not important, you might eliminate reference to relationship: "This is the new policy."

Second, when you think about the audience, should the writing be formal or informal? Official business documents normally use formal language: "The terms of the contract shall be executed in accordance with the provisions outlined herein." Letters and memos to acquaintances are more informal: "Charlene, I can't imagine why you are interested in this contract."

Third, do you want to imply a friendly or distant relationship? For acquaintances, you want a friendly tone: "Jack, I missed you on the 18th green Friday." When stating policies or reprimanding, you probably want distance: "The organization's progressive discipline procedures require a three-day suspension."

Fourth, consider what is culturally and legally acceptable in an organization. Sexist and racist language must be avoided. Some topics may be taboo. Also, match the climate of the organization, whether it is formal or informal.

WRITING

After the initial planning, get your ideas down on paper. Brainstorming, outlining, and writing a rough draft are all possible elements of this process. For shorter documents, such as letters and short memos, certain steps may not be necessary or may be combined with others. For example, if you're writing a simple, direct letter, such as an inquiry, you may not need to brainstorm or outline. However, after creating a rough draft, you would still want to edit for content, tone, organization, punctuation, and grammar.

Brainstorming

Sometimes ideas are easier to work with when they are written out. Simply write ideas down without criticizing them—brainstorm! Don't worry about word choice, content,

or organization. Just write out the major concepts you want presented in the document. This step is important for longer documents, such as proposals and recommendation reports. You may be able to combine brainstorming with outlining if your ideas flow logically. However, you may wish to get all your ideas down on paper before eliminating any of them. In this instance, brainstorming and outlining are separate, distinct steps. Whatever process you adopt as a writer, you should recognize that there is no single "right" or "best" way to create a successful document. You should do what works best for you.

Outlining

Now arrange your ideas in a patterned, logical order. In this stage, you may want to take advantage of computer programs designed to help writers organize ideas in an outline form. You might also use the layout of other documents that have been created for similar purposes in your organization as guides. Organize the main ideas logically to make the outline easy to follow. Main headings (introduction, body headings, and conclusion) will go under Roman numerals (in formal outline format), while sub-headings and paragraph topics will be preceded by capital letters and Arabic numerals, respectively. If you've never outlined a document before, try it. You may be surprised at how easily your rough draft will flow once the outline is completed. The following is an example of a correct outline format.

THE INTERVIEW PROCESS
    I. Introduction
   II. Research the Company
        A. Company websites
        B. Company publications
        C. Company employees
  III. Dress for Success
        A. Business suit
        B. Minimal jewelry and make-up
  IV. Be Prepared
        A. Categories of interview questions
        B. Questions for the interviewer
        C. Extra résumés and copies of references
   V. Conclusion

Drafting

The next step is writing a rough draft to flesh out the outline. The goal of this draft is to provide clear explanations for each idea and to support claims. Because this is only a rough draft, be more concerned about getting ideas down on paper than writing them perfectly. At this stage in the process, don't agonize over whether your spelling, grammar, and punctuation are correct. Concentrate on larger issues, such as organization (helped in large part by your outline), content (ask yourself whether assertions are supported by facts), and writing style (determined by the relationship you have or wish to establish with your reader).

REVISING

Some professional writers believe that more time should be spent on revision than on any other element of the writing process. As one business professor said when asked how he managed to write so well, "Oh, I don't know. After the 20th revision, it just sort of flows." Even very skilled writers revise their writing numerous times before they're satisfied. However, other writers revise very little on paper because most of their revision takes place in their heads before they write it down. Either way, revision must take place in some form, or you will always submit rough drafts as final copies.

Although shorter documents like memos might not require revisions as extensive as longer documents, all first drafts will improve with revision. For both long and short documents, revise for organization, content, style, format, punctuation, and grammar.

Organization

First, ensure that the main point is clear: Have you told the reader what he or she needs to know or do? The big point should be placed in a prominent position, preferably at the beginning or end of the document. Examine how you've arranged your ideas. The overall organization of the document should make sense to the reader. Review for the following:

- **Are the main points easy to identify?** Do headings and topic sentences make it easy for the reader to follow your principal ideas?
- **Are all points that are relevant to the purpose covered?** Are irrelevant points eliminated?
- **Is the overall organization of main ideas sequential and easy to follow?** Do you use the appropriate organizational pattern, such as a chronological, spatial, or alphabetical sequence? Do you have enough headings to guide the reader?
- **Are paragraphs logical, well organized, and easy to follow?** Are paragraphs organized to support topic sentences? Are relevant concepts included and irrelevant concepts deleted? Are paragraphs short and easy to read?

Content

Second, consider the content: Is the material in the document up-to-date and accurate? Review the document for the following:

- **Are ideas clearly explained and claims adequately supported?**
- **Are sentences logical, simple, clear, and complete?**
- **Does the content clarify what the reader is supposed to know or do?**

Without adequate and appropriate content, all other considerations become pointless, so be sure that your document says what it needs to say.

Style and Tone

Third, carefully review the style and tone of the document: Is it appropriate for your relationship with the audience?

- **Is the writing conversational?** Are sentences simple and easy to read?
- **Is the tone appropriate for the nature of the message and the relationship with the audience?**

Remember to use a conversational style for all your business documents, even more formal ones like long reports. If you find that your sentences are confusing or somewhat vague and abstract, but you're unsure about how to sound more conversational, try this trick. Simply say out loud whatever it is you're trying to convey the way you would say it if your reader were sitting across from you. Then delete any colloquialisms or slang, and write it down.

PROOFREADING

All other considerations in the writing process that we've discussed so far will be for naught if you fail to proofread your document. Nothing will destroy your credibility faster than a sloppy, error-ridden document. And don't forget that you need to proofread after each revision your document goes through because you may have created new errors. Delay proofreading until larger revisions are complete. To successfully proofread a document, you should be familiar with rules of punctuation and grammar. Many word processing programs can aid your proofing with built-in spell-checkers, as well as grammar, punctuation, and style-checkers. By all means, use these programs; however, keep in mind that computer programs are not foolproof. Even the spelling programs miss words that are spelled correctly but used incorrectly. Hence, after using these word processing aids, you should visually proof for overall format and mechanics.

Format

Why is format so important if your content is good? When documents are presented to readers in the correct format, they appear more credible. Your use of correct format shows that you are aware of cultural norms in business, you respect those norms, and your respect extends to your reader. Using the incorrect format slows your reader down as he or she tries to decipher just exactly *what* your document is. Make sure you've used the correct format for your intended audience (memos for internal audiences and letters for external audiences, for example).

When writing longer documents, be sure to break up the text for your reader by supplying main headings and subheadings, if necessary. Be sure the headings are grammatically parallel and useful to your reader by providing an accurate description of the content within each section. Visually, your document should be easily scannable, with headings and subheadings consistently placed and sized. Making an effort to fulfill your reader's expectations about document format will reflect well on you as a writer and on your company as a whole.

Proof for the organization's preferred layout first. Ask yourself the following questions:

- **Do I have all the elements of the expected format for the document in question?**
- **Are my headings and titles accurate and descriptive?** Are they parallel? Are page numbers included? If references are included, are they correctly formatted?
- **Is the document visually appealing?** Have I used the right amount of white space?

Mechanics

Next, proof for mechanical writing errors by checking the following:

- **Punctuation.** Review your use of commas and your punctuation of compound sentences. Sophisticated punctuation-checkers on some word processors can identify various common errors; some of these programs may even be customized.
- **Spelling.** If possible, use a spell-checker on a computer. In addition, check your word usage and the spelling of names.
- **Sentence structure.** Ensure that you have complete sentences; avoid run-on sentences. Some style-checkers may have special subroutines to help you detect these problems.
- **Subject–verb and noun–pronoun agreement.** Avoiding linking plural forms with singular forms and vice versa. Most grammar-checkers have become particularly good at picking up these errors.
- **Numbers and word usage.** Be aware of the style guidelines for your organization. Some style-checkers will allow you to customize the computer program for checking numbers. Most style programs allow you to modify (or create) a list of troublesome words that they will then highlight in your document.

Many writers miss errors in their own documents. When possible, have someone else read your documents for errors. When that is not possible, you might try a number of methods to catch typos and other errors. Some people like to read hard copy. Others catch errors more effectively on computer screens. Reading the content out loud is effective for many people. You might even try reading the document backwards. After making corrections, reread the sentence or section to ensure that it reads correctly. In the final analysis, you must find a system that works best for you to eliminate errors.

SUMMARY

The writing process, when systematically approached, can result in an improved business document. First, a writer should think about what sorts of ideas belong in the document. Thinking about the audience, having a clear purpose, and aiming for an appropriate style and tone are important considerations during the planning stage. The writing stage consists of brainstorming, outlining, and drafting. Next (and often most importantly), revising for organization, content, style, and tone is sure to improve the document. The final step in creating a sound business document is to proofread for format and mechanics.

For some documents, such as proposals or audits, you may find more success if you follow each of these steps in succession. Other documents may require a less formal process, allowing you to combine steps or perform some of them simultaneously. However, if you concede the necessity of the writing process and give proper attention to it, you should be capable of creating a document that is complete, logical, and visually appealing.

CHAPTER 7

Letter Style and Format

One of the most frequently written documents in the business world is the letter. Company business letters, as opposed to memos, are external documents, meaning that they go outside the company; therefore, they represent the company and, no matter what the message, should do so favorably. Personal business letters are ones written on your own behalf, rather than on behalf of your company. In either case, the formatting guidelines in this chapter apply.

In chapter 8, we discuss letter content and organization, including discussions of appropriate tone for specific types of business letters. However, in this chapter, we give objective guidelines for letter format and the different parts of the letter. Appropriate format can be just as important as content because readers expect documents to be formatted in ways that are familiar and widely accepted. Failing to use these formats can alienate and confuse your reader. Having to determine the exact nature of your document slows down the reader, and, therefore, your message may not get the attention or reaction you desire. Employing acceptable formats shows respect for your reader and lends credibility to your writing.

PARTS OF THE LETTER

Business letters have standard elements that readers will expect to find. The generally agreed-upon parts to a letter include the letterhead or heading, the date, the inside address, the salutation, the letter text, the signature box, and optional notations. Because the conventions for letters are widely known, subtle (and some not so subtle) messages may be conveyed by altering the degree of formality within the various sections of a letter.

Letterhead or Heading

Most business letters are written on company stationery already pre-printed with company letterhead. However, sometimes you may need to write a personal business letter or one on your own behalf. A letter of application and some claims letters are two examples of personal business letters. If this is the case, you should not use company letterhead. Instead, create a personal heading, consisting of your street address, city, state, and zip code. In certain situations, you may want to include a phone number, though generally the address is enough.

Avoid abbreviations in your heading; spell out words such as Street, Avenue, and Road. You should, however, use P.O. Box for Post Office Box and the two-letter postal state abbreviation if you would like to abbreviate the state. You have the option of using either the postal state abbreviation or writing out the state name in full. The following examples show the proper format for personal headings:

1234 Elm Street   *67 Bayswater Avenue*
Riverview, OH 34567   *Dallas, Texas 76576*

Date

The next item to appear on a business letter is the date. If you're using letterhead stationery, this will be the first part of the letter that you'll need to provide. If you're using a heading, single or double space after the city, state, zip code line, and type your date. The date is best written one of two ways: month, day, comma, year, or day, month, year (no punctuation). The latter form is the convention for European and most other international correspondence, and the former is widely used in the United States. Here are examples of both:

June 26, 2000
26 June 2000

In order to maintain a professional and businesslike document, it is best not to use only numbers for the date (6/26/01).

Inside Address

The inside address is the name and address of the person or organization to whom you're sending the letter. It's best to send letters to individuals if possible. However, sometimes you may not know the name of an individual at the business to which you're writing. In this case, address your letter to the department or the company when that's the only information you have available.

The inside address is organized from small to big, or from most specific to least specific. In other words, begin with the person's name (smallest), move to position title, department, company name, address, city, state, and zip code (biggest).

On the first line of the inside address, type in a polite title, such as Mr., Ms., Mrs., Miss, or Dr., followed by the individual's first and last name. When you're not sure how a woman prefers to be addressed, use Ms., which doesn't imply a marital status. If the person's name is not gender specific (Chris, Pat, Terry), omit the polite title, and use only the person's first and last names. You may follow the name with a comma and the person's position title if that title is fairly short, such as Manager or Director. If the position title is long, such as Chief Executive Officer, put it on the next line.

Sometimes, you will write letters without knowing to whom to address them. If this is the case, put the department on the top line followed by the rest of the inside address. You may even have a situation where you will simply address the letter to an organization. The following are examples of inside addresses:

Ms. Judy Warman, Manager   *Chief Technical Officer*
Accounting Department   *Caprock Computing Services*
Family Service Association   *376 Broad Street*
456 Main Street   *Chicago, Illinois 38756*
Anytown, TN 56789

Salutation

The salutation, or greeting, should in most cases match the first line of the inside address. When addressing an individual, use the word *Dear*, followed by the polite title and the person's last name and a colon. (Note: A comma after the greeting is not appropriate in formal U.S. business letters, but is the norm for European correspondence. Hence, you can convey a certain intimacy and informality with the comma following the salutation to a well-known business associate.) Again, when unsure of the person's gender, use *Dear* and the person's full name with no polite title.

Dear Mr. Holden:

or

Dear Chris Perry: [with unknown gender]

When you are addressing several people, the accepted greeting is *Ladies and Gentlemen*, not *Dear Sirs* or *Gentlemen*. The latter greetings are old-fashioned, evident by the fact that they ignore the distinct possibility that some of the people in your audience will be women.

If you haven't used an individual's name, but have instead addressed your letter to a department or organization, use that in your greeting. For example, if the first line in your inside address reads *Customer Relations Department*, then your greeting will look like this:

Dear Customer Relations Department:

or

Dear Customer Relations Director:

An alternative would be to use only the organization's name and address in the inside address and put the targeted department or person in an attention line, followed by the greeting *Ladies and Gentlemen.*

Family Service Association
456 Main Street
Anytown, TN 56789

Attention: Accounting Department

Ladies and Gentlemen:

If you use an attention line, be sure that the greeting matches the first line of the inside address (if you don't use *Ladies and Gentlemen*) and not the attention line; otherwise, you've defeated the purpose of the attention line. However, if you know the person's name, it's simpler to put it in the inside address and use it in your greeting.

Letter Text

Most business letters have at least three paragraphs and oftentimes more. There are exceptions: letters of congratulations and those of thanks are often one or two paragraphs long because the writer wants to appear less formal and more personable.

Usually, your first paragraph will begin either very directly or with a sentence that provides a context for your reader, particularly if there has been previous communication between you and your audience. You should also provide a general-purpose statement, which explains why you are writing.

Your second and subsequent body paragraphs will provide the reader with specifics. Certain letters, such as inquiries and replies, benefit from lists in the body; these should be set off from the rest of the text and usually contain the most important information you mean to convey. Use fairly short paragraphs so that the letter will be easy to scan through quickly.

Your final paragraph will reiterate your purpose or sum up what you've said. Often in this paragraph, you will set up the next step in the communication process. Finally, most letters close with a goodwill statement, which does just what it implies—creates or maintains goodwill. However, it's not a good idea to thank someone in advance if you're asking for a favor of some sort. Instead, express appreciation for the reader's time and possible assistance.

Signature Box

The signature box consists of a complimentary close, your signed signature, and your typed signature. Several different complimentary closes exist for the many different relationships you have with your readers. Some informal closes would be *Cordially, Best wishes,* or even simply, *Best.* More formal closes consist of *Sincerely, Sincerely yours, Yours truly,* and *Respectfully.* Choose the close that is most appropriate for the relationship between you and your reader. Closes consisting of more than one word, such as *Yours truly,* should have only the first letter of the first word capitalized; all others should be lower case. Always follow the close with a comma. (Note that some European and most international business correspondence will have longer phrases and sometimes sentence fragments for the close. The important point here is that the current or desired relationship with the reader, as well as cultural norms, should dictate your style of complimentary close.)

After the close, use five spaces, leaving four blank lines between the close and your typed signature (you will type on the fifth line) to allow enough room for your hand-written signature. Don't use a polite title in front of your name, unless your name isn't gender specific; if this is the case, put the polite title in parentheses:

(Mr.) Pat Pynes

or

Patrick "Pat" Pynes

When you sign, sign only your name and not the polite title. Try to sign your letter conservatively; in other words, avoid flashy ink colors and illegible signatures. Follow your typed name with a position title only if you are writing on behalf of an organization. Don't use a position title for personal business letters. Here is an example of the signature box:

Sincerely,

Dylan Holden
Manager

Optional Notations

Various notations have evolved for signaling specialized information within business letters. These notations are optional, but can be very useful. The most common notations include the attention line, the subject line, the enclosure reference, the copy acknowledgment, and the typist acknowledgment.

Attention Line

The attention line is used infrequently because it is much easier to simply put an individual's name, or a department or company, in the inside address and match the greeting to it. However, you may wish to have your letter read by a specific individual who may no longer be in a certain position or department. In this instance, leave the person's name out of the inside address, and situate an attention line, double-spaced below the inside address and above the greeting. If the individual has moved to another position or department, he or she should still receive your letter. The following is an example:

Personnel Director
Personnel Department
Federal Express Corp.
New York, NY 39678

Attention: Ms. Sarah Quintanilla

Dear Personnel Director:

Subject Line

Some letters benefit from the use of a subject line to alert the reader to the subject of the letter. The subject line is appropriate only for certain types of letters, such as inquiries, claims, adjustments, replies, and sales letters. It would be inappropriate to use a subject line in letters of application or persuasive requests.

If you do choose to use a subject line, it's generally situated double-spaced, after the last line of the inside address, followed by a double space and a greeting. Type the word *Subject* or the abbreviation, *Re* (regarding), followed by a colon. The subject line is like a title; all of the major words are capitalized. Try to be as specific as possible in the subject line, without being wordy (eight to ten words or fewer), so that your reader will immediately know the exact nature of the letter, and so that it can be easily filed and retrieved for future reference. The following is an example of a subject line:

Subject: Request for Adjustment on Defective Software

or

Re: Hotel Reservations for 1993 Conference

Enclosure Reference

If you include anything for the reader along with your letter, type an enclosure notation, double-spaced, after your typed signature and along the left margin (no matter what format you use). If you are including only one item with your letter, the word "enclosure" is sufficient. However, you should list those items enclosed or include a number if you are sending more than one so that the reader knows if he or she has received the necessary documents. The following is an example of each form:

Enclosure

or

Enclosures: Pamphlet and Map of City

or

Enclosures: 2

Copy Acknowledgment

The copy notation is set double-spaced after the enclosure notation. This notation indicates the other people to whom the letter will also be sent. Often you will see the letters *cc*, meaning carbon copy, before the list of names; another option might be *xc* for extra copies or *pc* for photocopies because carbons are rarely used these days. If necessary, include the person's position title or department after his or her name. Here is an example of a copy notation:

cc: *P. Smitten, Personnel Director*
D. Castor, Sales Division

A special copy notation is sometimes used for confidential correspondence, when you receive a copy of a letter without the knowledge of the addressee. In this case, you would see the notation *bc*, meaning blind copy.

Typist Acknowledgment

If someone else types your letter for you, he or she may include his or her initials and yours double-spaced after the copy notation. Your initials will appear first, in all caps, followed by a colon or slash and the typist's initials in lower-case letters. This infor-

mation is particularly helpful for retrieving word-processed documents or filed letters in an office with a large typist pool. The following is an example of a typist notation:

> *GED:yh*

Subsequent Page Headings
Occasionally, you may need to go on to a second or third page. It is best if you can limit most letters to one page, but some letters, such as sales letters, often require several pages. If this is the case, you should include the person's or organization's name that appears in the inside address, a page number, and a date. The following forms are acceptable and should appear at the top of the subsequent page:

Mr. Henry Wood
April 7, 2001
Page 2

Mr. Henry Wood	*April 7, 2001*	*Page 2*
Mr. Henry Wood	*-2-*	*April 7, 2001*

LETTER FORMAT

There are three basic letter formats used in business, with modifications acceptable for all: full block, modified block, and simplified. Which format you choose often depends upon your audience. For example, most business letters employ the full block style since it is easy to type and read. However, you may choose to use a modified block style with indented paragraphs for more formal letters such as letters of application or persuasive requests. The simplified format is becoming more acceptable in the business community, but be aware that the appearance of the letter will be rather stark and impersonal, so it's best used in less formal situations.

Whatever format you choose, certain spacing guidelines will be standard. If you're using a personal heading, begin typing anywhere from 1 inch to 2 $1/2$ inches from the top of the page. Your side margins should be 1 inch to 1 $1/4$ inches, and you should leave at least an inch at the bottom of your page, though most letters will leave more space. If you're using letterhead stationery, type your date two to three spaces after the last line of the letterhead. With a personal heading, use double or single spacing after your heading and type the date.

Between the date and inside address, you may leave as many spaces as are needed to center the letter vertically on the page. It is not necessary to leave an inch at the bottom of the page on most letters. Simply adjust your spacing so that the letter doesn't appear top or bottom heavy.

Your inside address will be single-spaced, as will all sections in your letter, with double spacing between sections. Use a double-space after the inside address to the greeting, or to the attention and subject line(s). Use a double-space after the greeting to the first line of the letter; use a single-space within paragraphs, and a double-space between paragraphs.

Again, use a double-space from the last line of the letter to the complimentary close, aligning the close with the date, if you're using modified block format. From there, leave four blank lines (type on the fifth line), and type your name. This spacing will leave you enough room to sign your name.

Use a double-space after your typed name to the enclosure notation, a double-space from there to the copy notation, and a double-space again from there to the typist notation. These notations are always flush left, no matter what format you use.

Full Block

Full block is the most commonly used letter format because it is easy to both write and read. With full block, all sections (except the letterhead) are flush against the left margin, including the heading (with personal business letters), date, and signature box. Paragraphs are usually not indented. On the next few pages are several examples of full block format (see Figure 7.1 and Figure 7.4).

Modified Block

Modified block uses many of the elements of full block with some parts of the letter indented. In general, with modified block, everything is flush left, except the heading, date, and signature box. These should be situated a few spaces right of center, and all should be aligned together. Often, these paragraphs are not indented, but a further modification would be to indent paragraphs three to five spaces. This format looks more formal and is considered more traditional, so if these are the features you're looking for, then this format might be to your liking. The letters in modified block format are displayed on the following pages (see Figure 7.2 and Figure 7.3).

Simplified

This format is becoming more accepted but is still less commonly used than the full and modified block formats. The word *simplified* means the letter gets to the point without some of the formalities one normally associates with the business letter. This is one for-

XYZ CORPORATION
6789 Broadway Avenue
Kansas City, MO 34567
(234) 555-8910

}DS

July 20, 200-

}variable spacing acceptable

Ms. Melanie Wadsworth
Assistant Manager
ABC Publishing   }SS
234 Zoar Street
Mytown, NM 10111

}DS

Subject: New Brochures for Public Relations Department

}DS

Dear Ms. Wadsworth:

}DS

XXXXXXXXXXXXXXXXXXXXXXXXXXXXXXXXXXXXXXXX.

}DS

XXXXXXXXXXXXXXXXXXXXXXXXXXXXXXXXXXXXXXXXXXXXXXXXXXX
XXXXXXXXXXXXXXXXXXXXXXXXXXXXXXXXXXXXXXXXXXXXXXXXXXX
XXXXXXXXXXXXXXXXXXXXXXXXXXXXXXXXXXXXXXXXXXXXXXXXXXX
XXXXXXXXXXXXXXXXXXXXXXXXXXXXXXXXXXXXXX.

}DS

XXXXXXXXXXXXXXXXXXXXXXXXXXXXXXXXXXXXXXXXXXXXXXXXXXX
XXXXXXXXXXXXXXXXXXXXXXXXXXXXXXXXXXXXXXXX.

}DS

Cordially,

} four blank lines

Laura Blessing
Manager

}DS

Enclosure

}DS

LB:gek

FIGURE 7.1 Full Block Format with Letterhead

XYZ CORPORATION
6789 Broadway Avenue
Kansas City, MO 34567
(234) 555-8910
}DS

July 20, 200-

}variable spacing acceptable

Ms. Melanie Wadsworth
Assistant Manager
ABC Publishing   }SS
234 Zoar Street
Mytown, NM 10111
}DS
Subject: New Brochures for Public Relations Department
}DS
Dear Ms.Wadsworth:
}DS
XXXXXXXXXXXXXXXXXXXXXXXXXXXXXXXXXXXXXXXXX.
}DS
XXXXXXXXXXXXXXXXXXXXXXXXXXXXXXXXXXXXXXXXXXXXXX
XXXXXXXXXXXXXXXXXXXXXXXXXXXXXXXXXXXXXXXXXXXXXX
XXXXXXXXXXXXXXXXXXXXXXXXXXXXXXXXXX.
}DS
XXXXXXXXXXXXXXXXXXXXXXXXXXXXXXXXXXXXXXXXXXXXXX
XXXXXXXXXXXXXXXXXXXXXXXXXXXXX.
}DS

Cordially,

four blank lines{

Laura Blessing
Manager
}DS
Enclosure
}DS
LB:gek

FIGURE 7.2 Modified Block Format with Letterhead

} 1-2 1/2"

234 Blake Road
Yourtown, VA 12345
February 27, 200-

}variable spacing acceptable

Mr. Thomas Huffhines
Customer Relations Department   }SS
XYZ Company
678 Morris Avenue
Riverview, MA 91011
}DS
Dear Mr. Huffhines:
}DS
XXXXXXXXXXXXXXXXXXXXXXXXXXXXXXXXXXXXXXXXXXXXXXXXXX
XXXXXXXXXXXXXXXXXXXXXXXXXXXXXXXXXXXXXXXXXXXXXXXXXX
XXXXXXXXXXXXXXXXXXXXXXXXXXXXXXXXXXXX.
}DS
XXXXXXXXXXXXXXXXXXXXXXXXXXXXXXXXXXXXXXXXXXXXXXXXXX
XXXXXXXXXXXXXXXXXXXXXXXXXXXXXXXXXXXXXXXXXXXXXXXXXX
XXXXXXXXXXXXXXXXXXXXXXXXXXXXXXXXXXXXXXXXX
}DS
XXXXXXXXXXXXXXXXXXXXXXXXXXXXXXXXXXXXXXXXXXXXXXXXX
XXXXXXXXXXXXXXXXXXXXXXXXXXXXXXXXXXXXXXXXXXXXXXXXX
XXXXXXXXXXXXXXXXXXXXXXXXXXXXXXXXXXXXXXXXXXXXXXXXX
XXXXXXXXXXXXXXXXXXX.
}DS
XXXXXXXXXXXXXXXXXXXXXXXXXXXXXXXXXXXXXXXXXXXXXXXXX
XXXXXXXXXXXXX.
}DS
Sincerely,

four blank lines {

Lisa Wilson

FIGURE 7.3 Modified Block Format with Heading

} 1-2 1/2"

234 Blake Road
Yourtown, VA 12345
February 27, 200-

}variable spacing acceptable

Mr. Thomas Huffhines
Customer Relations Department   }SS
XYZ Company
678 Morris Avenue
Riverview, MA 91011
                      }DS
Dear Mr. Huffhines:
                      }DS
XXXXXXXXXXXXXXXXXXXXXXXXXXXXXXXXXXXXXXXXXXXXXXXXXX
XXXXXXXXXXXXXXXXXXXXXXXXXXXXXXXXXXXXXXXXXXXXXXXXXX
XXXXXXXXXXXXXXXXXXXXXXXXXXXXXXXXXX.
                      }DS
XXXXXXXXXXXXXXXXXXXXXXXXXXXXXXXXXXXXXXXXXXXXXXXXXX
XXXXXXXXXXXXXXXXXXXXXXXXXXXXXXXXXXXXXXXXXXXXXXXXXX
XXXXXXXXXXXXXXXXXXXXXXXXXXXXXXXXXXXXXXXX
                      }DS
XXXXXXXXXXXXXXXXXXXXXXXXXXXXXXXXXXXXXXXXXXXXXXXXXX
XXXXXXXXXXXXXXXXXXXXXXXXXXXXXXXXXXXXXXXXXXXXXXXXXX
XXXXXXXXXXXXXXXXXXXXXXXXXXXXXXXXXXXXXXXXXXXXXXXXXX
XXXXXXXXXXXXXXXXXXX.
                      }DS
XXXXXXXXXXXXXXXXXXXXXXXXXXXXXXXXXXXXXXXXXXXXXXXXXX
XXXXXXXXXXXXX.
                      }DS
Sincerely,

                      }four blank lines

Lisa Wilson

FIGURE 7.4 Full Block Format with Heading

WILKINS AUTO PARTS
5678 Poolville Lane
Ourtown, IN 12345
(567) 555-9101

}DS

May 17, 200-

}variable spacing acceptable

David Charles
Accounting Department   }SS
Loggins Distribution Company
Sometown, KY 20212

}DS

APRIL ORDER OF SIDEVIEW WINDOWS

}DS

XXXXXXXXXXXXXXXXXXXXXXXXXXXXXXXXXXXXXXXXXXXX
XXXXXXXXXXXXXXXXXXXXXXXXXXXXXXXXXXXXXXXXXX.

}DS

XXXXXXXXXXXXXXXXXXXXXXXXXXXXXXXXXXXXXXXXXXXX
XXXXXXXXXXXXXXXXXXXXXXXXXXXXXXXXXXXXXXXXXXXX
XXXXXXXXXXXXXXXXXXXXXXXXXXXXXXXXXXXXXXXXXXX.

}DS

XXXXXXXXXXXXXXXXXXXXXXXXXXXXXXXXXXXXXXXXXXXX
XXXXXXXXXXXXXXXXXXXXXXXXXXXXXXXXXXXXXXXXXXXX
XXXXXXXXXXXXXXXXXXXXXXXXXXXXXXXXXXXXXXXXXXXX
XXXXXXXXXXXXXXXXXXXXXXXXXXXXXXXXXXXXXXXXXXX.

}DS

XXXXXXXXXXXXXXXXXXXXXXXXXXXXXXXXXXXXXXXXXXX.

}four blank lines

William Scotts
Assistant Manager

}DS

Enclosure

FIGURE 7.5 Simplified Format with Letterhead

mat that is used almost exclusively on behalf of a company; rarely would you use simplified format for a personal business letter.

In keeping with the full block format, type the letter flush left. Use a double-space after the letterhead, and type the date. After the date, type the inside address, leaving off a polite title before the person's name. Instead of typing the greeting after the inside address, include a subject line (without the word *Subject*) in all caps. From there, use a double-space to the first line of the letter. Try to work the person's name into the first paragraph, usually by first name only. Obviously, this is a very informal, conversational format and can come in handy if you're unsure of an individual's gender.

Type the letter as usual, using the same spacing as discussed above. However, eliminate the complimentary close after the last line of the letter; instead, space five times, and type your name. Sign the letter in the space provided. See Figure 7.5 for an example of a letter using the simplified format.

SUMMARY

The standard parts of the business letter serve necessary functions, as can the optional parts of the letter, depending upon the situation. Business writers should be familiar with the three most common letter formats: modified block, full block, and simplified. Choosing one format over the other two reflects the type of message conveyed and the intended writing style. Letter style and format are important considerations in business letters. Using commonly accepted formats for your letters will lend credibility to your writing and will reassure your readers of the care you've taken in creating them.

CHAPTER 8

Types of Business Letters

Business letters serve many functions. Because the content and style of these letters can determine their effectiveness, you should become very familiar with the different types. Although there are many specific types of letters, a handful of general categories may be used to classify them: (1) direct and good news, (2) bad news, (3) goodwill, and (4) persuasive letters. Letters may be organized in one of two basic ways: deductively or inductively. In either case, your task as a writer, and as a representative of your company, is to consider the reader's point-of-view at all times. When your message is neutral or positive, your letter may be organized deductively. In other words, begin with a direct statement about the purpose of the letter. However, many business letters are by nature negative, such as refusals to inquiries or negative adjustment letters. If this is the case, you should use an inductive method of organization, employing a buffer and always maintaining a positive tone, no matter the message.

Tone is directly related to the style and the language that you choose to use. With the exception of formal reports, business documents should in general be written in an informal, conversational style. In most cases, avoid jargon and long, pretentious words unless your reader expects them. Most business writing is scanned; long paragraphs, sentences, and words tend to slow down a quick assessment of your message. In keeping with a conversational style, feel free to use contractions; write as you would speak at your best. Do not, however, use bad grammar, slang, or obscenities.

Another way to improve your overall tone is to remain positive throughout by avoiding any unnecessary negative wording. Look for negative words and phrases in your letter, and rephrase them positively. Even in bad-news letters, such as refusals, you should phrase your message as positively as possible. In the business world, you don't want to risk alienating others, many of whom are current or potential customers or associates. When writing a personal business letter that may potentially offend your reader (such as a claims letter or refusal), remember that you're more likely to gain satisfaction or retain goodwill by using positive wording throughout your letter. If you can remember the most important element of letter writing, you should avoid any major pitfalls: keep the reader in mind at all times!

DIRECT AND GOOD-NEWS LETTERS

We put these two types of letters together because good-news letters, such as positive replies to requests and positive adjustments, follow much the same pattern as other direct letters. The most common direct and good-news letters are the inquiry, the routine claims, the positive reply, and the positive adjustment.

In general, these letters are organized along similar lines. First, you will begin directly by including a statement of purpose in your introductory paragraph. (Sometimes, however, you may want to begin with a statement of goodwill followed by your purpose statement.) Next, you will provide details in your body paragraphs. All of these letters often employ lists within the body to guide the reader to the most important information. Such lists may consist of questions, answers, or detailed information. The list should be set off from the rest of the text by a double-space before and after and should be indented. Your final paragraph will set up the next step in the communication process, express appreciation, and perhaps include a response date and reason, depending on the type of letter.

Inquiry

There are two ways to write letters of inquiry, and the one you choose depends upon your audience and the nature of your request. Many inquiries ask for information that the reader is more than happy to supply because he or she stands to benefit. These letters are direct and to the point. However, you may find yourself in a situation where you're asking a favor of the reader; he or she will have to take time out of a busy schedule to collect whatever information you need and send it to you. The reader in this situation doesn't directly benefit from answering your letter. You will probably want to soften the request with goodwill statements, an explanation of the importance of a response, and a sincere expression of appreciation. The following are guidelines for writing effective inquiry letters.

1. If necessary, begin with a statement of goodwill—this is often a compliment to the company or to its goods or services.
2. Provide a general purpose statement. For inquiries in which the reader will benefit, this can be your opening sentence. Your purpose sentence should be stated in general terms; provide details in the body of the letter.
3. Use a polite tone; don't be demanding, or your letter might never get a response.
4. Provide specifics in your body paragraphs, using a list to draw attention to the most important part of the letter. Arrange your list in descending order of importance; in other words, put your most urgent question first, and end with your least important.

5. If the reader is doing you a favor by responding, indicate how important the information is and why. Doing so will motivate the reader to answer your request promptly.
6. Your list should follow a few guidelines: (1) Be grammatically and structurally parallel. If you begin with questions, use questions throughout; if you begin with phrases, use them consistently. (2) Include only one idea in each item on your list so as not to overwhelm your reader. (3) Don't include requests that you can fulfill yourself. (4) Be clear and precise; don't make your reader puzzle over your request.
7. Provide a response date and a reason as to why you need your request fulfilled by such a time.
8. You may want to include a statement of goodwill in your final paragraph, even in those letters where the reader will benefit from responding. Without this goodwill statement, the letter may sound clipped and demanding.
9. Set up the next step in the communication process.
10. Express appreciation for the reader's time.

See Figures 8.1 and 8.2 for letters of inquiry.

Direct Claims

Claims letters ask for an adjustment for defective merchandise and poor or faulty service. Claims letters are more difficult to write than most inquiries because they are negative by nature. If you're motivated enough to sit down and write the letter, then you're probably fairly angry and upset. However, it's never a good idea to write an angry, abusive claims letter. You might feel temporarily vindicated, but you will eventually calm down and feel foolish. A calm, positive tone will always get better results than a hostile one.

Realize that most companies reply favorably to claims letters; most of the time, it's simply not in their best interest to respond negatively. However, if your situation is unu-

THE OPTICAL STORE
5012 Main Street
St. Louis, MO 33110

January 18, 200-

Mr. Bob McQueen
Sales Director
Bausch & Lomb, Inc.
1399 3rd Avenue
Seattle, WA 71936

Dear Mr. McQueen:

| background information purpose statement | In the December 25 issue of <u>JAMA</u>, you ran an ad for fashion Bausch & Lomb extended-wear lenses. Please send me information about these lenses; I am interested in selling them to my patients. |

specific details

Many of my patients have astigmatisms and have difficulty wearing lenses that are comfortable for longer than a few hours at a time. Also, several patients have requested deep colors, including purple and solid black lenses.

lead-in to list

Could you please answer the following questions for me?

list of questions

1. Do these lenses have at least a 40 percent water content?

2. How much would the lenses cost compared to standard lenses during a year's time?

3. What sort of guarantee do you offer?

goodwill statement; response date and reason

I have always felt comfortable prescribing your products to my patients. Please respond by February 14 so I can place an order before my supply of sample lenses runs low.

Yours truly,

Dr. Cara Simpson

Dr. Cara Simpson

FIGURE 8.1 Sample Letter of Inquiry

2658 50th Street
Bismark, ND 89076
February 24, 200-

Customer Service Department
Quincy Sports Equipment
4500 Desert Ridge
Cincinnati, OH 45277

Ladies and Gentlemen:

background
information
purpose
statement

Please send me information about your Softsides Thermal Knee Supports. My tennis coach has suggested that I gather some information about different types of knee supports, and you may have what I've been looking for.

specific
details

I have had problems with my right knee, and I might have to give up tennis unless I find the right support. I need a knee brace that gives moderately firm support, is flexible, and reduces swelling.

lead-in to
list

I would appreciate your answering the following questions:

list of
questions

• Are these supports recommended by doctors and athletic trainers? I am specifically interested if tennis trainers have recommended them.

• Do these supports reduce the shock experienced when playing on hard court surfaces such as clay and cement?

• How do these supports retain therapeutic body heat?

• What is the warranty on the supports?

response
date and
reason

Please reply by March 10 because I wish to practice before my next tournament scheduled on March 30.

Sincerely,

Joella Galindo

Joella Galindo

FIGURE 8.2 Sample Letter of Inquiry

sual, you may need to take a more indirect, persuasive route (to be discussed later in the chapter). For most claims letters, follow these guidelines:

1. Begin with a general statement describing the problem and making your request. Be sure to *specifically* state your request in this first paragraph. Remember, this is a **deductively** organized letter.
2. In the body of your letter, provide details to clarify the problem. If a product is defective or broken, be specific and precise in describing the defect. Give the reader any information that might help in expediting your adjustment, such as model numbers, serial numbers, copies of warranties, sales slips, and date and place of purchase.
3. Be clear about what you would like to have done: a replacement, a refund, or an apology. Be reasonable in your request; don't expect a refund on a product that you've used routinely for some time.
4. Maintain a positive tone throughout, no matter what your personal feelings in the matter. However, you should also attempt to sound confident of receiving what you request; avoid an apologetic tone.
5. Close courteously, perhaps by offering a statement of goodwill. If you've never been disappointed by this company in the past, there's no reason to assume that you will be this time. Let your reader know when you need to hear back and why.

Figures 8.3 and 8.4 are examples of direct claims letters.

Positive Reply

Responding positively to inquiries, whether they be sales orders or requests for information or action, is easy and pleasurable. Because you convey good news, you can follow a direct method of organization.

1. Indicate in the first paragraph that you are fulfilling the reader's request. In some cases, such as with acknowledgment of order placements, it is appropriate to thank the reader for his or her letter.
2. Remember to stay focused on the reader and not on the benefits gained by the company.
3. In the body of the letter, provide specifics. These will differ based on the type of reply. For order acknowledgments, let the reader know when the shipment can be expected, and provide any specifics about payment that the reader may need to know. Also, alert the reader to any new products that you know he or she may be interested in. If you're fulfilling a request for information, answer the reader's questions in the order in which you received them, using a list for increased readability. Include any additional information that the reader might find relevant and helpful.
4. Close by offering further communication and expressing appreciation.

See Figures 8.5 and 8.6 for examples of positive reply letters.

MUNCY
TOOL
COMPANY
5446-A Humphrey Road
Lubbock, TX 79456
806-789-5643

April 17, 200-

John Lodge, President
Airfreight Lines, Inc.
27908 Elm Drive
New Orleans, LA 45367

STEEL PIPE DELIVERIES

description of problem; specific request

John, over the past three weeks, deliveries of steel pipe to my company have arrived late. I have spoken with several of your drivers and a line-haul dispatcher but have not received a clear reason for these late shipments. Would you please look into these delays and get back to me?

specific details

All of my inbound freight must arrive as scheduled because we operate on a just-in-time inventory schedule. Any overdue shipments create a materials shortage, resulting in assembly downtime and excessive production expenses. I simply cannot afford late deliveries.

request

I would appreciate your looking into the matter for me. I'm curious as to why the shipments have been late, but even more importantly, I want problems cleared up so that the shipments arrive on time. In addition, if a representative from your company would notify us as to the status of all future shipments, we might be able to make acceptable adjustments in the production department.

goodwill statement; response date and reason

I have been doing business with your company for many years and have always been satisfied with the service that you have provided. My next shipment is due on May 15; please contact me within two weeks.

Justin Hayward, President

FIGURE 8.3 Sample Direct Claims Letter

76989 Avenue Y
Apartment B
Harlingen, TX 78551
October 31, 200-

Mr. Bill Tucker
Tucker's Garage
1515 MacArthur Road
Mission, TX 78572

Dear Mr. Tucker:

description
of problem;
specific
request

The afternoon before my wife and I drove from Harlingen to Dallas, our car's air conditioner failed to cool well. I brought the car to your garage where your serviceman charged me $65 (receipt enclosed) to add Freon to the air conditioner. The next morning, halfway through our trip, the air conditioner failed again. I request a refund of the $65 charge.

specific
details

When we arrived in Dallas, after a very hot, uncomfortable ride, the head serviceman at Robinson Chevrolet examined the air conditioner. He said that during the service we had received from your establishment, a cap was left off one of the tubes at the lower level, allowing Freon to drain out. After adding more Freon, the Robinson Chevrolet serviceman replaced the missing cap; we returned to Harlingen in a cool car.

goodwill
statement;
request;
response date

In the past, I have been pleased with your service. I have an appointment with you for routine maintenance in mid-November. I know you have a reputation for being fair, and I look forward to receiving my $65 refund in time to use for my November's servicing.

Sincerely,

Ken Bennett

Ken Bennett

Enclosure

FIGURE 8.4 Sample Direct Claims Letter

DEXTER SHOE SOURCE

1345 Central Drive
Dallas, Texas 76044
1-800-345-7689

October 8, 200-

Mr. Victor Sondreggor
3240 Hill Avenue
Lubbock, Texas 79407

Dear Mr. Sondreggor:

indication
that the
reader's
request will
be fullfilled

We are so pleased that you have enjoyed the shoes you ordered through our mail order catalog. Your fax was forwarded to the Service Department, which is working right now to fill your latest order and to send you another catalog, as you requested.

specific
details

Our soft-leather Dexter men's model "Rugged" is built especially for customers who do a lot of walking. This shoe has been through rigorous testing, and it has proved to be a favorite with people like you who walk a minimum of a few miles a day. You'll be pleased with the design because we have the endorsement of the American Podiatric Society, which oversees the design of all our shoes.

goodwill
statement

Thank you for choosing soft-leather Dexter. You should have your shoes and our Fall catalog within a week. We wish you many more miles of comfortable walking in these good-looking shoes.

Yours truly,

Dianne Anderson

Dianne Anderson
Sales Supervisor

FIGURE 8.5 Sample Positive Reply Letter

AMERICAN PHILLIPS CORPORATION
1511 Main Street   New Haven, CT 06711   (290)393-4012

July 20, 200-

Ms. Irene Locke
8301 McRae Drive
Orlando, FL 59814

Dear Ms. Locke:

thanking the reader —

Thank you for your letter of July 4 and your order for additional office supplies. We always look forward to hearing from you.

specific details —

To confirm your order, the following lists the items we plan on shipping to you:

1. one dozen blue ball-point pens (model 53)
2. five dozen legal pads (model S-39)
3. one desk pad set (model D-8)
4. two steel file cabinets (model U-3051)

description of new product line —

I would like to point out that our new line, the Executive Power Products, will be available in the next few weeks. I will send the catalog describing these products to you as soon as possible.

goodwill statement; offer for further communication —

You can expect the office products you have ordered to arrive within a week. The order will be packed and sent via UPS in a few days. Again, thank you for your order. If I can be of further service, please call me. My extension is 234.

Sincerely yours,

Gail Estevez

Gail Estevez
Customer Service Representative

FIGURE 8.6 Sample Positive Reply Letter

Positive Adjustments

Whenever possible, try to respond favorably to claims letters by giving the reader what he or she requests. Obviously, it's bad for business to absolutely refuse a customer's request for action. Even if you can't fully comply with the customer's request, you can attempt to soften the blow by offering some sort of compensation. However, when it's possible to respond favorably, follow these guidelines:

1. Immediately state your willingness to comply with the reader's request. Maintain a positive, courteous tone by thanking the reader for his or her letter. However, avoid a submissive tone peppered with repeated apologies.
2. In your body paragraphs, describe what you will do to honor the reader's claim. Your tone is important; you want to sound helpful without sounding overly apologetic. Yet you want to avoid sounding as though you somehow blame the reader for the problem (even if you think that's the case). If you feel that the reader was in some way responsible for the problem, provide a non-threatening, objective account of how you believe the problem occurred. This explanation can ensure that there is no repetition of the event.
3. Close by indicating the next step in the process, whether yours or the reader's.
4. Re-sell the company by reminding the reader of your positive adjustment and by expressing appreciation for the customer's continued patronage. Don't apologize again, but avoid an outright sales pitch.

Positive adjustment examples are shown in Figures 8.7 and 8.8.

BAD NEWS LETTERS

The most difficult letters you will probably write in your career are those conveying bad news. How pleasant it would be if we could always respond positively to all requests, whether they be for time, information, or money. Obviously, this is impossible. Sometimes we must refuse requests because of personal reasons, and other times we must refuse because of policies beyond our control. In any event, bad-news letters are by their very nature negative, yet we should try to absorb the shock of the message by providing a buffer, offering alternatives, and maintaining a positive tone throughout. Because the purpose of the letter (the refusal) is delayed, we say that the letter is indirectly, or **inductively,** organized.

Two categories under which most bad-news letters fall are refusals to inquiries and negative adjustments.

Refusal-to-Inquiry Letters

1. Avoid plunging in with the bad news. Instead, begin with a **buffer.** The buffer will usually take up the entire first paragraph and can take many forms. The best way to write your buffer is to find some common ground that you and the reader share. This could be stated in several ways: an expression of appreciation for the reader's letter, an indication of your understanding of the situation, or an agreement with the reader. The buffers we use are as varied as the situations that require them. What's important is that you put yourself in the reader's place

JAVA, INC.
5896 Stamford Street
Houston, TX 06904
(215) 428-0093

December 20, 200-

Mr. Anthony Baldwin
6890 Pearson Drive
Ft. Worth, TX 79352

Dear Mr. Baldwin:

indicaiton
that the
reader's
request will
be fullfilled

Thank you for your letter of December 10. We will do everything to ensure your satisfaction with your Model 5930 Norelco Coffee Brewmaster. Our technicians examined the coffeemaker and discovered a faulty brew valve.

explanation
of the
problem

The technicians determined that the discontinuous brewing process you detected was the result of water deposits forming around the brewing valve. You live in a hard-water area of the country, so more deposits have collected around the valve than usual. The valve has become so encrusted that we feel it would be best to replace your Brewmaster. For future reference, cleaning your Brewmaster every three months with vinegar and water or a commercial cleaning product will keep hard-water buildup to a minimum.

the next
step in the
process

I have enclosed a gift certificate for a new Brewmaster; the certificate is redeemable at the many department stores and appliance stores that carry our products.

expression of
appreciation
for the
reader's
patronage;
"resale" of
your
company

Please accept our appreciation for your patronage and patience. As soon as you redeem the gift certificate, you can once again enjoy the finest brewed coffee in the world!

Yours truly,

Frank Belden

Frank Belden
Customer Representative

Enclosure

FIGURE 8. 7 Sample Positive Adjustment Letter

COMPU-TODAY | **Computer School**
7653 Avenue P Suite #34
Pensacola, FL 56698 (789) 321-6698

April 21, 200-

Mr. John Vera
6754 Prestwick Street
Pensacola, FL 56699

Dear Mr. Vera:

indicaiton that the reader's request will be fullfilled

Thank you for writing to us about our Introduction to Computers course. We are always glad to receive feedback from students who enroll in our courses so that we can more easily review and improve the quality of our courses. We will be glad to do what we can to correct the problem you had with your instructor.

explanation of the problem

We currently employ a full-time staff of personnel who are responsible for actively seeking quality instructors to teach our courses. Though we at times misjudge such quality, we have been pleased by the majority of letters and comments we have received concerning our technical programs.

the next step in the process

After reviewing the specific course you mentioned in your letter, we can certainly understand your dissatisfaction with the results it produced. The instructor you had is no longer with our school, and we hope you will consider taking the course again (free of charge, of course) under a different and better-qualified instructor.

"resale" of your company; more details about the next step in the process; offer for further communication

We believe that basic computer knowledge is vital in today's work environment and that the benefits you would receive under proper guidance would reward the extra time spent retaking the course free of charge. Simply fill out the enclosed registration form and indicate the term that is most convenient for you if you decide to accept. We have also included a catalogue of other excellent technical courses that we will be offering soon. If I can help you in any other way, please feel free to call me.

Sincerely,

T. J. Spencer

(Mr.) T.J. Spencer
Dean

Enclosure

FIGURE 8.8 Sample Positive Adjustment Letter

and ask yourself what you would need to hear. While the buffer is essential if you want to write an effective refusal letter, it shouldn't be too long. One brief paragraph is enough, or you run the risk of truly alienating your reader by raising his or her hopes and then dashing them later in your letter.

2.   Give your reader the bad news in the second paragraph. There are some guidelines to follow here. Again, lead into the bad news by providing an objective explanation for the refusal. Avoid red-flag words such as *unfortunately, regret,* and *unable.* Work to rephrase negatives into positives; it's sometimes difficult, but it's worth the effort. Stick to factual explanations since they're less likely to inspire hostility than more emotional ones. If possible, offer an alternative to the request such as another source of information, or a more convenient date or time. By doing so, not only do you retain the reader's goodwill, but you make the refusal easier. Instead of dwelling on what you *can't* do, you can focus on what you *can* do for the reader.

3.   Finally, close in a friendly, positive manner. Don't repeat the bad news. Offer a statement of goodwill in the form of future interest or continued patronage. If you offer some sort of action, follow up on it immediately.

See Figure 8.9 for a refusal to an inquiry.

Negative Adjustments

1.   Begin on neutral ground with a buffer, perhaps by conceding the customer's inconvenience. Keep the buffer brief and neutral.

2.   In your second paragraph, provide a factual explanation before refusing. As with a positive adjustment, avoid an accusatory tone. If possible, provide an alternative solution: a discount coupon, a replacement instead of a refund, or a store credit. To avoid negatives, focus on what you *can* do for the reader.

3.   Finally, instead of repeating the refusal in your last paragraph, re-sell the company. This is easier to do if you're offering an alternative of some kind. Your last paragraph should not refer to the customer's claim, but rather should focus on the company, the customer's future patronage, and your appreciation for his or her business.

See Figure 8.10 for negative adjustment letters.

GOODWILL LETTERS

The purpose of these letters is simply what the name implies—goodwill. By letting your customers or clients know that you care about them enough to offer thanks or congratulations, you are indirectly creating new business for the future. The secret to writing an effective goodwill letter is sincerity. You should avoid an open sales pitch; your tone should be one of understated warmth and friendliness.

There are three basic types of goodwill letters we will discuss: thank-yous, congratulations, and letters describing new products or services.

967 Oakland Street
Lubbock, TX 79416
February 15, 200-

Mr. James Pickens
Executive Director
Texas Tech University
Ex-Students Association
P. O. Box 4009
Lubbock, TX 79409

Dear Mr. Pickens:

buffer

As a proud graduate of Texas Tech University, I was pleased to receive your letter. Your continued communication with the alumni shows the bonds between Texas Tech and its graduates. The funds donated by alumni are a link between past and present Texas Tech students. I thank you for the opportunity to help educate future generations.

neutral opening that provides explanation

refusal

alternative proposal

With the education I received from Texas Tech, I was able to succeed in the corporate world and to later start my own business. Though my company has been successful, in recent months, I have experienced a dramatic decrease in business. Because I am currently trying to improve my company and its services, I am not able to offer you the $500,000 you requested. However, I am willing to make a smaller contribution of $20,000. If my financial position improves, I may be able to make another contribution to Texas Tech.

goodwill statement

Although I contribute to other charitable and non-profit organizations, I consider scholarships for Texas Tech students my most beneficial investment. If I can help you in any other way, please call me at 795-2312.

Sincerely,

Dorothy Reis

Dorothy Reis

FIGURE 8.9 Sample Refusal Letter

Friendly Ford

89976 Erskine Avenue
Las Vegas, Nevada 67786
1-800-789-8754

April 21, 200-

Ms. Dee White
7865 Michigan Drive
Las Vegas, Nevada 67789

Dear Ms. White:

buffer ———— Thank you for your letter regarding your 1999 Ford Taurus. We appreciate loyal customers like you and value your ideas.

explanation ———— Your car was carefully examined by our top technicians. They discovered nothing to be wrong with the car and agreed that nothing under the warranty covers tires when they

refusal ———— blow out. We are unable to replace your car, but we can replace the tires. If you will bring your car to us by the end of the month, we will gladly replace your tires at a "Preferred

alternative solution ———— Customer" price of only $75 per tire.

goodwill statement; next step/offer for further communication ———— Daily driving does put a great deal of wear and tear on vehicles as well as on tires, so please continue to check your tires before driving each day. Providing our customers great driving value is second in importance only to ensuring their safety. We are certain you will be satisfied with your replacement tires and hope to see you soon. Please call me, and I will set up your appointment with the service department.

Yours truly,

George Thomas

George Thomas
Service Department Manager

FIGURE 8.10 Sample Negative Adjustment Letter

Thank-you Letters

Before you begin writing the letter, think about your relationship with the reader. If you're well-acquainted with the reader, use a first name only in the greeting (Dear Susan); however, don't assume that all goodwill letters are this casual. If your reader expects to be addressed more formally, do so (Dear Mr. Coleman). The following are some guidelines for the thank-you letter.

1. Open with sincere thanks. Because most goodwill letters are brief, your first paragraph may consist of only one sentence.
2. Following your expression of thanks, provide details, such as how a donation of time or money has benefited others (be specific without being long-winded) or how much a customer's patronage means to you and your company. Try to personalize the letter so that your reader knows you aren't sending a form letter. This also holds true if you're writing a thank-you letter for an employment interview.
3. Focus on the reader, not yourself or your company.
4. Make your tone sincere, not gushy. People will be offended by what they perceive as insincerity or condescension.
5. In closing, repeat your thanks, and end with a compliment to the reader, if you wish.

Figures 8.11 and 8.12 are examples of thank-you letters.

Congratulations

The letter of congratulation is organized in much the same way as the thank-you letter. Begin with your expression of congratulations; be sure to specifically mention the reason for your congratulations. Provide details in the middle of your letter: What has the reader accomplished that deserves congratulation? End with a statement about the reader's future, such as "Best wishes for a successful career with Westover Enterprises." One of the most important points to remember about goodwill letters such as thank-you and congratulatory letters, is to focus on the reader. Practice the "you" attitude in these letters.

See Figure 8.13 for a congratulations letter.

New Products or Services

This type of goodwill letter is a bit tricky to write because you want to avoid an open sales pitch; your main purpose is to inform. When you're letting current customers know about new services, such as extended hours or in-home estimates, your letter may be straightforward. Begin by announcing the new service, then provide details, and finally, thank the customer for his or her patronage.

You must be careful to avoid an all-out sales campaign when you're informing customers about new products. Because people *buy* products, you want to refrain from seeming as though profit is your main motive. However, people need to know about *new* products, so this type of letter simply informs others about the availability of the product. For example, if you worked for a drug company, you would want to inform

UNITED WAY

5110 Darcy Street
Suite 12-E
San Jacinto, Texas 79360
(204) 555-2391

April 21, 200-

Mr. B. T. Bell
2980 5th Street
Austin, Texas 83129

Dear Mr. Bell:

thank you statement

We at the United Way wish to express our deepest thanks for your generous donation of $50,000.

details

Your donation has already been put to effective use. As your letter requested, we divided the money between a daycare center for developmentally disabled children and a shelter for battered women. Both establishments have purchased new (and much-needed) equipment, and they still have funds to run for several more months.

With your donation, you have ensured that people in great need will have a higher quality of life than they would have had without you. As grateful as we are, no letter can completely express our thanks to you. We invite you to visit the children's center or the women's shelter so that you can see for yourself the good that is coming from your donation.

repeat the thanks; sincere compliment

Once again, thank you for your donation. People like you exemplify the word "generous."

Sincerely yours,

Yolanda Alvarado

Yolanda Alvarado
Administrator

FIGURE 8.11 Sample Thank-You Letter

Young Business Professionals Organization

Box 56 ◈ University of Texas-Pan American
Edinburg, TX 78512 ◈ (956) 435-9807

December 29, 200-

Mr. Gary Poffenbarger
CEO, English Imports, Inc.
1245 Doniphan Street
Houston, TX 78954

Dear Mr. Poffenbarger:

thank you statement — I would like to extend my most sincere thanks for your speaking to us at our last meeting.

details — Most of us in the organization have little or no "real world" big business experience. To hear someone like you who has accomplished so much in his career is fascinating and gives us vision for our futures. Many of our members commented enthusiastically how you vividly illustrated the concepts that they have learned in class. We can now better relate classroom learning to how it applies to the business world.

repeat the thanks — Again, we truly appreciate the time you gave to our organization. Thank you!

Sincerely,

Malena Rivera

Malena Rivera
Secretary

FIGURE 8.12 Sample Thank-You Letter

MATTHEWS, PETERS, & WILKINS
Attorneys-at-Law
8396 McIntosh Drive
Denver, CO 53691
(316) 555-6193

August 23, 200-

Mr. Oscar Martinez
Senior Partner
Todd, Tisdale, Ellis, & Martinez
1501 Montgomery Avenue
Denver, CO 53653

Dear Mr. Martinez:

expression of congratulations — On behalf of my entire firm, I would like to congratulate you on your promotion to Senior Partner. A promotion of this sort is truly a well-deserved feather in your cap.

details — I still recall meeting you when you were a recent law school graduate. Even then, you displayed drive and dedication to hard work. I've always known that you would move up in the ranks because of your work ethic and your belief in the justice system. The many favorable comments about your work from lawyers throughout the region attest to your talent and integrity.

statement pertaining to reader's future — Once again, Counselor, I extend my most heartfelt congratulations. I look forward to seeing you at the Courthouse.

Sincerely,

G. Elizabeth Hanna

G. Elizabeth Hanna
Attorney-at Law

FIGURE 8.13 Sample Congratulations Letter

COOKCRAFT, INC.
5959 Homestead Road
San Francisco, CA 09654
1-800-987-6543

June 1, 200-

Mr. George Winston
The Gourmet Shoppe
9645 Selkirk
Lubbock, TX 79876

Dear Mr. Winston:

announce-
ment of new
product

As a loyal merchant of our cookware, you'll be interested to learn about our most recent addition to the Cookcraft line.

description
of benefits
to the reader

The new Cookcraft Tube Cake Pan is the latest in our line of non-stick, professional-grade bakeware. Because of numerous requests for this type of pan from our merchants (including you), we've added what we hope will become a top seller. Whereas most commercial bakeware can withstand temperatures of only 400 degrees Farenheit, our Bakezoid 2000 can handle temperatures as high as 500 degrees, which will translate into increased durability and more satisfactory baking results every time.

description
of how the
reader can
see/obtain
the new
product

You'll be receiving brochures describing our full line in detail within the next two weeks. We at Cookcraft value your past patronage and want to ensure you the earliest opportunity to view our latest product. If you have any questions, we would love to hear from you on our toll-free phone line.

Sincerely,

Paula Sorenson

Paula Sorenson
President

FIGURE 8.14 Letter Announcing New Product

doctors and pharmacists of any new or improved drugs on the market. These people have a right to know about this new product in order to do their job more competently.

Begin a letter of this type by announcing the new product. In the body of your letter, focus on the benefits to others, rather than the profits to be made from selling the product. End by indicating how the reader can obtain the product. Throughout the letter, stick to facts, and avoid the emotional, excitable tone indicative of the sales letter.

See Figure 8.14 for a letter announcing a new product or service.

PERSUASIVE LETTERS

Persuasive documents of any kind require much thought and effort because you are trying to convince someone to do something such as buying a product or service, donating time or money, or replacing damaged or defective merchandise. Therefore, your letter should be **inductively,** or indirectly, organized. You will want to state your case before asking for anything. Three basic types of letters are persuasive in nature: the sales letter, the persuasive request, and the persuasive claims letters.

With all three types of persuasive letters, certain guidelines apply: gain the reader's attention, define the problem and the proposed solution (in general terms), explain how the reader can help, and end with an action-oriented close.

Sales

The sales letter is an open solicitation for a company's products or services. Because most sales letters are mass-produced, writers often attempt a personal, friendly tone to offset the fact that these letters are unable to target an individual reader. Sales letters often employ short (sometimes one sentence) paragraphs and make ample use of white space. People are more likely to read something they can quickly scan through, as opposed to long, difficult paragraphs. Other devices used in sales letters are bold style, lists, capitalization, exclamation points, and lots of numbers and figures. The tone of the sales letter is usually excited and very focused upon the reader. The following is a list of guidelines for writing an effective sales letter.

1. Begin with an attention-getting statement. Often, attention-getters are phrased as questions ("When was the last time. . .?"), as startling facts ("Did you know that. . .?"), or as anecdotes ("You're walking to lunch one day, when . . .")
2. Limit your paragraphs to only a few sentences; one-sentence paragraphs are not unusual in sales letters.
3. Introduce your product or service, focusing on its most attractive features (limit these to two or three). Use facts and figures whenever possible to back up your claims; people are much less likely to believe you when your claims are unsubstantiated or exaggerated.
4. Talk about what your product or service can do for the reader. Maintain a focus on your reader. Use lots of action verbs and colorful adjectives and adverbs.
5. Use repetition to emphasize your point.
6. Next, discuss price. Unless a low price is one of your best selling points, wait to discuss it until the middle or end of your letter. Compare your price against those of your competitors. If your price is higher, focus on the greater benefits your product has to offer as opposed to those of your competitors.
7. Finally, motivate your reader to act immediately. Be clear as to how the reader can begin to enjoy your product, and be sure that what you're asking the reader to do is easy and immediate. Try to convince the reader that he or she should act now; if you fail to do this, the reader will probably put the letter away and never get around to responding.

See Figures 8.15 and 8.16 for examples of sales letters.

Persuasive Request

A persuasive request differs from a sales letter in that you are not trying to sell something, but are trying to persuade someone to donate time, money, products, or services. The organization of the persuasive request is also somewhat different, as is the tone. Paragraphs will be longer and more focused. You will want to avoid the excitable tone and attention-grabbing graphics of the sales letter. Overall, the tone will be more formal than the sales letter is, but not stuffy or pretentious. Aim for the friendly, warm tone used for other business letters. Here is a list of guidelines for the persuasive request:

1. Begin with an attention-getter *relevant* to the subject at hand.
2. Describe the problem and the possible solution. It is best if you outline the solution in general terms rather than specifically targeting the reader early in the letter. For example, if your university needs a new computer room, and you need a donation of equipment, describe the computer room and how it would function for the students' benefit.
3. Next, focus on how the reader can help with the problem. Remember to target the *reader's* concerns rather than your own; they may be different.
4. Discuss both tangible and intangible benefits to the reader. Tangible benefits include tax breaks or memberships for donations; intangible benefits would be prestige, exposure, and goodwill.
5. Your close should be action-oriented. Set up the next step in the process. Be assertive without being obnoxious. For example, if you close by simply saying, "I hope to hear from you soon," you probably won't. But if you say, "I'll contact

Skip-a-Stitch, Inc.
4826 SINGER LANE • MIDLAND, TX 79703
(915) 683-9077

June 17, 200-

Ms. Ruby Kendall
Cook Smart
479 Fayette
Syracuse, NY 13202

Dear Ruby:

attention-getter

Have you ever played golf on a hot, humid day and realized that the only place to get a drink, the clubhouse, was still six holes ahead?

introduction of new product

Now I have a solution to this problem. I tie a bottle of Gatorade to my golf bag with one of my new products. The product, a **bottlebag with a drawstring,** is designed for carrying wine, but it meets my needs on the course as well.

benefits to the reader

Ruby, I know you sell some interesting items in your shop, and I think this unique pouch would be a fine addition to your stock. This high-quality bottlebag is handmade from a washable suedecloth. Your customers can choose a **red or a green bag with either a designer emblem or a three-colored stripe.**

I have enclosed a sample of my product that is monogrammed with your name. You can offer this personal touch to your customers in **old English style or script.** Take the bag to the golf course or to picnics, and see how handy this bag can be. I have also enclosed color samples.

discussion of price; motivation for reader to act immediately

I would like to offer you *25 bottlebags for the wholesale price of $4.00 per bag!* I will let you have *additional bags for only $3.80!* The monogramming I mentioned above would cost $5.50 per bag. You will find that this is an exceptional offer when you *retail the bags for $6.75 each!* As an incentive for responding quickly, I will even give you a *10% cash discount* if you order by July 10. Please use the enclosed postage-paid envelope for easy return.

goodwill statement

If you find that the bottlebag will not fit your type of merchandise, keep your bag as a gift. Since the Boston convention, I have found you to be a valued friend. I hope you can also be a valued customer.

Sincerely yours,

Darren Patrick

Darren Patrick, Owner
Enclosures

FIGURE 8.15 Sample Sales Letter

VISION
Computers

2344 White Oak Drive
Arlington, TX 74214
(215) 768-0098

October 31, 200-

Ms. Jana Morris
Texas Tech University
234 Horn Hall
Lubbock, TX 79406

Dear Jana:

attention-getter

Do you sometimes wonder why computer companies make it impossible for a college student to own a computer without first taking out a loan? Do you hate not having the ability to e-mail your friends or surf the web from your home?

introduction of new product

Vision has instituted a new way to help college students obtain a computer without rendering them penniless. It's called our ***Smart-Buy*** plan, and with this program, you could have your very own computer in your home in less than seven days. I'm not talking about an ancient computer; I'm talking about the **top-of-the-line 900mhz Millennium Centura.** This computer's not only fast, but it also has a 14 gig hard drive, which means you can download all sorts of things from movies to music via the Internet.

benefits to the reader

I know you have heard of offers from other computer companies that sound too good to be true. The Vision difference is that we actually keep college students' needs in mind. We want you to have all the ***conveniences*** that a personal computer has to offer. Would you like to pay bills from your house? Would you rather buy your textbooks cheaper at home without the inconvenience of having to drive down to the bookstore? If so, then this is the way! Over **3.5 million** households in the U.S. alone have a personal computer, and 3 million of them are connected to the Internet. **YOU COULD BE NEXT!**

discussion of price

motivation for reader to act immediately

I would like to offer you our product at an incredible price. The Millennium Centura can be ***yours for only $1080.00.*** Now, this is no one-time payment. You can pay as little as only $45.00 a month! Can you believe it? What could possibly be better? If you send us the enclosed postage-paid application by November 1, we'll throw in a brand new **Canon S200 bubble jet printer absolutely free!** This incredible deal also includes a **three-year warranty** with on-site parts and labor.

FIGURE 8.16 Sample Sales Letter

Ms. Jana Morris
Dell's Smart-Buy Plan
Page 2

emphasis of
sales point
by repetition

You might be thinking that this offer is too good to be true. There must be a catch. How much is tax and shipping and handling going to cost over the price? NOTHING! That's right, the **tax and shipping charges are already included** in the low price. A monthly payment of $45.00 is all you pay for a brand new top-of-the-line Vision computer.

goodwill
statement

I hope this brings your wish of having a computer of your very own into a reality. Please respond today so you don't miss out on this chance of a millenium.

Sincerely,

Heather Stover

Heather Stover, Sales Consultant

P.S. Don't forget the opportunity to get a new printer for free! Send in the enclosed reply today!

Enclosure

FIGURE 8.16 *continued*

you next week to get your feelings on this matter," you let the reader know that you're serious about his or her help. On the other hand, saying something like, "I'll be at your office at 8:00 Monday morning to collect your donation" is both presumptuous and demanding.

6. Try to end your letter with a thought-provoking sentence that may provide the final push that the reader needs to comply with your request. For example, if you're requesting a donation of equipment from an alumnus, you might say something like, "Here's your opportunity to help future businesspeople achieve the kind of success you've realized in your career."

See Figures 8.17 and 8.18 for examples of persuasive requests.

Persuasive Claims

Most companies respond positively to an initial claims letter, either because the product is under warranty or simply because it's more economically feasible to grant the customer's request than to refuse and risk losing a customer. However, you might find yourself in a situation where your product is no longer covered by a warranty, yet you feel that the damage or defect is in no way your fault, and you want satisfaction. If this is the case, the direct approach might not work to your advantage. Instead, try the indirect approach by explaining your situation before asking for action. Use the following guidelines to write a persuasive claims letter.

1. Use a neutral beginning by explaining what happened in general terms. Avoid an accusing tone. You should compliment the company if you've been happy with it in the past. Your opening might sound something like this: "We have used Delilah luggage for years and have come to expect a reliable and durable product. However, recently we purchased a large, soft-sided suitcase from your Topper line that had a rip in the lining. We didn't discover the rip until we had had the suitcase for a month-and-a-half. When we took the suitcase back to Winan's Department Store, where we had purchased it, the salespeople claimed that it was too late to get a refund, and they were unable to replace it because they were out of stock."
2. In the body paragraphs, provide more details, such as dates, model numbers, serial numbers, and names. Send copies of receipts, sales slips, warranties, or any other relevant paperwork.
3. State your case factually; accuse no one, even if you feel that you've been taken advantage of.
4. Confidently request exactly what you would like done. Let the reader know how you feel without using an angry tone. You can express your feelings of disappointment, dismay, or anger if they're expressed calmly.
5. State when you would like to hear back from the company, or give a date by when you need your request granted.
6. If possible, end with a goodwill statement to indicate your continued good faith in the company.

Figures 8.19 and 8.20 are examples of persuasive claims letters.

AUSTIN ORGAN DONORS
1235-B 50th Street
Austin, Texas 73546
(512) 555-1231

March 28, 200-

Mr. Kevin Mellington
Assistant Manager
Foleys, Inc.
3420 Phillips Avenue
Austin, Texas 73254

Dear Mr. Mellington:

attention-getter; problem solution

Seven out of ten people will be involved in a serious accident sometime in their lives. In an accident in which a vital organ is damaged, a suitable organ must be found as soon as possible. With a new computer, our organization will be able to locate an acceptable organ or donor within minutes.

description of proposed solution

This computer will help preserve the quality of life for people in Austin and the surrounding community. The computer will match the victim's needs to a compatible donor through blood type, age, and location in a matter of minutes. The computer's networking abilities will allow us to choose the most acceptable donated organ before it decomposes. The end result is that countless precious lives will be saved.

description of how the reader can help

You can do something to help save those lives! Your donation of a Dell Power Edge 4400 Dual Xeon Processor will benefit our organization and our community. The cost of your donation will amount to $10,000, or about $30 a day.

list of benefits to the reader

Your contribution will benefit you and your company in many ways. First, you have the self-respect that comes from knowing that you gave to a worthy cause. Second, you will receive community recognition for your contribution. Third, your contribution to a non-profit organization is tax deductible.

action-oriented closing; thought-provoker

I would enjoy meeting with you in person to discuss my proposal. Please contact me within the next two weeks, and I can stop by your office at your convenience. Remember, the lives of seven out of ten people are in your hands.

Yours truly,

Scott Anderson

Scott Anderson
Director

FIGURE 8.17 Sample Persuasive Request Letter

FAIRS & FESTIVALS

8202 Pynese • Eumenclaw, Washington 98203 • (509)555-7711

March 12, 200-

Ms. Betty Warman
Everett Parks Department
2nd Avenue SE
Eumenclaw, Washington 98204

Dear Ms. Warman:

attention-getter; problem; solution

Is Christmas important to you and your family? Do you look forward to all of the traditions that you associate with the holiday season? I am sure that these are traditions that you hold very dear. If these traditions were removed, would you feel that something was missing from your life? The citizens of Eumenclaw face this very prospect; unless someone steps forward, we face the loss of the Eumenclaw Feast.

description of proposed solution

Our company has a plan that will allow our citizens to continue enjoying the Eumenclaw Feast. Fairs & Festivals is capable of organizing, planning, and managing the acts and vendors, but, quite frankly, finding the proper location is a problem. We believe that a smaller version of the Feast will succeed in the right location. The recreation fields in Eumenclaw are ideal for the number of visitors anticipated, with adequate space for parking and access to bus services.

description of how the reader can help

list of benefits to the reader

Ms. Warman, I mentioned that someone should step forward to help this community. The Parks Department can be that someone. By sponsoring the Eumenclaw Feast, the department will help keep alive a tradition that benefits all of the citizens of our city. Local vendors and performers will benefit from the tourist traffic; citizens will enjoy the food, entertainment, and fellowship. The logo of the Parks Department will be prominently displayed. Visitors will have the opportunity to see the good work of your department. As a result, interest will increase in the facilities and programs of the Eumenclaw Parks Department.

action-oriented closing; thought-provoker

Fairs & Festivals has completed all of the preliminary work on the plans for the festival. To complete the plans for this popular event, we need a suitable site. I invite and encourage you to consider sponsoring the Eumenclaw Feast through the Parks Department. I will contact you by phone next Monday to discuss the matter further. This is your chance to save a valued tradition.

Sincerely,

Mark Key

Mark Key

FIGURE 8.18 Sample Persuasive Request Letter

1593 Montana Avenue
New York, NY 36591
May 15, 200-

Ms. Jennifer Trask
Customer Relations Director
Woodlands Toy Company
P O Box 1113
Oakland, CA 12459

Dear Ms. Trask:

compliment — Last month, I purchased a toy rocking horse from your Galloping Cowpoke collection for my nephew. I've bought your products before and love their educational, yet whimsical, qualities. I'm pleased to tell you that my nephew, Joshua, fell in love with "Skippy," as he calls it.

explanation of what happened; details — The rocking horse I purchased is labeled Model 135, and it was manufactured at your Green Bay plant. The toy is advertised as being intended for children from one to three years of age; my nephew is two years old, but the runners cracked and broke apart as though they were unable to support my nephew's weight. Joshua is heartbroken that Skippy has been "put out to pasture."

request of what the writer would like — I am enclosing a copy of the sales receipt. The manager of the toy store from where I bought the rocking horse told me to contact you because his store no longer carries this model, and he was unable to make an exchange. I would like to make an exact exchange with you.

response date; goodwill statement — My nephew enjoyed playing with Skippy, and he is looking forward to receiving "Skippy II." I would like him to have the new rocking horse by early April. Over the years, my family has played with many fine toys produced by your company, and my nephew will continue the tradition. Feel free to call me at (801) 733-7707 if you need more information.

Sincerely,

Madelene Wheeler

Madeline Wheeler

Enclosure

FIGURE 8.19 Sample Persuasive Claims Letter

67543 Avenue of the Americas
Washington, DC 12543
February 15, 200-

Mr. Rocky Rogers
Customer Relations
American Airlines
5668 Bellaire Street
New York City, NY 10076

Dear Mr. Rogers:

compliment — On January 28, I flew from Washington, DC, to Tulsa on your airline. When possible, I have used your airline on all of my business trips during the past 15 years because of your exceptional service.

explanation of what happened; details — When I arrived in Tulsa, however, I was disappointed to find that my suitcase had been ripped during the flight. Although the contents of the suitcase were not damaged, the suitcase itself was ruined. The rip was seven inches long and was irreparable. I had to purchase a new suitcase for $150 while in Tulsa. A copy of the receipt is enclosed; I would

writer's request — like to request that your company reimburse me for the cost of this new suitcase.

goodwill statement; response date — I have enjoyed many miles of travel on your airline over the past 15 years, and your company has always provided efficient, courteous service at a reasonable price. Please respond by February 28 because I am planning a family reunion in Canada and would like to receive reimbursement for the suitcase before completing my itinerary for that trip.

Sincerely yours,

Rick Drost

Rick Drost

Enclosure

FIGURE 8.20 Sample Persuasive Claims Letter

SUMMARY

Because business letters are by far the most common external documents in the business world, it's important to be familiar with standard formats and basic letter types. Include specific information that the reader will want to know or will find helpful. If your letter has a generally upbeat message, maintaining a positive tone will be easy. However, with letters that are persuasive or that convey bad news, you will need to double-check your tone to ensure you are maintaining the reader's goodwill. Remember: business letters will be viewed in a larger context because many of them represent the company's image. Take care to make this representation one of competence and professionalism.

CHAPTER 9

Memos and E-mail

Unlike business letters, which comprise much of the correspondence that goes outside an organization, memos and e-mail are the chief means of communication among workers within that organization. Depending on their purpose, memos and e-mail can be less formal and shorter than letters because readers are probably familiar with the subject.

MEMOS

In their short form, memos can be used to communicate an array of information, from vacation requests to policy changes. Generally, what distinguishes a short memo from a memo report (discussed in the next chapter) is length rather than the nature of the message itself. Short memos are usually kept to a page and therefore do not make use of headings and sub-headings. Rather, these memos rely on brevity to convey their messages.

In addition to their obvious purpose of relaying all types of information among workers, memos have another, equally important role: they are also used to determine, in part, promotions and pay raises. Therefore, it is imperative that you learn the art of memo-writing, not only to ensure the success of the document itself, but also to ensure the success of your own future. To establish a reputation for sloppy memo-writing may be to stop a career in its tracks.

Because memos are filed for future reference and often used in determining pay raises and promotions, writers must heed guidelines for effective writing as discussed in previous chapters. However, attention to tone becomes especially important in memo-writing. Most people, at some point in their careers, will write memos directed at a variety of audiences: subordinates, peers, superiors, groups, and individuals. And these memos will encompass a variety of topics: announcements, policy changes, requests, inquiries, and so on. It's essential that you learn how to match the tone of the memo with the message it conveys. A serious tone should accompany a serious message, while a lighter tone would be more appropriate for less-serious messages. Failure to match the tone and the message will often result in alienation of your audience.

Despite these warnings, we're not suggesting that you avoid emotion in your memos. Used properly, emotion can be very effective in conveying urgency and a sense of the importance of the situation. For example, if you write a memo encouraging employees to become more physically fit, you might end the memo with "Your continued good health is important to me—let's work together to remain a healthy and happy company!" Or if you've had an ongoing problem with employees taking extra-long breaks, you might write "I'm not happy that my directives are continually being ignored. I hope that this will be my final warning." Your message has been received, but your emotion is kept under control.

Finally, while you will write a variety of business documents throughout your career, the memo is by far the most frequently written document. Your command of the craft of memo-writing will be an important stepping stone in your climb up the corporate ladder.

Format

In general, you will have access to pre-printed memo paper, which will either have the company letterhead or the word "memorandum" printed across the top of the paper. The headings To, From, Date, and Subject will appear, usually double-spaced. All you will need to do is fill these in. Oftentimes, you will send memos to individuals; follow the person's name with his or her job title, either on the same line or single-spaced directly underneath the name.

Subject Line

The subject line plays an important part in the memo because the memo is filed by the subject line. Therefore, you must take care to create a subject line that is specific enough so that the memo is easily retrievable, yet not so long and involved that any actual message becomes unnecessary. For example, a memo announcing new summer hours in the production division should have a subject line more specific than simply "New Summer Hours." When? Where? The memo stands a good chance of becoming lost. However, the subject line "New Summer 2002 Hours in the Production Division because of Budget Cuts and Decreased Sales" is too long and awkward. The best subject line in this case would be "New Summer Hours in Production Division." This gives enough information for the memo to be adequately filed, and yet is brief and to the point.

Signing Off

One other aspect of memo format is initialing or signing off. Beside your typed name on the "From" line, be sure to either initial or sign your name to indicate that you have approved the final, typed copy of the memo. Signing off the memo is similar to signing your name in the signature box of a letter.

Spacing

Most short memos are single-spaced within paragraphs and double-spaced between paragraphs. Of course, you will want to follow the accepted format used in-house, whether it calls for single or double-spacing. You should use either a double or triple space after the subject line and begin your memo. Memos employ the full-block format; therefore, paragraphs are not indented. Figure 9.1 shows the typical memo format.

Types of Memos

Memos fall into five general categories:

1. informative and instructional
2. direct requests
3. good-news
4. bad-news
5. persuasive

Informative and Instructional

Because these memos are usually very straightforward in terms of content, they are short and to the point. Be sure to use a **deductive** method of organization. The first paragraph should provide a context for the reader (if applicable) and a purpose statement. Often, the introductory paragraph for these types of memos need not contain more than one or two sentences.

The second paragraph will provide specifics for the reader. If a list would aid in readability and serve to emphasize the importance of any part of your message, use one. Remember to keep paragraphs brief; lengthy text tends to intimidate, and readers are likely to skip over important details.

If your message requires that you go on to subsequent body paragraphs, do so. Just remember to be as concise as possible without shortchanging your reader.

Your concluding paragraph should briefly sum up your message, or, if you prefer, include a statement of goodwill; oftentimes, in a very short memo, one sentence will suffice. Lastly, you should offer further communication so your reader knows that you are open to questions or suggestions. Figure 9.2 is an example of an instructional short memo.

Direct Request

The direct request memo is organized much like the informational and instructional. In other words, use **deductive** order (provide a context and a purpose statement), clearly stating your request in the first paragraph. Provide specifics or an explanation in the second and subsequent paragraphs, and finally, include a goodwill statement and offer for further communication. Figure 9.3 illustrates a direct request memo.

Good-news

The good news about good-news documents is that they are easy and fun to write. Begin **deductively,** with the good news in the first paragraph—perhaps even the first sentence. Your subject line can reflect your purpose; there is no need to soften the message either in the subject line or in the first paragraph, as in a bad-news memo.

LETTERHEAD OR MEMORANDUM

TO:
    }DS
FROM:
    }DS
DATE:
    }DS
SUBJECT:
    }DS or TS

XXXXXXXXXXXXXXXXXXXXXXXXXXXXXXXXXXXXXXXXXXXXXXXXXX
XXXXXXXXXXXXXXXXXXX.
    }DS
XXXXXXXXXXXXXXXXXXXXXXXXXXXXXXXXXXXXXXXXXXXXXXXXXX
XXXXXXXXXXXXXXXXXXXXXXXXXXXXXXXXXXXXXXXXXXXXXXXXXX
XXXXXXXXXXXXXXXXXXXXXXXXXXXXXXXXXXXXXXXXXXXXXXXXXX
XXXXXXXXXXXXXXXXXXXXXXXXXXXXXXXXXXXXXXXX.
    }DS
XXXXXXXXXXXXXXXXXXXXXXXXXXXXXXXXXXXXXXXXXXXXXXXXXX
XXXXXXXXXXXXXXXXXXXXXXXXXXXXXXXXXXXXXXXXXXXXXXXXXX
XXXXXXXXXXXXXXXXXXXXXXXXXXXXXXXXX.
    }DS
XXXXXXXXXXXXXXXXXXXXXXXXXXXXXXXXXXXXXXXXXXXXXXXXXX
XXXXXXXXXXXXXXXXXXXXXXXXXXXXXXXXXXXXX

FIGURE 9.1 Typical Memo Format

Memorandum

TO: All Employees

FROM: *LA*
Lilly Abercrombie, President

DATE: February 14, 200-

SUBJECT: New Parking Stickers

background information

As many of you now know, our company parking policy will be changing in two weeks. I would like for you to know the new procedure so that your cars are not mistakenly towed from our parking lot.

Sometime this week, please make sure to do the following:

specific details

1. Choose your reserved space (please indicate first, second, and third choices so that we may better accommodate everyone) from our parking lot.

2. Drop by my office (#345) to fill out a Parking Intent Form.

3. Pick up a parking sticker from the Parking Control Office starting next Monday, February 20.

offer for further communication

We can all look forward to more convenience and better safety with the new parking system. Please feel free to call if you would like to discuss the new procedure further.

FIGURE 9.2 Sample Instructional Memo

WAITE MANUFACTURING COMPANY, INC.
806 Lincoln Avenue
Lubbock, TX 79416
(806) 796-2689

TO: Joanna Deines
                Department Supervisor

FROM: Shannon Bruton *SB*
                Division Superintendent

DATE: October 25, 200-

SUBJECT: Recognition of Lawrence A. Lecuyer's Retirement

context;
purpose
statement

After 43 years with our company, Mr. Lecuyer will be retiring next month. I feel that we should honor Mr. Lecuyer's long years of service and am asking for your feedback about what type of function we should have.

specific
details

Our employees should decide what kind of function they would prefer. This special occasion can take the form of a formal banquet, a picnic, or a reception. It can be a family affair or for employees only. I also need to know what the best dates and times would be for the event.

Finally, there is the matter of a retirement gift for Mr. Lecuyer. It would help me tremendously if you could provide me with information about his interests, needs, and other relevant information.

offer for
further
communic-
ation

I would appreciate your assistance in acquiring this information for me. If you have any questions, please feel free to contact me anytime.

FIGURE 9.3 Sample Direct Request Memo

CHARLES R. HOLLISTER AND ASSOCIATES
Accounting Specialists
100 Van Wyk
Peoria, IL 52109
120-742-2398

TO: Penny Partlow, Marketing

FROM: Candy Katz, Personnel

DATE: March 15, 200-

SUBJECT: Vacation Request Granted

purpose statement — I am delighted to let you know that your request for vacation at the end of the month has been granted.

details — To clarify, your scheduled vacation week will begin on Monday, March 27. That week opened up when our District Director, Ralph Moss, postponed his trip to our offices. My records also show that you have reserved a week of vacation starting on Monday, July 3.

goodwill statement; offer for further communication — I understand that you and your family are headed to Disneyland to attend a family reunion. Have a great vacation! Feel free to come by my office if you have any questions about the new schedule.

FIGURE 9.4 Sample Good News Memo

Provide details in your body paragraph(s), and close with a goodwill statement. Think of a statement of goodwill as something like a cheer: you're showing your approval for this particular person or group. Goodwill statements might sound something like "We're proud to have you on our team!" or "Your group is doing great work—keep it up!" If your good-news message involves a positive change from the status quo (for example, an increase in pay or more accrued vacation hours), you should also offer further communication so readers know they can have any questions answered. Figure 9.4 shows an example of a good-news memo.

Bad-news

Bad-news documents are usually not fun to write and, therefore, are not very easy to write. As in a negative letter, such as a refusal, your memo will be **inductively** organized; it should provide the reader with a **buffer** before getting to the bad news. The buffer works to soften the blow of the bad news. Generally, a buffer will be a short introductory paragraph and will help to absorb the shock of the message. Word your buffer neutrally by finding some common ground between you and your reader. Keep your buffer brief. If you continue on for several paragraphs before providing the bad news, the reader may be in for an even bigger shock because he or she has come to think that the memo doesn't contain any bad news at all. Therefore, it is best to keep the buffer to one brief paragraph.

In addition to supplying a buffer, you should also be sure that your subject line does not reflect the bad news (or your buffer becomes unnecessary). For example, a memo refusing a worker's request for specific vacation time should not have a subject line that reads, "Refusal to vacation request." Instead, it might read simply, "Spring vacation request." As with any bad-news memo, you should try to use positive wording and, if it's in your power, attempt to mitigate the negative situation with positive action.

Bad-news memos will often be longer than the three types of memos previously discussed. Because you are conveying bad news, in order to avoid alienating your audience and appearing uncaring, you should spend more time providing details as to why the situation exists and what can be done, if anything, to improve it. If you fail to do this, you will appear to be callous and dismissive. Remember your tone at all times!

As always in business writing, use short paragraphs that are easy to scan. Finally, end with a goodwill statement that shows your concern, and offer further communication. In bad-news memos especially, the reader needs to know that he or she can come to you with questions or suggestions. Figure 9.5 is an example of a bad-news memo.

Persuasive

A persuasive memo, like a bad-news memo, should also be inductively organized, though not for the same reason. With bad news, you should provide a buffer to soften the blow, as discussed above. With a persuasive request, you should try to "hook" the reader before supplying any specifics or making your request. If it helps, use a modified version of Monroe's Motivated Sequence as discussed in chapter 15. Use an attention-getting statement to "hook" your reader, and then briefly describe your problem and a possible solution. As in a persuasive letter, all this information can go in an introductory paragraph.

Next, describe how the reader(s) can help with the solution to the problem. For example, if insurance premiums are rising for your company because of an increase in health claims during the last year, you can suggest that perhaps these premiums will

NEWSOME COMPUTERS
1123 Haley Blvd.
Chippewa Falls, WI 54729
1-800-567-7890

TO: Beverly Bevers, Director of Personnel

FROM: Carl Goldman, Department Supervisor

DATE: April 15, 200-

SUBJECT: Office Renovations

buffer — You are aware that the annual meeting of the Board of Directors was held yesterday. The main topic of discussion was the proposed renovations to expand our office space.

bad news — Our goal of having individual offices is a valid one. However, after several hours of discussion, the Board voted down our proposal. Newsome Computers' $500,000 annual budget will not be able to cover the $400,000 renovations that we had proposed. Some of the projects that will instead be covered are the hiring of two additional secretaries and the purchase of 12 new Supercab pickups for company use.

details/ explanation

description of what can be done to improve the situation — The Board has granted us $50,000 to improve our current office conditions. Perhaps we could buy partitions to separate our employees' workspaces until next year. At that time, we can once again propose a more permanent solution to the office situation. Also, the Board has agreed that each of our office workers deserves a private phone line. The amount of funds needed for this project is well within the annual budget.

goodwill statement; offer for further communi- cation — I have really appreciated collaborating with you on ways to improve our office, Beverly. Your presence here is a valuable asset to the company. If you can think of any other suggestions, please come see me.

FIGURE 9.5 Sample Bad News Memo

MEMORANDUM

TO: All Employees

FROM: Sammy Davila, President

DATE: December 1, 200-

SUBJECT: Participation in the Toys for Tots Campaign

attention-getter

As a child, were you lucky enough to have the kind of Christmas morning that kids dream of? Did you have a pile of beautifully wrapped presents that were delivered specially to you from Santa? Some children won't have this kind of Christmas unless we help through donations to the Toys for Tots Campaign.

problem and solution

All children deserve a Christmas filled with love, laughter, and the feeling that they're special. To help ensure that no child in our community feels left out on Christmas morning, please join me in participating in the Toys for Tots Campaign. Our local Marine Corps has asked for our company's help, and I have agreed to place collection bins throughout our office complex.

description of how the reader can help

To donate, please purchase a toy priced at $15 or higher, and place the unwrapped toy in one of the bins before December 20. The more toys that are donated, the better, of course; our minimum goal, though, should be one toy per employee. Just imagine how great it would be to put your generous Christmas spirit to such good use!

incentive for the reader to help

If you would like more information about the Toys for Tots Campaign, give me a call at extension 60. Please help several hundred children feel that they, too, are special enough for Santa to remember.

action-oriented close

FIGURE 9.6 Sample Persuasive Memo

decrease if employees will begin a regular exercise program and stop smoking. Obviously, you can't require that employees do either of these things, thus the persuasion is needed.

It helps if you can provide incentive for your reader(s): how will he or she benefit? Be specific! A general statement such as "It would be great if we could all start exercising and stop smoking. Let's do it!" probably won't get very good results. Instead, do what you can to help your audience get motivated: "We've been talking with Good Fit Health Clubs, and we're able to offer a 20 percent discount for all ABC employees who wish to join. Good Fit offers aerobics classes all day long, weight training, and best of all, a swimming pool. I'll be there—hope to see you there!" Then supply details about how employees can join the club. If possible, offer a stop-smoking seminar for those employees who smoke. If this is not feasible, you may be able to offer other, less-expensive incentives, such as a paid day off from work for each employee who quits smoking.

In addition to describing benefits for individual readers, you can also visualize for your audience how your suggested solution could help the business as a whole. People are often inspired to action by knowing that they aren't the only ones to benefit; appeal to their "let's stick together" attitude.

Finally, end your memo with an action-oriented close. This could appear as a statement of goodwill, as an offer for further communication, or both. If possible, indicate in a non-threatening way that you will be following up on your reader's response. This will force your reader to at least think about your request without tossing it aside for an indeterminate length of time. Figure 9.6 shows an example of a persuasive memo.

E-MAIL

An upper-level manager for a prominent hotel chain recently complained to us about e-mail. He reads over 60 e-mail messages a day and was appalled at their poor quality. Too many people in his organization don't capitalize or punctuate. The text is full of grammar and spelling errors; some messages are unintelligible. Many are too informal; some even include silly screen names that are inappropriate for business.

He said that because of poor e-mail communication, he had eliminated some employees from possible promotions. He believed upper-level managers should always communicate clearly and professionally. He also ignored some e-mail messages because he didn't have the time to interpret their meanings.

The informality in e-mail probably derives from its versatility and popularity. Many people use e-mail as a substitute for telephone conversations. They get in the habit of using an informal style that is okay with friends. However, that same casual style is inappropriate in the workplace.

We suggest that you get in the habit of using the same level of formality in writing e-mail messages as you do in writing hard-copy memos. Both kinds of media can be widely dispersed and provide a permanent record. In fact, because it is so easy to copy and pass on e-mail, the chance of wide dispersion is greater for e-mail than for memos. Don't write anything in an e-mail that you wouldn't want to appear on the front page of a newspaper.

We suggest that you use a similar format for business e-mail as you do for memos. In addition, use the guidelines we previously provided for writing informative and instructional, direct-request, good-news, bad-news, and persuasive memos.

The text format is basically the same for business e-mail as it is for memos. However, use the following guidelines or adaptations for business e-mail.

Omit the "Date," "To," and "From" headings. The date and address are already included in the e-mail. The "from" information is also provided. However, you may want to provide a signature box at the conclusion of your message.

Include a descriptive subject line. Follow the guidelines for subject lines for memos. The subject line will cue the reader to the topic and its importance.

Consider using a formal greeting. Because e-mail addresses often don't include the name of the receiver, you may want to identify a specific receiver with "Dear_____" or by simply writing his or her name at the beginning of your message.

Inform or hook the reader in the first paragraph. Some people set up their screens so they see only the first few lines of incoming e-mail. If the e-mail doesn't appear interesting, they delete it. To get the reader's attention, use memo guidelines for providing a purpose statement or a hook in the first paragraph.

Be concise and complete. Use the same approach as you would in a memo. The message should be short and to the point. However, you need to adequately cover the subject.

Use paragraph breaks. Use the same kind of paragraph breaks that you do in other written documents.

Review and revise your message. As with any other documents, e-mail messages should be professional and clear.

Check for spelling and grammar. Many e-mail programs make proofreading easy by providing spelling- and grammar-checkers.

Consider adding a closing that you might use in a traditional letter. Since an e-mail doesn't provide a way for you to sign your initials, you may want to add something like:

> **Regards,**
> **Tom**

> or

> **Sincerely,**
> **Theresa**

Provide an e-mail signature. Most e-mail programs provide the means to automatically add a signature at the conclusion of your e-mail. Typically, the signature includes your name, title, company, telephone, fax, and e-mail address, similar to the following:

> Terry Brockhaus
> Acquisitions Manager
> Double-T Press
> (806) 216–1011
> (806) 216–1012 (fax)
> tbrokhaus@pina.com

Send only to your target audience. Many people in business complain that they are overwhelmed with e-mail. You can help by sending and copying messages only to readers who need the message.

Avoid "inflammatory" comments. Because of its ease of use, e-mail can become too frank and even inflammatory. Don't send messages to let off steam. If you are angry, we suggest you send the e-mail to yourself first. Revise it until you've taken out offensive or accusatory language.

Do not use e-mail for private or personal communication. News media have reported how private "love letters" have been copied throughout a company and beyond. E-mail is a public form of communication. Some companies screen or archive e-mail. Therefore, you should not use e-mail to joke, gossip, or send private or confidential messages. Humor and sarcasm often don't translate well through e-mail. Managers should not use e-mail to discipline subordinates. Discipline is a private matter that should be handled face-to-face.

Do not answer at the bottom or on someone else's e-mail. If you answer at the bottom of the e-mail, when the sender gets your response, he or she may assume the mail was returned undeliverable and delete it. Answering on someone else's e-mail can be confusing. If you need to, you can attach the original e-mail to your own.

SUMMARY

Memos and e-mail are used daily in organizations. They not only perform a vital communication function, but also provide an enduring record for the organization. Although they tend to be short, you should write them with care. Other people will form impressions about you based on your memos and e-mail. Even though they may be written to one individual, they can become very public. Use the format and guidelines provided here as a basis for memos and e-mail, but adapt them to organizational norms and expectations.

CHAPTER 10

Short Reports

Short reports serve to inform the reader about a given topic, analyze the topic, and sometimes encourage the reader to act according to the writer's wishes. Short reports are often preferred over other types of documents because they are more detailed than letters and memos, but they are not as long and drawn out as formal reports.

Many authorities consider "short" reports to number five or fewer pages; some other authorities consider "short" to be 10 pages or fewer. What constitutes "short" is debatable, but most businesspeople agree that two of the most useful short reports are memo reports (a multi-page version of the memo) and letter reports. Each should be short enough to be read and understood in a single sitting.

Memo reports and letter reports are so named because they are longer, more detailed versions of their namesakes. These short reports can have a few extra features, such as headings, subheadings, footnotes or endnotes, and graphics.

The main difference between memo reports and letter reports is their format, which is determined by the intended audience. Memo reports, like memos, are internal communications (that is, they are kept within the company), and letter reports, like most letters, are external (they are sent outside the company).

Business writers are sometimes required by their employers to use a certain format preferred by the company. However, if no format is specified, the writer must determine the format based on whether the report will be internal or external.

A less obvious, but still important, difference between memo reports and letter reports is the tone. The same rules that apply to memos and letters apply here, as well: memo reports have a more conversational and relaxed tone than letter reports. Of course, the writer must always maintain a polite, respectful tone for the report to be well received.

MEMO REPORTS

The main purpose of a memo report is to officially note important business decisions or actions and to designate responsible parties. Since memo reports stay within the company, they are often written for the record to detail the particulars of the subject at hand. Memo reports go into more detail than short memos because the content tends to be more complicated or emotionally charged. For example, you would probably need a memo report if you had to detail several changes in a health insurance policy; you might also want a memo report if you had to discuss a company-wide cut in pay for your employees.

Format

The format of a memo report is similar to that of the memo, as discussed in the previous chapter. Maintain standard one inch margins; center the word "Memorandum" or the company letterhead; follow with the typical "To/From/Date/Subject" heading (make sure to include handwritten initials after the "From" line); single-space the text; and leave your paragraphs flush left. Double-space between paragraphs as always.

Memo reports are long enough that the reader will benefit from headings, subheadings, and graphics. As with many documents, the spacing of the memo report differs from company to company, but most firms either use a double space or triple space above headings and a double space below. Major headings identify major concepts; these are typed so that they visibly stand out from the rest of the text. They can be centered, underlined, boldfaced, or completely capitalized. The subheadings are considered to be more minor, so they should have a somewhat less dramatic impact and should always appear flush left. Figure 10.1 shows the differences in the levels of headings of a memo report.

Remember, while this example shows different headings, sometimes you will not need more than a single level. Always include text between headings; it is an incorrect format to have two headings (one major, one minor, for example) with no text between them.

Every page after the first should include some key identifying information or **header.** A half-inch from the top of the page, type the reader's name, the topic you are writing about, and the page number. This information should appear on three separate lines, with single-spacing between. Next, use a triple space below and continue typing the rest of your memo report.

Since memo reports are detailed, graphics like tables and figures break the monotony of the printed page and allow the reader to absorb analytical information. Review chapter 5, "Designing Visual Aids," for guidelines in setting up graphics.

WADSWORTH ENTERPRISES
4568 Main Street
Lubbock, Texas 79408
806-567-4444

TS{
TO: Michael Alexander, Chairman
DS{   RC
FROM: Rachel Caroline, President
DS{
DATE: May l, 200-
DS{
SUBJECT: New Summer Hours
                 DS or TS{
                  INTRODUCTION
     DS{
XXXXXXXXXXXXXXXXXXXXXXXXXXXXXXXXXXXXXXXXXXXXXXXXXXX
XXXXXXXXXXXXXXXXXXXXXXXXXXXXXXXXXXXXXXXXXXXXXXXXXXX
XXXXXXXX

XXXXXXXXXXXXXXXXXXXXXXXXXXXXXXXXXXXXXXXXXXXXXXXXXXX
XXXXXXX.

     DS or TS{
                  MAJOR HEADING
DS{
XXXXXXXXXXXXXXXXXXXXXXXXXXXXXXXXXXXXXXXXXXXXXXXXXXX
XXXXXXXXXXXXXXXXXXXXXXXXXXXXXXXXXXXXXXXXXXXXXXXXXXX
XXXXXXXXXXXXXXXXXXXXXXXXXXXXXXXXXXXXXXXXXXXXXXXXXX

XXXXXXXXXXXXXXXXXXXXXXXXXXXXXXXXXXXXXXXXXXXXXXXXXXX
XXXXXXXXXXXXXXXXXXXXXXXXXXXXXXXXXXXXXXXXXXXXXXXXXXX
XXXXXXXXXXXXXXXXXXXXXXXXXXXXXXXXXXXXXXXXXXXXXXXXXXX
XX
     DS or TS{
Subheading
     DS{
XXXXXXXXXXXXXXXXXXXXXXXXXXXXXXXXXXXXXXXXXXXXXXXXXXX
XXXXXXXXXXXXXXXXXXXXXXXXXXXXXXXXXXXXXXXXXXXXXXXXXXX
XXXXXXXXXXXXXXXXXXXXXXXXXXXXXXXXXXXXXXXXXXXXXXXXXXX
XXXXXXXXXXXX
     DS or TS{
Subheading
     DS{
XXXXXXXXXXXXXXXXXXXXXXXXXXXXXXXXXXXXXXXXXXXXXXXXXXX
XXXXXXXXXXXXXXXXXXXXXXXXXXXXXXXXXXXXXXXXXXXXXXXXXXX
XXXXXXXXXXXXXXXXXXXXXXXXXXXXXXXXXXXXXXXXXXXXXXXXXXX
XXXXXXXXXXXX

FIGURE 10.1 Sample Memo Report Format (two heading levels)

Rachel Caroline
New Summer Hours
Page 2

TS{

MAJOR HEADING

DS{
XXXXXXXXXXXXXXXXXXXXXXXXXXXXXXXXXXXXXXXXXXXXXXXXXXXXXX
XXXXXXXXXXXXXXXXXXXXXXXXXXXXXXXXXXXXXXXXXXXXXXXXXXXXXX
XXXXXXXXXXXXXXXXXXXXXXXXXXXXXXXXXXXXXXXXXXXXXXXXX
    DS or TS{
Subheading
    DS{
XXXXXXXXXXXXXXXXXXXXXXXXXXXXXXXXXXXXXXXXXXXXXXXXXXXXXX
XXXXXXXXXXXXXXXXXXXXXXXXXXXXXXXXXXXXXXXXXXXXXXXXXXXXXX
XXXXXXXXXXXXXXXXXXXXXXXXXXXXXXXXXXXXXXXXXXXXXXXXXXXXXX
XXXXXXXXXXXX
    DS or TS{
Subheading
    DS{
XXXXXXXXXXXXXXXXXXXXXXXXXXXXXXXXXXXXXXXXXXXXXXXXXXXXXX
XXXXXXXXXXXXXXXXXXXXXXXXXXXXXXXXXXXXXXXXXXXXXXXXXXXXXX
XXXXXXXXXXXXXXXXXXXXXXXXXXXXXXXXXXXXXXXXXXXXXXXXXXXXXX
XXXXXXXXXXXX
    DS or TS{
Subheading
    DS{
XXXXXXXXXXXXXXXXXXXXXXXXXXXXXXXXXXXXXXXXXXXXXXXXXXXXXX
XXXXXXXXXXXXXXXXXXXXXXXXXXXXXXXXXXXXXXXXXXXXXXXXXXXXXX
XXXXXXXXXXXXXXXXXXXXXXXXXXXXXXXXXXXXXXXXXXXXXXXXXXXXXX
XXXXXXXXXXXX
    DS or TS{

CONCLUSION

    DS {
XXXXXXXXXXXXXXXXXXXXXXXXXXXXXXXXXXXXXXXXXXXXXXXXXXXXXX
XXXXXXXXXXXXXXXXXXXXXXXXXXXXXXXXXXXXXXXXXXXXXXXXXXXXXX
XXXXXXXX

FIGURE 10.1 *continued*

Knowing the rules of creating an outline can come in handy as you format your memo report. If you use major headings, you must have at least two. If you have only one heading level, most companies prefer that the report have at least three headings. How many headings you have (and how many levels there are) is determined by how detailed you make your memo report.

Types of Memo Reports

The two most frequently written memo reports are the recommendation memo and the periodic or progress memo. Both kinds focus on issues that are of great importance to a business' functions and operations.

Recommendation Memo Report

Also called a justification memo, the recommendation memo suggests changes in policies and procedures and justifies why the changes should be implemented. Recommendation reports should focus on specific benefits to the company, such as gains in money, time, or efficiency.

Recommendation memo reports should be set up deductively, as are most memos. The first section, sometimes given the heading "Recommendation" or "Introduction," should remind the reader why you are writing the report: Did the reader request the report, or did you want to initiate changes? The first section should also clearly state your recommendation and summarize the benefits to your company.

The middle sections of the report should provide specific details. Here is where you are likely to have a table or other specific information to support your ideas. Discuss concrete ideas about how the changes can be implemented. The better defined your ideas are, the more likely your memo report will be taken seriously. The middle sections may also identify any previous efforts for change, but your main focus should be on what you think the company should do in the future.

The concluding section, often labeled "Summary" or "Conclusion," wraps up your main ideas and repeats your recommendation. To maintain a helpful tone, end with an offer for further communication. Figure 10.2 shows a recommendation memo report.

Periodic and Progress Memo Reports

Both the periodic and progress memo reports are summaries that detail the current status of a project. They are similar in that they discuss what has taken place over a given period of time. However, progress reports focus on the specific activities and accomplishments of the group; periodic reports summarize the general events that took place over a period of time (usually either a month or a quarter). Both types of reports should be well detailed and answer in advance any questions the reader might have.

There is no one correct format for the body of the periodic or progress memo report. Many formats exist; you should check with your supervisor to see which format your firm prefers. Generally, though, these types of memo reports begin with the heading set in standard memo format with a company letterhead or "Memorandum" at the top of the page, followed by the "To, From, Date, Subject" heading. You may include major and minor headings within the text as needed. Figure 10.3 shows a sample progress memo report.

DILLARDS DEPARTMENT STORE

2061 Slide Road
Lubbock, TX 79407
806-789-9652

TO: Beverly Crane
Store Manager

FROM: Roy Jo Sartin *Ray*
Customer Relations Manager

DATE: October 19, 200-

SUBJECT: Recommendations for Improving Dillards's Image

INTRODUCTION

background information; specific reccommendation

As you requested, I have examined the image of Dillards Department Store in Lubbock. I interviewed Dillards' customers, the customers of other department stores, and Dillards' employees, and I believe I can offer some concrete suggestions to improve our image.

The main problem with Dillards' image is that our employees are perceived as being unprofessional, abrupt, and ill-informed about the merchandise that they sell. I recommend that we hold two workshops to improve both our employees' professionalism and knowledge about the merchandise.

middle sections have specific details, concrete ideas; focus should be on what the company should do in the future

PROFESSIONALISM WORKSHOP

While Dillards' own customers enjoy the goods and clothing we provide, they often find our salespeople to be overbearing. Other stores' customers also listed this as a reason they avoid our store; our employees often come across as being unprofessional and abrupt. These brusque attitudes can be remedied by training in customer courtesy.

Etiquette Plus, a company based in Midland, specializes in workshops that improve etiquette and professionalism in retail salespeople. Its "One-Day Wonder Workshop" offers intense training in customer courtesy and professional attitudes and techniques. Personnel from Etiquette Plus lead the workshop any day of the week, even on Sunday.

For an organization the size of ours, Etiquette Plus offers a special rate of $20 per attendee for the One-Day Wonder Workshop. For all of our salespeople to attend the workshop, this amounts to a significant cost; however, any cost pales in comparison to the benefits our store will enjoy when our public image improves.

FIGURE 10.2 Recommendation Memo Report

Beverly Crane
Improving Dillards's Image
Page 2

MERCHANDISE WORKSHOPS

Several of our customers think that our employees are not as knowledgeable or caring as the salespeople in other stores. Several Dillards' employees told me that they do not feel properly trained or knowledgeable in their respective areas of assignment in our store. I recommend that we hold workshops within individual departments in our store, led by experienced salespeople with knowledge in that certain area.

For example, Penny Harris has worked in the Ladies' Suits and Dresses section of our store for 15 years. She expresses interest in leading a workshop to teach newer employees in that area about sizing and accessorizing professional outfits to fit customers' needs. Similar workshops could be organized in each specific department; if our Lubbock store does not have experienced salespeople in some departments, the Dillards' store managers in Amarillo have informed me that they will be glad to help.

CONCLUSION

summary of
main ideas;
recommenda-
tion; offer
for further
communi-
cation

Workshops that focus on professionalism and knowledge about merchandise are definitely needed to improve the attitudes of our employees and to enhance the image of Dillards Department Store here in Lubbock. I recommend that we contact Etiquette Plus and schedule the "One-Day Wonder Workshop" within the next month. Penny Harris and I can have leaders organized to hold merchandise workshops by the end of next week.

With your approval, I will begin planning these activities as soon as possible. Please let me know if you have any questions.

FIGURE 10.2 *continued*

GODDARD
CONSTRUCTION
76890 67th Street
Seattle, WA 98124
1-800-723-7890

To: Mr. Keith Kerr, President

                         RC
From: Robert Carroll, Foreman

Date: June 1, 200-

Subject: Progress on the Seattle Coastal Mall

INTRODUCTION

background information

As we discussed in our weekly meeting last Thursday, the Seattle Coastal Mall is now becoming a reality. I am pleased to update you on the progress made in May on the mall's construction. Of particular importance to the project at this point are the concrete foundation and the planning of the parking lots.

middle sections will focus on activities and accomplishments; provide details

CONCRETE UPDATE

Currently, we are one week ahead of schedule. We began pouring the concrete foundation just this morning. The Seattle climate has been dry for the past month, allowing our concrete contractors to begin work sooner than we had anticipated. Dennis L. Walters, our head concrete contractor, has informed me that his workers will probably be finished pouring concrete by the middle of June. Considering that we should allow the concrete to set for maximum hardness, we should count on starting the next phase of development by early July. The contractor has guaranteed the foundation cost, and it will fit within the proposed budget for the project.

Mr. Walters has further suggested that we consider adding decorative concrete fountains around the main interior entrances of the mall's three largest department stores. He has done decorative work of this nature before for other malls in the Washington State area, and he showed me some pictures. I believe that the fountains add a classy touch, and the sound of falling water is known to be soothing to shoppers. He has priced the fountains at $2,000 each.

PARKING LOT UPDATE

The architect's blueprints indicate that this mall will have a grand total of 900,000 square feet of shopping space (including the food court). Most malls of this size have parking lots with anywhere from 4,000 to 7,000 parking spaces. We can easily fit 5,000 spaces in the leveled areas that are designated P1, P2, P3, P3a, and P4. It is possible, however, to further level the south side of the mall parking area; in this case, we could fit in 6,000 parking spaces total.

FIGURE 10.3 Sample Progress Memo Report

Keith Kerr
Seattle Coastal Mall Update
Page 2

As you can see from the surveyor's report, the west side of our mall will rest at the foot of Franklin Peak. We can fit extra spaces around the natural terrain of the mountain and landscape to accentuate the natural beauty of the mountain. This will make the shape of parking lot P4 irregular, but the mall will seem to blend in nicely with nature. Plus, any additional west-side spaces we can fit in will ultimately benefit the stores' profits.

As is standard with any project involving parking lots, we will pave the lots after the heaviest trucks have finished hauling building materials to the construction site. I estimate that the parking lots will be paved by August 1. Of course, the painting of the spaces will be one of the last steps to finishing the mall; I will keep you posted as to when I estimate the painting to begin.

CONCLUSION

wrap-up of
ideas

offer for
further
communic-
ation

All in all, I am pleased with our progress at this early date. If we can maintain our current pace, the mall should be open in time for the Christmas shopping season (early November). Feel free to call me if you have any suggestions, particularly about the concrete fountains and the parking lots' capacities. I look forward to talking with you again.

FIGURE 10.3 *continued*

LETTER REPORTS

Letter reports, as opposed to memo reports, are intended for an external audience and are therefore written in letter format. Generally, these reports are written in a more formal style than memo reports because business clients comprise the audience. However, a personal tone, as identified by the use of "you" and "I," is still appropriate for this type of report.

Two basic types of letter reports are progress reports and analytical or recommendation reports. In both cases, the format will resemble the format used for all business letters, as discussed in chapter 7, "Letter Style and Format." Also appropriate is a report written in manuscript style and accompanied by a letter of transmittal addressed to the client, although this particular format is more formal and would usually be used with a longer report requiring more information.

As in most reports, deductive order is advisable. Occasionally, writers may use inductive order if they feel that their recommendation, for example, requires special justification. These reports will lead up to the recommendation, which will follow after a detailed and specific discussion of the reasons for that recommendation.

In general, however, you will want to open by providing a context for your reader. If the client has requested the report, then a simple "As you requested . . ." is the most direct way to open the letter. If you are providing an unauthorized report, identify yourself and state your purpose in your introduction.

Your body paragraphs will provide specifics. Lists come in handy in many business documents and will be especially helpful in a letter report. Use short paragraphs, keep your language simple, and be sure to explain everything fully. If your report covers more than two pages, you should include headings (as discussed earlier) to help your reader understand your material more easily.

In your conclusion, reiterate your purpose and offer further communication. Use a traditional close, and be sure to indicate any enclosures following your typed signature. Refer to chapter 7, "Letter Style and Format," for typical letter format.

Types of Letter Reports

There are three major types of letter reports: (1) progress reports, (2) analytical or recommendation reports, and (3) external proposals.

Progress Reports

A progress report can either be one authorized by the client or one that you volunteer to provide. In either case, these reports supply the client with important information regarding work on a particular project. They are generally sent out to the client on a fairly regular basis, agreed upon beforehand, to keep the client updated.

You will want to include a brief introduction stating the purpose of the report; be sure to include specifics, such as the name of the project and the span of time that this particular report encompasses. If the report will require more than a page or so of information, you should use headings to guide the reader.

With interim progress reports such as these, you will concentrate more on updating the client on work accomplished thus far, as opposed to analyzing results of the project. You can save the analysis for the long manuscript report usually provided for a client after work on the project has been completed. Therefore, your headings will reflect work accomplished to date.

You should follow your discussion of work accomplished by outlining any problems encountered thus far. Often, these reports will also provide the client with an updated schedule indicating future plans.

Analytical or Recommendation Reports

We have combined these two categories because often an analytical report will include a recommendation, but this is not always the case. After work on a project is completed, you will probably provide your client with an analysis of the entire project. An example of an analytical report that doesn't provide a recommendation would be an audit report: you are analyzing data and interpreting it for your client, but you probably aren't recommending any particular action. On the other hand, if you are a lawyer, you might be asked to analyze various aspects of purchasing some land for development and to recommend action.

PROPOSALS

Proposals can be either external or internal reports. Internal proposals are much like the recommendation reports discussed in the previous chapter. External proposals, however, are unique in that they will almost always compete with other companies' proposals. For this reason, you should keep in mind that your external proposal is a persuasive document. Most external proposals are sales proposals, or bids for business. Therefore, in order to be successful at securing new business, you must be able to produce a well-written document.

Another type of proposal is a bid for funding. Non-profit organizations must often ask for funding from the government or from private foundations in order to continue operating. The basic organizational structure of the proposal remains the same, with a shift in focus to the benefits that this organization provides to the community. While most funding sources will provide you with specific guidelines for format and content, you can refer to the *Program Planning & Proposal Writing* handbook, published by The Grantsmanship Center, for explicit instructions on general proposal format and organization.

External Proposals

An external proposal is a company's bid for business from another company. A proposal of this type will always compete with other companies' proposals to secure the winning bid. Therefore, an external proposal is an important persuasive document and should be given the attention such a document deserves.

When an organization encounters a problem it cannot solve alone or when it solicits bids for contract work, it sends out what is called a **request for proposals,** or **RFP.** The RFP describes the nature of the problem or desired work and requests businesses to respond with proposals outlining their particular plans for solving the problem or completing the work. Most RFPs give specific instructions about how these proposals should be structured and what content should be included. You should always follow the guidelines given in the RFP; failure to do so will almost always guarantee a rejection. However, most proposals are similar in content even when the organization or format differ from company to company.

The secret to good proposal writing is to state your case (yours is the best company for the job at hand) succinctly yet thoroughly. The best proposal will not skimp on content, especially because your specific audience usually dictates what that content should be. However, most external proposals, with the exception of some government proposals, are relatively brief and always to the point. Thus, letter-report format is often used for these reports because they go outside the company, yet are rarely long enough to warrant formal-report format (to be discussed in the next chapter).

To be successful, a proposal should rely on three elements to persuade the reader: (1) facts, (2) emotion, and (3) credibility. Facts, such as statistical data, testimonies, illustrations, and examples, are essential if your proposal is to be a serious contender in securing the bid. These facts support your assertions and prove your points. For example, if you state that your company has a proven record in improving morale for other companies, you must back up that statement with proof: What other companies have you helped, and to what degree have you improved morale for those companies?

Although you must certainly rely primarily on factual data to convince your audience, don't ignore the influence that emotion plays on your reader. In order to appeal to a reader's emotions, you must first assess your reader's priorities. For example, if your hotel chain is submitting a proposal to a company looking to contract for all its employees' travel needs, you would do well to first determine the company's desired image. Does the company stress its family orientation? If so, you might highlight the family-friendly features of your hotels. Does the company wish to appear prosperous? In that case, you would underscore your hotels' luxury features. Taking the time to discover your reader's priorities can have a major impact on your reader's final decision.

Finally, don't fail to consider the credibility of the proposal itself. You may have the best plan for a company, but if your proposal is sloppy, poorly thought out, incorrectly formatted, or riddled with errors, you will not get the bid. Everything else being equal, what might push the decision in your favor is the care you've taken with the document itself. Answer all the reader's questions. Be sure to use the guidelines given in the RFP. If a group is writing the proposal, make sure that someone has taken the time to proofread for a consistent writing style throughout. Proofread any time changes are made in the document.

The following are guidelines for writing a successful external proposal. Keep in mind that, while the content remains essentially the same, different companies will give different guidelines for proposals in their RFPs. Always use the company's guidelines when writing your proposal.

I. Introduction

In a letter report, this section will begin immediately after the greeting. In this section, you should summarize the company's problem and your proposed solution. In one or two paragraphs, show the efficiency and effectiveness of your solution. Finally, tell the reader what to expect in the pages that follow. Usually, this introductory section will not have a heading.

II. Technical Plan

The technical plan is the core of the proposal and should be specific and concrete. You may include visuals in this section. Be sure to review the chapter on visuals for the correct formatting of visuals in documents. Label the section **Technical Plan** with a heading. The technical plan includes the following specific sections:

1. Statement of problem—In this section, you need to give a detailed description of the company's problem and its need for your product or service. Don't skimp on this section. In order to persuade your reader that your company is the best one for the job, you must first prove that you possess a good understanding of your reader's needs.
2. Technical description—This section describes the specific steps you will take to complete your proposal's objectives, being specific and concrete throughout. Use subheadings or a numbered list to organize this section.
3. Facilities description—This section describes any facilities or equipment you may require in order to implement your proposal.
4. Exceptions—No one company can do everything, and your reader knows this. In this section, you must address what you cannot do that your reader may expect you to do. For example, because you cannot control customer dissatisfaction due to employee error, you may not be able to guarantee that your product or service will completely eliminate the company's problem.

III. Management Plan

The management plan describes who will manage the project, should your company win the bid. Usually, this section will discuss specific individuals who will be involved in the project at various stages. Be sure to focus on these individuals' roles *within the confines of this particular project.* It's not necessary to delve into these people's backgrounds at this point in the proposal. You will have ample opportunity to do so in the next section, organizational qualifications. Use the heading **Management Plan** for this section.

IV. Organizational Qualifications

The organizational qualifications section is an important one because it is here that you address your company's ability to complete the project for which it is bidding. You should describe your company's past successes (include names of specific companies that you've helped), its tenure in the community, and other relevant facts about your company that may serve to convince your reader. Here you also provide background information about key employees at your company and/or the employees who would be involved in the implementation of the project, those discussed in the management plan. In discussing individuals, you might provide their years with the company, other companies they worked for previously, and educational background. Label this section **Organizational Qualifications.**

V. Cost Analysis

The cost analysis section is one of the most important parts of the proposal, simply because companies ultimately must be concerned with the bottom line. While your dollar bid doesn't necessarily have to be the smallest of those companies bidding, you must provide ample justification for all expenses incurred. Other factors such as company longevity, expertise, and service can help justify a higher bid and will, in fact, often win out over lower bids. Depending on the size of the project, the cost analysis can be separate from the rest of the proposal, albeit submitted along with the proposal. Be sure that this section is clear, explicit, and thorough. Also, it's important to give your reader a time frame for the budget: in other words, indicate for how long your dollar bid is valid. Label this section **Cost Analysis** or **Budget.**

VI. Conclusion

Label your final section **Conclusion** or **Summary.** Provide a brief summary of your proposal—the company's problem and how you intend to solve it. Be sure not to introduce any new information in this section. Use your conclusion as one last opportunity to persuade your reader to accept the terms of your proposal. Try to end with a thought-provoking final statement, something pithy to keep you in the reader's mind.

The most important aspect of the external proposal to keep in mind is that it is a persuasive document and will be one among many. Ensure your success with a document that is clear, thorough, and professional.

For any of these external reports, a letter report could be appropriate, although if the material you're presenting is particularly long and complex, you might consider using a more formal format for the report along with a letter of transmittal. Many experts agree, however, that letter reports can be as long as 10 pages or more. Use your judgment: if the report seems jumbled and confused, you probably need to use a formal report format so that your reader(s) can easily comprehend your message. For the majority of external reports, however, the letter format is most appropriate. See Figure 10.4 for an example of a proposal letter report, and Figure 10.5 for an example of a recommendation letter report.

Summary

Short reports carry advantages over other types of reports; a short report allows room for details but is concise enough to be easily read in a short period of time.

Different types of short reports serve different purposes. The memo report can note business decisions within a company; the most common memo reports are classified as either recommendation or periodic or progress memo reports. Letter reports maintain a more formal style than memo reports and are suitable for audiences outside your own company. The most common letter reports include progress reports, analytical or recommendation reports, and external proposal reports. Know when and why to use a memo report, as opposed to a letter report, and remember that in either case, your company's reputation will be reflected in the professionalism of the document.

Cash Register Systems
For Hamburger King

Prepared For:

Mr. Dave Markland
Hamburger King CEO

PREPARED BY:

Molly Cowell, Vice President of Client Services
Jennifer Benson, Information Systems Manager
Troy Clifton, Technical/Support Representative
Techno Cash Registers, Inc.

November 17, 200-

FIGURE 10.4 Sample Proposal Letter Report

Techno Cash Registers, Inc.
3459 University Avenue • Austin, TX 79512
(512) 234-9876 • tchnoreg@aol.com

November 17, 200-

Mr. Dave Markland, CEO
Hamburger King
4567 Bowman Road
Upper Saddle River, NJ 07458

Dear Mr. Markland:

briefly discuss the problem and the solution / *provide purpose or statement*

According to recent reports, Hamburger King has had a decrease in efficiency of orders over the last few months. We feel that this problem is because your cash register system is outdated. Our company, Techno Cash Registers, has dedicated 22 years of service to the Austin area. We now feel that we are ready to expand our business to include your national restaurant chain, and we feel we can correct your problem of inefficient orders. We would like to take this opportunity to help Hamburger King by installing new cash registers to increase order efficiency.

Techno Cash Registers has established a solid and trustworthy reputation since its inception 22 years ago. We have serviced local businesses here in Austin and have received zero complaints since the beginning of our business. We are committed to providing the best service possible to our customers. Our current customers include many small locally owned businesses in Austin and throughout central Texas. We also provide emergency service to any business in need. We have provided excellent service to our current clients and feel we can provide Hamburger King with the same satisfaction and quality service.

discuss content of upcoming sections

The following is our proposal, which outlines the details of how Techno Cash Registers can install new cash registers in Hamburger King Restaurants to increase the efficiency of orders in your establishments. Our plan will explain how well our system works, the benefits it can bring to Hamburger King, the amount of training employees will require to operate the system, and the cost to install the system. At Techno Cash Registers, we are confident that our system will greatly benefit your establishments and will increase order efficiency.

TECHNICAL PLAN

discuss the problem in detail

Hamburger King maintains an excellent level of quality of food and service to its customers. However, there seems to be a problem with your cash register systems. As our economy grows, so does our technology. It is very important for a successful restaurant chain like yours to keep up with new technology to enhance effectiveness and efficiency. Currently, you are running on a touch-button system that serves the purpose. I think with our new specialized registers, you will save money and provide better customer satisfaction.

FIGURE 10.4 *continued*

Mr. Dave Markland
Cash Register Proposal
Page 2

We have been specializing in point of sale register systems for the retail industry for 22 years. Our experience has given us the background we need to give you even better service than larger cash register companies can provide. We currently hold accounts with companies for over 75 percent of the industry in Austin.

mention the
solution

We have managed to provide faster service to customers and, on average, have increased profits by $23,000 for small companies. I think we can help you make an extra $600,000 per year by updating your cash register systems with our newest technology and innovative software designs. Our touch screen systems are much more user friendly than many push button systems and use the latest technology available.

I propose that you allow Techno Cash Registers to begin installing new advanced systems in Hamburger Kings throughout the country. The following will describe the process we will go through upon your agreement to this proposal.

Latest Technology

use either a
list or
subheadings
in the
Technical
Plan to
discuss in
detail your
proposed
solution

Our system uses touch-screen monitors with small CPUs underneath them. This will optimize the small amount of space our clients have available. These touch screens are user friendly, allowing the representative to quickly access any orders or food items without searching for specific buttons. We recommend you use Premio workstations, which are run on a Pentium III with a speed of 850 MHz. These workstations will not only give you immediate access to the network but will provide you with the fastest-responding equipment currently available on the market. These machines are being used by such major food chains as Pizza Hut, Long John Silvers, and Taco Bell. The new register system will also have compact remote printers that will enable the clerk to print out a customer receipt, send a copy to the kitchen printer, and print an extra copy for management files.

System Design and Installation

Our systems are based on each individual client's needs. We design our own software to enable us to individualize each register system. We will meet with experts from your corporate offices to design the best layout for Hamburger King and its product menu. This layout will allow us to specify what the user will see on the touch screen. For example, when the customer service representative begins an order, the system will then allow him or her to specialize orders. Once a hamburger is selected, the screens will automatically change to allow the user to select toppings. This will save time because the user will not have to search for a button if the customer wants to add pickles or to omit onions, for example.

Also, customer satisfaction will be enhanced because you will eliminate any mistakes. Each workstation will be connected to your server, allowing each general manager to review sales and check on what items are selling successfully. The process will not only cut down on inventory and disposal costs but will also save the managers time by providing a detailed inventory list. Managers will appreciate this service when they order additional inventory.

FIGURE 10.4 *continued*

Mr. Dave Markland
Cash Register Proposal
Page 3

Thus, to provide the ideal system for your needs, we will follow this procedure:

- meet with Hamburger King's corporate office representatives to evaluate your individual needs
- custom design our Premio workstations for Hamburger King
- install workstations (installation will take four hours per restaurant) during Hamburger King's non-peak hours.

Training

Techno Cash Registers will provide extensive training on this easy-to-use system. After the installation of registers in a restaurant, our trainers will come into the restaurant and provide a two-and-a-half hour training course for employees and managers. We are certain that this is sufficient time to effectively train all employees of the establishment. It has been our experience that our training program provides more self-confidence, more efficiency, and more effective use of the system by all users. Beyond the initial course, our company will provide at no extra charge an additional on-site training session if needed.

Facilities Description

describe equipment or facilities you will need to implement your proposal

A small area is needed for the new registers on the counter tops. As compared to the desktop units you are now using, our units will take up considerably less space. Each new register will require a maximum space of 14" x 13" x 13" for the touch screen, CPU, and the remote printer for receipts and printed copies. We feel that this small amount of space is preferable to the amount of space wasted on the larger, out-of-date registers used in your restaurants. The locations for the registers will be determined by each of your general managers and Jennifer Benson, our Information Systems Manager. Ms. Benson will be meeting with each management staff four weeks prior to installation to ensure a smooth transition.

Exceptions

discuss what you cannot do/provide that the reader might expect

We feel that the new registers we have recommended will provide you with an advantage over many other fast food chains, but compliance by all employees and managers is the only way to ensure this. It's very important that all managers work closely with employees and our staff to provide the best possible transition to our system. To maximize the effectiveness of our system, we recommend that attending the training session be mandatory for all employees. We realize that special accommodations will have to be made due to hours of operation, but we can provide this new technology at a time that is convenient to you.

FIGURE 10.4 *continued*

Mr. Dave Markland
Cash Register Proposal
Page 4

MANAGEMENT PLAN

this section
tells who will
oversee the
process, step-
by-step

Molly Cowell, our Vice President of Client Service, will be your contact person for this project. Molly has worked with Techno Cash Registers for five years and is familiar with all of our systems. She will be there to answer any of your questions or concerns and provide you with the general information you need. Molly will schedule the necessary times for implementation and training of your new cash register system.

Jennifer Benson, our Information Systems Manager, will be responsible for the installation of your new system. She will work closely with you to ensure this process takes place quickly and efficiently. Jennifer has over 20 years experience installing and running cash register systems. Should your system experience a hardware problem, Jennifer will be there as soon as possible to fix it.

Finally, our Technical Representative, Troy Clifton, will be running the training sessions. Each session will take approximately two and one-half hours to ensure that all of your employees are comfortable with the system. These training sessions will be scheduled at your convenience through Molly Cowell. Troy will also be your contact person in case you have any technical questions regarding your system.

describe how
well qualified
your
company is
to handle
the task; be
specific

ORGANIZATIONAL QUALIFICATIONS

Techno Cash Registers, Inc. has been in business for 22 years. During these 22 years of serving Austin businesses, we have developed an outstanding reputation. We have installed over 300 cash register systems to date and have had no complaints.

One reason businesses are so satisfied with our systems is our expertise and understanding of their needs. We understand the importance of having all machines up and running every day. Our service and technical representatives are on call 24 hours a day to serve you. All of our representatives are thoroughly trained in all areas of our systems. Before our representatives can go out into the field, they must pass a month of intensive training in all possible failure areas that customers might experience. I'm sure you will agree that our representatives are leaders in their fields.

Like Molly Cowell, Jennifer Benson, and Troy Clifton, all other members of the Techno Cash Registers' team are highly educated and experienced in cash register systems. Our employees go through a rigorous six-month course to be certified to work with our company. Ms. Cowell, Ms. Benson, and Mr. Clifton have nearly 45 years of combined experience with the company. Additionally, they have degrees in Marketing, Finance, and Management Information Systems from Texas Tech University and Brigham Young University. If you consider all of our education and experience in this field, you will find our representatives are able to address any concerns that may arise.

FIGURE 10.4 *continued*

Mr. Dave Markland
Cash Register Proposal
Page 5

describe costs involved in the implementation of the plan; consider inflation, if necessary

COST ANALYSIS

The cost to install the new touch screen system is $10,450 per establishment. This amount covers the cost of three touch-screen monitors, three CPUs, software, labor for installation, and manuals used in training employees. This fee is minimal when compared to the cost of losing business due to inefficient ordering processes. Reports show that Hamburger King is losing $2500 per month because of its inefficiency. Our cost to install the registers is a one-time cost that will bring you benefits now and well into the future. The only additional fee that will be incurred is the option of monthly maintenance checks for a small monthly fee of $50 per store. Your peace of mind is easily worth this amount.

Keep in mind that the one-time cost of installing the registers will be returned to your business within one year after installation because efficiency will increase, resulting in increased profits for Hamburger King. The estimated figures of increased profit do not reflect the increase in service that customers will notice, which will also greatly benefit each of your restaurants.

CONCLUSION

provide persuasive statements

offer further communication

Techno Cash Registers guarantees that it can increase efficiency in Hamburger King while also improving customer service. Your fast-food restaurants will benefit from our new register system, and these benefits greatly outweigh the cost of installing the system in the restaurants. By accepting our proposal and joining with Techno Cash Registers, Hamburger King can once again become a leader in the fast-food industry by providing efficient service as well as excellent food. We look forward to hearing from you in the future and hope we can work together as a team to make Hamburger King as successful as it deserves to be.

Sincerely,

Molly Cowell

Molly Cowell
Vice President of Client Services

FIGURE 10.4 *continued*

SAN DIEGO INTERNATIONAL DIVERSITY GROUP
2009 MAIN STREET ■ SAN DIEGO, CA 90876 ■ 1-800-456-8734

November 28, 200-

Dean Amber Adams
Box 34
College of Business Administration
University of California-San Diego
San Diego, CA 90456

Dear Dean Adams:

provide background

As you know, the proposed expansion of your college has resulted in much discussion and excitement within the community. As a member of the San Diego International Diversity Group, I believe that the College of Business Administration would be strengthened if it were to focus more strongly on foreign students.

state your recommendation

The program I am recommending within this report will encourage students to put forth their best efforts so that they will stay in the United States and hopefully recommend your university to friends in their homelands. Your college has already taken steps in the right direction by way of the new International Business major and the establishment of an International Business student organization. There is already interest within the existing international student population, and we can use the momentum that is building to make an expanded program successful.

describe what will follow in this report

The purpose of this report is to recommend a basic plan that U of C can use to help recruit and retain international students. I will outline proposed activities and will discuss my organization's role in achieving recruiting goals.

middle sections provide specific details about the proposed plan

Outline of Proposed Activities

Your college should follow a design that is similar to the program currently under the direction of Cynthia Miller in the College of Human Sciences. Of course, we will need to make some changes based on characteristics unique to the College of Business, such as the number of international students in your program and the types of classes that tend to most challenge them.

FIGURE 10.5 Sample Recommendation Letter Report

Dean Amber Adams
International Students' Retention Program
Page 2

The following list highlights specific recruiting and retention tactics that could work for your college:

1. Pre-college recruiting—One of our representatives would accompany your undergraduate recruiter with the express purpose of talking with resident international high school and junior college students. Our representative could give a speech about the benefits of a U of C business degree and would pass out brochures aimed at international students.

2. Pre-college preparation—Once an international student has applied to and been accepted at U of C's College of Business, we can help them with a program of pre-college preparation. The summer before their first fall semester is to begin, international students would specifically be invited to attend a skills-sharpening seminar put on by my organization that focuses on study skills, test taking, computer skills, and time management.

3. Clustering—To foster the notion of community among your College's international students, the College can adopt a policy of "clustering." That is, three or four spaces in each class could be set aside for "clusters" of international students who have already gone through the skills-sharpening seminar. Since they will already know each other, they will tend to get together as outside study partners and will lend moral support to each other.

4. Tutoring—We could organize upper-level business students to be tutors for lower-level international students. Tutors should be available for all subjects, not just for business classes. The tutors would be paid an hourly rate by your College.

5. Academic monitoring—A representative from my group could help organize grade files for all international students. The files would track each semester's grades. Also, progress report forms could be sent to professors of international students after the first six weeks of the semester. Acting to solve an academic problem (through student-professor discussions, tutoring, etc.) before it becomes too serious is a good way of helping to retain international students.

6. Scholarships—One of our representatives would work in conjunction with your Undergraduate Office to make available a list of scholarships for international students.

Implementation

My group would like to be designated to direct an International Students Program. We have been active with helping international students get settled in San Diego since 1979, so we have a good understanding of students' needs. We enjoy working with these fine young people.

FIGURE 10.5 *continued*

Dean Amber Adams
International Students' Retention Program
Page 3

My group would devote six hours per week to program duties. The position would entail an annual fee of $1000. If the College were to receive outside funding for this program, we would be compensated at a rate of 10 percent, and remaining funds would finance tutors, scholarships, and program expenses (brochures, etc.).

Summary

The San Diego International Diversity Group would put forth a strong effort to represent U of C well because we truly believe that there is no College that is better.

If you would like to discuss these ideas further, please contact me at 674-8140, extension 210. I look forward to hearing from you.

Yours truly,

Vladamir Ivaneski

Vladamir Ivaneski, President

conclude with a goodwill statement, summary, and offer for further communication

FIGURE 10.5 *continued*

CHAPTER 11

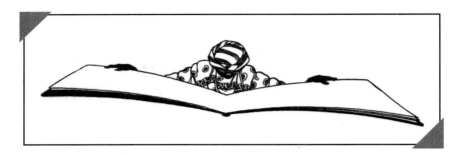

Long Reports

As you have already seen, many situations in business today require the use of reports. So far, we have discussed the shorter, less formal type of report. However, you will often find yourself faced with a decision about what type of report to write: formal or informal. Many factors distinguish a long, formal report from a shorter memo or letter report. One of these factors is length. Most experts agree that reports longer than approximately 10 pages should include the components associated with a formal report. With a report of this length, readers will benefit from a more stylized format, making reading and understanding of the material easier.

Another factor influencing the decision to use a more formal approach is your intended audience. Reports meant for a large audience, or for people with whom your relationship is more distant or formal, should follow a formal report format.

Oftentimes, certain individuals or groups within your organization will request reports that require such a format. Many formal reports go outside the organization, however. Depending on the nature of your business, some clients expect a final, formal report that details and analyzes the results of a project. Even if you have provided periodic progress reports throughout the duration of the project, you must usually provide this long report that will either interpret results or provide a recommendation. These external reports are especially important because they will represent the company's image.

The content of the report will also determine its formality. As previously stated, longer reports going outside of the organization will be more formal, as will internal reports that cover complex material. The longer and more complex your content, the more your readers will need the components of a formal report to guide them in their reading and understanding of the material. Controversial subject matter or material that may meet with hostility should also be couched in such a format because doing so will help you to appear more objective and professional.

In addition to your format, choosing an appropriate style and tone is essential in achieving a formal quality to your report. Your language should be more formal and distant. Nonetheless, your style should remain readable; in other words, formality does not require an overblown vocabulary. However, you should strive to keep your personality out of the report; any sort of glibness will not be appreciated. Avoid colorful or "creative" language, keep your personal opinions to yourself, avoid contractions, and maintain a serious tone at all times or you risk alienating your audience or not being taken seriously.

Language alone, however, will not ensure objectivity. As with all business documents, you must learn to present facts and arguments in a logical way. Use credible sources, back up any assertions you make with evidence, and avoid fallacious reasoning.

FORMAT

Formal reports tend to be long and traditional in style and tone. The reader expects the report to be broken into different sections and will read the most "important" sections (as he or she sees fit) first. For this reason, you as a writer must make the report sections distinct. The following discussion presents the different report sections in their traditionally correct order. Remember, though, to follow the format preferred by your company.

Cover

Usually, the cover page is made of lightweight cardboard or heavier-than-normal paper. Some companies have standard covers; if yours does not, include the title of the report and your name and department. Be as specific as you can when naming the report.

Title Page

The title page includes the following:

1. title of the report
2. name, title, and address of the intended audience
3. name(s), title(s), and business address of the person or group responsible for preparing the report
4. date of submission

The above information should be spaced evenly on the entire page. If the report is short, or if it is intended to be an internal communication, the title page can take the place of the cover.

Letter of Transmittal

This letter, typed on company stationery, introduces your report to the reader if you are unable to hand the report directly to the person who authorized it. Discuss the scope of the report, how you went about finding data, and any limitations of the report in your opening paragraph. The next few paragraphs discuss your most important findings, give any possible suggestions for future research projects, and acknowledge assistance (financial or other kinds) given to you. In your closing paragraph, offer further communication and, if you choose, urge the reader to action.

Table of Contents

One of the last pages you will write, the table of contents is a list of page numbers for the headings of your report. Use outline form when listing the headings. The table of contents lists all parts of the report that immediately follow this page. Connect the heading to the page number with leader dots (horizontal dots with a space between them). To increase readability, try to have at least one heading or subheading per page; the table of contents will thus have almost every page listed on it. The wording shown on the table of contents page should exactly match the wording of the headings used within the report.

Abstract or Synopsis or Executive Summary

The abstract or synopsis (the terms are used interchangeably) is a brief summary of the report. Roughly 10 percent the length of the report text, the abstract or synopsis should contain no new information, graphics, computations, or minor details. You can either describe what the report will cover or state the main ideas.

An executive summary is sometimes used in place of an abstract or synopsis. The executive summary is usually no longer than two pages, but it may be highly detailed; it can contain headings and graphics. Ideally, the executive summary is complete enough so that the reader can base an educated business decision on the summary alone.

The abstract or synopsis, or executive summary, is a helpful part of a long report. In shorter reports (those with fewer than 10 pages), it may be omitted on the basis that the report itself is not too long to be read in a single sitting.

Report Body

Remember that your word choice should include smooth transitions between the individual parts of the report text. Your main ideas should also be obvious to the reader. By using headings, you can guide the reader through your train of thought; different levels of headings will help maintain a hierarchy of ideas. Use different fonts, underlining, and capitalization, but be consistent from the level of heading to the same level of heading. Also, be consistent in spacing above and below the headings. Most writers use triple space above and double space below, but some choose to double-space both above and below. Consistency is the key here.

The introduction is the first section of the actual report body. Like the abstract or synopsis, or executive summary, it identifies the report's purpose, often in reference to a specific issue or problem. The introduction gives the reader an idea of how the report will be organized and defines key terms.

The body of the report is composed of the sections that immediately follow the introduction. Here is where the detailed information that backs your ideas will be found. Use different levels of headings as needed. Keep each heading level grammatically parallel and detailed enough so the reader can find the information of most interest to him or her. Include all graphics in the report body. As mentioned in chapter 10, **Short Reports,** make sure you discuss within the text why the graphics are relevant.

The final section of the report's text is the summary or conclusion. This section will repeat your findings, summarize your analysis of the topic, and make recommendations.

Appendix

An optional supplement to the report, the appendix includes information of interest to the reader that he or she might find distracting within the text. Different items that could appear here include multi-page graphics, statistical formulas, computer printouts, and glossaries. Each type should appear in its own appendix, labeled with a capital letter and a descriptive title. List each appendix in the table of contents.

Reference List

The reference list alphabetizes the sources that were cited within the report, along with pertinent bibliographic information. Business journals most often use the American Psychological Association (APA) format or a derivative of this style of citation. See Figure 11.1 for an example of a formal report.

TYPES OF REPORTS

There are three major types of reports: (1) formal informational, (2) analytical or recommendation, and (3) proposals. Each of these reports serves different functions and follows certain conventions. A detailed discussion of proposals may be found in Chapter 10.

Formal Informational Report

The focus of the formal informational report is on facts. The main goal of the writer is to present technical or academic information as clearly as possible. The reader is left to consider the information and draw his or her own conclusions. **Periodic** or **annual reports** are the most commonly written type of formal informational report.

These reports are issued on a regularly timed basis. As the name implies, annual reports are published once yearly; periodic reports are usually published monthly or quarterly. Use the formal report format when the report is going outside the company or when your intended audience is a superior whom you don't know well. Your tone for this type of report will be more formal than if you were writing a periodic or annual report in a memo format.

Formal periodic or annual reports should include the following information:

1. a discussion of routine duties of the writer(s)
2. a summary of new duties undertaken during the period that is being discussed
3. a proposed list of activities for the upcoming period

Periodic or annual reports sometimes focus on recent problems that have unexpectedly cropped up. Since this is an informational report, though, recommendations are usually omitted so the reader can analyze and proceed as he or she desires.

Analytical/Recommendation

This type of report is so named because some analytical reports merely interpret and analyze data while others may also offer recommendations. In either case, as a writer, you must learn how to accurately gather, interpret, and analyze data for your audience.

In using secondary sources, or material already published, you must keep several things in mind. First, use credible sources. Generally, articles in periodicals will offer more credibility than books, simply because of their currency. Journal articles, as opposed to magazine articles, will engender more confidence because they are written by and intended for experts in the field. You should become familiar with the top journals in your discipline and refer to them for source material.

Secondly, know where to find secondary sources. Your local public or university library will likely have pertinent periodicals and books in addition to general reference books such as *Business Periodicals Index* and *Standard and Poor's Register of Corporations*. Be aware that many libraries now offer computer databases on which to conduct searches, thus making your search relatively easy. The internet is also an excellent source of information.

Your place of business may also provide a library; company reports, facts, and figures can hold the key to a successful report.

Finally, you need to be prepared to READ. A big part of collecting data is reading what's out there and culling pertinent information. If you fail to do a thorough job here, you could end up embarrassing yourself by either repeating what's already been done or by overlooking evidence that completely refutes your premise. Once you've done a bit of reading, you'll begin to see trends of thought or similar results so it won't be necessary to read everything on the subject. However, two or three sources of information will generally not be enough to provide you with a clear picture.

Another way to gather data is through primary sources, such as surveys and interviews (by you) with experts, whether face-to-face or over the phone. Surveys can be used when you're asked to write a report about how your company's employees feel about a particular subject (for example, flexible scheduling); outside sources would be little help in providing data in such cases.

You can also gain important information and credibility by interviewing experts in the field (whatever that may be). Expert testimony is an especially convincing method of persuasion; people tend to place a great deal of faith in the opinions of experts. Think of how lawyers use expert opinions to convince a jury and how advertisers use them to sway an audience. It works!

Interpreting and analyzing your information is not really the "next" stage in the report process because you already do both as you read. However, you will probably

report title ——————— COMPUTER SOFTWARE SYSTEMS FOR
BUSINESS COMMUNICATIONS

Prepared for:

intended
audience ———————————

Ms. Grace DeBord
Information System Supervisor

Prepared by:

Diane Carlson, Advertising Director
writer(s) ——————— Shane Gunkel, Systems Analyst
Tony Rutledge, Budget Director

date of ——————————— April 18, 2000
submission

FIGURE 11.1 Sample Formal Report

also called
the Abstract,
it summa-
rizes the
main ideas
of the report

SYNOPSIS

Finding a software system to transform a network of Pentium III processors into a communication highway is an integral part of business success. The chosen software system should include such things as a word processor, modem, fax, bulletin board, and calendar. Profs is an e-mail system with communication applications that has been used for many years, but it has now been overshadowed by new software systems that can be run on PCs rather than mainframes. OS/2.2.1, used in client-server networking, is a very integratable system enhanced with a Windows 2000 package and multimedia accessories. Windows NT is a brand-new, peer-to-peer networking software system capable of working among several applications, such as DOS and Windows, and easily connected with other networks, making this a powerful communication tool with good system support. Another peer-to-peer networking system is Windows for Workgroups 7.0, which also has a large battery of communication tools and allows for the sharing of resources and data. Windows NT and Windows for Workgroups 7.0 were chosen as the best options in communication software systems to be considered for Meca Advertising Company.

ii

FIGURE 11.1 *continued*

TABLE OF CONTENTS

Page

virtually
every page
beginning
with the text
is listed
because you
want at
least one
heading or
subheading
to break the
monotony of
the printed
page

iii

FIGURE 11.1 *continued*

COMPUTER SOFTWARE SYSTEMS FOR BUSINESS COMMUNICATIONS

the introduction section indicates how the report will be organized

The success of computers in business communications and operations lies in the selection of a useful software system that meets the needs of the company and its employees. With the purchase of Pentium III processors for each workstation, Meca Advertising Company should invest in a software system to run a network with bulletin board, modem, fax, calendar, and word-processing capabilities. The IBM Profs system will provide a base line of comparison, since this was an important operating system for businesses several years ago. IBM's OS/2 2.1 operating system uses a server–client foundation for its networking capabilities and is widely used in the business community. A new operating system by Microsoft called Windows NT has a peer-to-peer networking foundation and offers many applications. Another very popular operating system that uses a peer-to-peer networking foundation is Microsoft's Windows for Workgroups 7.0.

NETWORKING WITH IBM PROFS OPERATING SYSTEM

detailed information appears here, as will graphics, if needed

subheadings can also appear in the middle sections

IBM's Professional Office System (Profs) is defined by Cheryl Gerber (January 11, 1993) as an electronic mail software system with home-based applications for schedules and calendars. Profs has a higher cost because, according to Michael Vizard (August 23, 1993), it is a mainframe-based system which IBM has ceased to support. He quotes David Ferris, president of Ferris Networks, Inc., as saying, " 'It's much cheaper to run e-mail on a PC in terms of cost-per-seat than on a mainframe' " (p.2). Because of the high cost and mainframe support needed, the Profs software system would be less than desirable for our company.

Instead, using a software system that runs in a local area network (LAN) will improve efficiency, communications, and cost reduction, according to Anne Fisher Lent (1994). She says LANs allow for sharing of resources and files, eliminating repeated effort, sending messages electronically, and sharing hardware and equipment. There are two kinds of LANs that can be used in setting up a business' software system among its personal computers: server–client and peer-to-peer.

SERVER–CLIENT NETWORKING WITH IBM'S OS/2 2.1

Lent (1994) explains that a client-server network links each personal computer to a file server, which is a central computer that regulates the use of data and the availability of that data to certain users. Tracey Capen (1993) says IBM's OS/2 2.1 operating system can support a server–client network, common outlying equipment, and Windows 2000 applications. He adds that the Windows 7.0 package that comes with OS/2 2.1 includes Word for Windows; Windows accessories, such as Media Player, Calculator, Paintbrush, Sound Recorder, and Notepad; and Windows File Manager, which allows a user to move files at a quicker rate than using the drive icons in OS/2 2.1. In addition, he mentions that IBM's Multimedia Presentation Manager/2 is included with OS/2 2.1, and this would make OS/2 2.1 an effective multimedia tool for Meca's business presentations and reports. Capen (1993, p. 36) states that OS/2 2.1 is "a complete 32-bit, multitasking, multithreading operating system" that is fast and flexible when moving between whole programs or

FIGURE 11.1 *continued*

between parts of programs. However, he notes that two big drawbacks to this system are its lack of built-in peer-to-peer networking capabilities and its difficulties running applications that need communication port drivers. OS/2 2.1, he reports, can be installed with disks or CDROMs, uses 18 MB to 31MB of hard disk space, needs at least 8MB of RAM for suitable performance, and costs $225.

OS/2 2.1 would be a satisfactory system when looking at cost, installation needs, and document applications, but it lacks a good communication application. Strong communication capabilities are needed in order for Meca's Creativity and Budget Departments to interact with Meca's clients around the nation. Meca Advertising Co. needs the ability to send faxes of ideas, plans, and billing statements, and to be interconnected with suppliers. Also, Meca would be better suited to a peer-to-peer network, and OS/2 2.1 cannot provide this type of network.

PEER-TO-PEER NETWORKING POWER
WITH WINDOWS NT

Lent (1994) describes a peer-to-peer network as a group of personal computers that do not operate under a single system, even though each computer is comparable in its ability to share files and applications with other computers in the network. Dale Lewallen, Scot Finnie, and Ed Bott (1993, p. 119) have assessed Microsoft's operating software system called Windows NT and have found it to be a very functional and productive system that will have "support for multiple hardware platforms, built-in peer-to-peer networking, and point-and-click connectivity among DOS, Windows, Windows for Workgroups, and Windows NT PCs." They note that Windows NT will also include Microsoft Mail, Schedule Plus, and Remote Access server, which allow access to network resources of different configurations and locations. Also, they say that the technology used in Windows NT will safeguard against the entire system collapsing when one program collapses, will allow for multitasking and multithreading, and will support a flexible and reliable security system.

All these capabilities will provide Meca Advertising Company with productivity and efficiency when running multiple programs in several applications and will provide reduced costs because, as explained by Lewallen, Finnie, and Bott (1993), a single computer will be able to have more than one user. However, they remark that 32-bit applications for Windows NT will be difficult to obtain because the system is so new, and although it is an easy system to install with either disks or CD-ROMs, it will require at least a Pentium III PC with 70MB of hard disk space and 12MB of RAM to run at an appropriate speed. Even though Microsoft quoted its retail price would be under $500, Windows NT would be an acceptable consideration for Meca's needs because it has many networking and communication capabilities in its basic package and can be used without upgrading every personal computer in the company. If this software system is chosen, a portion of Meca's new Pentuim III PCs will need to be upgraded by the Systems NT Department. This added expense will need to be considered as a part of the overall Windows package cost.

2

FIGURE 11.1 *continued*

PEER-TO-PEER NETWORKING
WITH WINDOWS FOR WORKGROUPS 7.0

According to Frank J. Derfler, Jr., and Steve Rigney (January 11, 1994), Windows for Workgroups 7.0 is an expandable operating software system with a peer-to-peer network fax and drive sharing, along with e-mail, calendar, and schedule applications. This also features a print configuration that is versatile enough to be used in either small or large networks. They report that Windows for Workgroups 7.0 contains software that allows for an integrated printer and telephone system.

Manager and File Manager, allow data and resources to be shared among users, and Windows for Workgroups 7.0 can be integrated to network with Windows NT users in a server–client configuration. In addition, they explain that Window for Workgroups 7.0 has a good security system and simple installation, requiring only 7MB of hard disk space and 3MB of RAM. They quote the price for Windows for Workgroups 7.0 as being $249.95 and $99.95 for the Workgroup Add-on for Windows, for those computers that already have an installed Windows package.

Windows for Workgroups 7.0 would be an excellent software system for our company's networking needs. This system would supply sufficient document and communication applications for a very reasonable price, especially when considering that Meca's hardware will satisfy the system's installation needs without any difficulty. Windows for Workgroups 7.0 will complement the activities of all departments in Meca Advertising Company and will allow communication both within the company and with those people and companies that Meca serves.

CONCLUSION

the conclusion repeats major findings, provides a summary, and might make recommen- dations

Today's business climate demands the use of computer software systems in order to be interconnected with others, both inside and outside the organization, for business success. An operating software system that has word processing and electronic communication capabilities is needed to utilize the potential benefits that a network of Pentium III PCs could bring to Meca Advertising Company. Since Meca's employees are most familiar with the Windows format, and the Microsoft operating systems seem most compatible with our needs and budget, the Windows NT or Windows for Workgroups software will be most beneficial to the success of Meca Advertising Co. in its business operations.

3

FIGURE 11.1 *continued*

these are the sources that were used in the text of the report; they most often appear in APA style (as shown here)

REFERENCES

Capen, T. (1993, August). OS/2: It's top technology, but where are the apps? <u>PC Computer</u>, pp. 36-39.

Derfer, Jr., F. J., and Rigney, S. (1994, January 11). Windows for Workgroups 7.0: The best Windows for all? <u>PC Magazine</u>, pp. 38-39.

Gerber, C. (1993, January 11). Attachmate E-mail links Profs to LAN systems. <u>Infoworld</u>, p. 32.

Lent, A. F. (1994, March). Compute's getting started with personal networking. <u>Compute</u>, pp. 63-71.

Lewallen, D., Finnie, S., and Bott, E. (1993, July). Windows NT: It's everything you every wanted in an operating system-or is it? <u>PC Computing</u>, pp. 119-152.

FIGURE 11.1 *continued*

want to take notes as you read to aid you in your final analysis. Look for answers to your central questions and find evidence for your assertions, particularly if you are recommending action. Avoid the temptation to overlook evidence that rebuts your claims; work instead to find data that will rebut the rebuttal.

When you must recommend action, you will often use numbers to back up your claims. Your reader will find these numbers easier to understand if you use tables and graphs to clarify the results. However, you cannot rely only on visuals; you must also discuss the numbers and interpret the results for your audience.

Some recommendations will rely on logical arguments rather than numbers. One way to persuade your audience with your logic and objectivity (and to organize your report) is to establish criteria and measure each possible solution by these same standards. Be sure that your recommendation is feasible for your audience, whether that is your company or a client. All your work will be for naught if your recommendation is too expensive or too complex. Also, be clear about how your plan should be carried out (although you don't necessarily have to get into specifics yet, know what those specifics are), and provide your audience with a general step-by-step process to work with so that your suggestions can begin to be implemented as soon as possible.

Finally, remember to maintain your objectivity and remain professional no matter what your personal feelings on the subject. By doing so, you will likely write a thoughtful, well-researched, and, ultimately, well-received report.

SUMMARY

Long, formal reports are common in real-life business writing. If your audience is large or unfamiliar to you, or if the content of the report is long and detailed, a formal report is the ideal choice over shorter, less-detailed types of reports. The different parts of the long report (including the cover, title page, letter of transmittal, table of contents, abstract or synopsis, body, appendix, and references) serve the purpose of guiding the reader through the report.

The most common types of long formal reports are the formal informational report, the analytical or recommendation report, and the proposal. Each report has a different purpose, but all should rely on solid, detailed facts. Remember that the formal report is a weighty document (figuratively and sometimes literally), and thus you should take care to give it the attention it deserves.

CHAPTER 12

Résumés

No other single document will have as much impact on the direction of your career than your résumé. Your résumé, while it won't get you the job, will almost always be the only way to secure the *interview* that will get you the job. Unfortunately, most students won't give their résumé the time and effort it requires to be the outstanding one that will open doors to opportunity. Before you begin to write your résumé, you must think and search your memory. An exceptional résumé will require hours of work, but will always be worth the effort.

For businesses, the résumé initially serves as a screening device. Remember that potential employers are looking for a reason *not* to grant you an interview. Your résumé should overcome reservations employers might have about interviewing you. Once the interview has been set up, the résumé guides the interview process. Realize that you provide some control over questions asked in the interview by virtue of the information you include on your résumé and how you present it. After the interview, your résumé helps justify the hiring decision. An outstanding résumé will represent you well to those who didn't have the opportunity to meet you during the interview.

Experts differ in their opinions regarding the format and length of the résumé, but agree on most major areas, such as skills listings, education, and work experience. We will attempt to inform you of the most widely held viewpoints and provide a cohesive picture of basic résumé requirements. All experts agree that before you can begin writing the résumé, you must target your job objective and know the product you're selling: yourself.

JOB OBJECTIVE

Many résumé writers make the mistake of writing a general résumé meant to target a variety of jobs. Not only does failure to target a specific job indicate sloppy thinking and laziness, but it also confuses the reader: just what is it that you're looking for? Remember, most initial scannings of the résumé last approximately 5 to 30 seconds. If *your* résumé doesn't immediately convey the necessary information, there is always another that will reveal the ideal candidate.

Targeting your job objective means deciding exactly which position you're interested in, and qualified for, and determining what attributes a potential employer seeks. This means that you will probably develop two or three versions of your résumé, subtly changing the focus in each one. For example, a recent graduate with a bachelor's degree in management might be qualified to work in sales, personnel, or administration. Each separate résumé will focus on training and experience in each discipline.

The job objective category isn't mandatory, but many people always include one on their résumés. In fact, it can be helpful to the reader who is seeking a candidate for a very specific position. The job objective category can be deceptively simple. Yet, a well-written, useful job objective takes time to compose. The job objective that you often see on résumés creates any number of problems. Most job objectives sound something like this: "Seeking an entry-level job in accounting." First of all, this statement does absolutely nothing to set you apart from the thousands of other applicants also seeking an entry-level position in accounting. Secondly, the statement implies that the position is merely a stepping-stone in your career. Remember, to the person who is hiring, every job is important. Thirdly, statements such as these focus on the *applicant's* desires rather than those of the company (and, therefore, the person doing the hiring).

To write a useful, effective job objective, focus on the reader's needs instead of your own. Although this category gives the appearance of stating your own career desires (and, of course, ultimately should), you must word it to appeal to the reader. For this reason, much of its focus should be on what you can offer the company in a particular position, not what you hope to gain from the position. The following is an example of an effective job objective:

"Seeking a management position in a retail setting that will allow me to increase profits while motivating employees to greater achievements."

Writing the job objective requires much thought, but spending the time necessary to create a meaningful one will pay off in the long run. Position your job objective category immediately after your name and address on your résumé.

PROFILE

Although experts differ slightly in their wording, all agree that because the résumé is organized in order of its strongest selling point, it should begin with a **profile** or **list of qualifications.** This profile should focus on qualifications that directly pertain to the job for which you are applying. Therefore, while the rest of the résumé might remain essentially the same, the profile should differ with each separate type of job. With a profile category on your résumé, you allow the reader to assess your skills without having to cull through the entire document to determine if you're a candidate for the position.

Here is my profile.

The profile, or list of qualifications, should pinpoint what you can do for this company in this position. Of course, all of your assertions must be backed up with specifics. In other words, it's not enough to say "Excellent management skills" without backing this statement up with concrete evidence. You don't need to go into great detail (in fact, you shouldn't), but realize that anyone who can type can write that statement on his or her résumé; it doesn't prove anything. Follow up with something like "Increased productivity and morale, and lowered absenteeism."

Most experts agree that the profile should be anywhere from 3 to 10 lines long. The general consensus is that 10 lines is bordering on too long. The ideal would probably be 5 to 7 lines.

In order to write a list of qualifications that will best highlight your skills, you need to brainstorm. Think about all the jobs you've held, including those that at first glance may seem insignificant. Next, review your coursework and other academic experiences. Look at all your honors and awards. Think about your activities, both in and out of school. Any unusual travel, as well as community service, should be reviewed. Think about special qualifications, such as language specialization and computer skills. As you review these experiences, allow yourself to simply freewrite. Don't think about grammar, spelling, and punctuation at this point. Once you've finished, look at what you've written, and choose skills provided by any and all of these experiences that will transfer to the job for which you are applying. From this list, write an effective profile. The following is an example of a profile:

PROFILE
Financial Operations: Financial and statistical-based analysis. Skilled in Lotus, dBase, WordPerfect, and MS Word. Background in project planning and market research. Skilled in working with wide range of individuals. Fluent in Spanish.

While the profile may be the most time-consuming and difficult part of the résumé to assess and write, it's an essential part of a résumé that will stand head and shoulders above the rest.

EDUCATION

Conventional wisdom has held that the strongest selling point of recent college graduates is the degree, and it should therefore be placed prominently at the top of the résumé. For the most part, this is still true, but be forewarned that your college education will win you favor for just so long. Most experts agree that after about two years in the workforce, you will be expected to have accomplished a number of impressive feats that will take prominence on a résumé.

The education category will be arranged in reverse chronological order, no matter what type of résumé you use (chronological, functional, combined, or electronic). Therefore, begin with your highest degree first, and work your way down. If you received both a graduate and undergraduate degree simultaneously, still list the higher degree first. The listing should include degree type (B.A., B.B.A., B.S., M.A., M.S., Ph.D., etc.); there is no need to spell out the degree type unless it's not readily understood by most people. Next, be sure to include your major; you would consider leaving this off only if it would be a detriment to the job for which you are applying. Follow with the year you received your degree or your expected date of graduation. Next, you should provide the institution name, followed by the location. Some people prefer to omit the city and state, and this is acceptable, particularly if you are applying for jobs within the general area. The following is an example of an education listing:

B.B.A., Finance, 2001
Old Dominion University, Norfolk, Virginia

Occasionally, a person may want to highlight the university if it's a particularly prestigious one. This can be done by listing the institution first or by bolding:

Harvard University, Massachusetts
M.B.A., 2002

or

M.B.A., 2002
Harvard University, Massachusetts

Some people are tempted to provide information about high school. This temptation should usually be avoided. However, there are exceptions: if you attended a prestigious private or public school, you might consider displaying that fact in your education category. Also, do so if you're applying for a job overseas, where listing high school information is the norm. If you wish to convey the fact that you were salutatorian or valedictorian, don't do so here; you can put that information in an "Honors" category. You don't want to leave the reader with the impression that you hit your peak in high school.

If you attended more than one school, most experts recommend not taking up space by listing all schools. List only the school you received your degree from, even if you have an associate's degree from a two-year college.

Include your G.P.A. if you so desire. However, it should be included only if it's higher than 3.0 (one résumé expert notes that even 3.5 isn't all that impressive anymore). If your G.P.A. isn't noteworthy, think about revealing your G.P.A. in your major or in your last two years. If you do so, be sure to label it correctly. Some companies will value work experience or financial independence over G.P.A.; with these companies, an average G.P.A. can sometimes be offset by professional work experience or evidence that you paid for all, or a majority of, your education. At any rate, you should drop your G.P.A. from your résumé after five years.

You may include in your education section any projects, courses, or theses pertinent to your college career and to the job for which you are applying. This is particularly helpful if you're weak in job experience.

WORK EXPERIENCE

Again, before you begin writing your work experience on your résumé, you need to do extensive brainstorming. Don't limit yourself to thinking only about long-term, paid work experience. Also think about volunteer experience, non-paid work, internships, self-employment, odd jobs, and temporary positions. All of these experiences taught you something, and many of these skills can be translated to the job market.

Once you've thought about all your work experience, you need to focus on what you accomplished on the job. Freewrite about your job duties, accomplishments, and results, keeping in mind that potential employers are much more interested in what you accomplished than in what you did day-to-day on the job. What did *you* bring to the job that no one else did? Thinking and writing about these accomplishments will take time. You should know, though, that employers will want to know more about the experience that taught you relevant skills, even if that experience was short-lived, than they will about the job you held for five years as fry-cook, if that experience taught you little.

Each listing under work experience should contain certain information: company name, job title, dates, accomplishments, and job duties. If the company you worked for is well known, such as IBM, there is no need to provide a description of the company's products or services. If, however, the company is not readily recognizable, think about giving a brief description. When you provide your job title, make sure that it's accurate. Again, highlight information that you want the reader to immediately notice, such as company name or job title. Generally, cities, states, and dates will not be bolded since this information is not key. Be sure to be consistent throughout your résumé, however. If you bold one company name, you must bold all company names. Be sure that you keep the same order, font size and type, and spacing for each item in this section.

Normally, you will order your job listings in reverse chronological order, beginning with your current or most recent job and working backward. However, there are ways to highlight certain jobs to make them stand out to the reader. A job that is directly relevant to your job search might go under a separate category entitled "Professional Experience," "Related Experience," or, more specifically, "Sales Experience." You also need to group together those jobs that you returned to every year, say in the summers. Simply write the date as, for example, "Summers 1998–1999." This saves space and implies loyalty and dependability. Remember to include temporary jobs, such as holiday work.

If you've held a variety of jobs that really didn't do much more for you than get you through school, you should list these jobs in a simple phrase, such as "Also worked as wait person, cashier, and groundskeeper, 1998–2000." This will let the reader know that you've been gainfully employed, but you don't waste space and the reader's time providing descriptions.

FIGURE 12.1 Suggested Action Verbs

achieve	contract	expand	market	provide	simplify
act	contribute	expedite	master	purchase	sort
administer	cooperate	facilitate	merge	raise	solve
advise	coordinate	file	minimize	realize	staff
allocate	correlate	finalize	moderate	receive	start
analyze	correspond	finance	monitor	recognize	stimulate
approve	create	forecast	motivate	recommend	streamline
assess	customize	form	negotiate	reconcile	strengthen
assign	decide	formulate	observe	record	structure
attain	decrease	gain	obtain	recruit	succeed
audit	delegate	gather	offer	redesign	summarize
authorize	deliver	generate	open	reduce	supervise
balance	demonstrate	handle	operate	reevaluate	supply
budget	designate	head	order	refer	support
build	design	hire	organize	regulate	surpass
calculate	determine	identify	originate	relate	survey
carry out	develop	illustrate	overcome	reorganize	tabulate
clarify	devise	implement	oversee	research	test
classify	direct	improve	participate	resolve	trace
coach	display	increase	perfect	restore	train
collaborate	distribute	initiate	perform	retrieve	transact
collect	document	inspect	place	reverse	transfer
communicate	draft	install	plan	review	transform
compile	earn	institute	predict	revise	treat
compose	eliminate	instruct	prepare	save	troubleshoot
compute	employ	integrate	present	schedule	unify
conceive	enable	justify	prevent	secure	update
conceptualize	enact	keep	process	select	upgrade
condense	enhance	launch	produce	sell	utilize
conduct	ensure	lead	program	separate	validate
consolidate	establish	locate	project	serve	verify
construct	evaluate	log	promote	set up	win
consult	examine	maintain	propose	shift	work
contact	execute	manage	prove	ship	write

As you type up your work experience on your résumé, remember to be consistent; use graphic devices, such as bolding, bullets, different font sizes and styles, and indentation to focus your reader's attention and aid in scanning; target accomplishments and results. Think about using action verbs such as *developed, increased, lowered, prepared, analyzed, maintained, repaired, established, organized, performed, assessed, achieved, earned, created, conceived, wrote, provided,* and *promoted,* just to name a few. A more complete list appears in Figure 12.1. These verbs denote action and imply results. Words like *best, highest, most, only,* and *first* will impress a reader. Also, use phrases like *resulting in,* or *which resulted in;* utilizing these phrases will force you to think about results. Remember, it's not enough to provide mere job duties; show the reader your potential, and **be specific.** The following is an example of an effective job listing:

Waldenbooks, Cincinnati, Ohio, 1998–2000

Assistant Manager
- *Managed 15 employees. Opened, closed, inspected work on each shift.*
- *Created additional sections of employee handbook, increased employee morale. Sold 15% over projected sales first year, 22% second year.*
- *Won Employee of the Year in region, 1999.*
- *Conceived and created successful "Spring Fashion Show of Books," 1998 and 1999, which continues today, resulting in a consistent 33% increase over projected sales for April.*

You'll notice that each sentence begins with an action verb. Because this person no longer works for this company, the verbs are in past tense. For your current job, use present tense.

Remember, you may have spent 85 percent of your time performing mundane tasks, but you'll want to focus on that 15 percent that was spent in accomplishing the unusual. Don't worry that your résumé targets that 15 percent; that's the indication of potential that employers are looking for!

ACTIVITIES, HONORS, AND ORGANIZATIONS

This section can encompass all three categories suggested, or it can be broken down into two and even three separate sections if you have a lot of information. Generally, you want to keep your lists fairly brief, so if you have more than about six items on any list, think about reorganizing them into separate lists. Conversely, it's never a good idea to include only one item on any list under these categories; one item tends to point out to the reader that you were not very active. Instead, leave the item off entirely, or combine it with other items under one category.

There is a rhyme and reason to the list(s) under this category. You'll want to list the items in order of importance. Be sure to list them in order of importance *to the reader.* You must see the résumé from the reader's point of view in order to list the items correctly.

The "Activities" section includes involvement in volunteer organizations, such as Big Brothers or Big Sisters; it can also list more personal types of activities, such as marathon running. While some experts contend that personal information should be kept out of the résumé, most agree that tidbits of your personal life will often spark interest during the interview. Talking about something that truly interests you during the interview can relax you and make the interview go more smoothly. It will also provide you with a point of reference in your follow-up letter that will immediately let the reader know that yours is not a form letter.

Honors include such things as awards, scholarships and fellowships, as well as valedictory and salutatory awards. Again, they should be presented in order of importance. It's helpful to include dates.

Organizations listed on the résumé should be relevant to the job for which you are applying. List academic organizations and professional associations if you are still an active member. If you're no longer an active member of a particular organization, omit this information unless you held office. If you feel that an organization doesn't add much to your résumé, leave it off. Although you might want to include your social fraternity or sorority, this is not a good idea because your reader may belong to a rival organization, in which case this item on your list could automatically disqualify you. The only time you should list a social fraternity or sorority is if you know you're sending the résumé to a brother or sister, and then you should display it prominently.

You should also omit any organization or activity that refers to your political or religious affiliation or your race. Remember, if you list these activities, you're providing the reader with information that he or she cannot legally ask you about in an interview or on an application.

REFERENCES

The "References" category has undergone a complete about-face in the past several years. While in years past, references on a résumé were mandatory, today, most employers do not want to see a list of references unless requested at a later date. The threat of litigation has caused employers to be very cautious about giving and requesting references.

If you choose to list your references, do so on a separate sheet of paper, and keep it with you in the event that it's requested. Three to five references are ideal. (Of course, always be sure that you have asked your references' permission to list them. Also, it's a good idea to ask each reference what he or she would say about you.) Include names, position titles, business addresses, and phone numbers.

If you don't want to list your references but would like to refer to them, you might put "References available upon request" at the bottom of your résumé. However, because employers know this to be true, this statement isn't usually necessary.

As you collect your references, keep in mind that personal references should be kept to a minimum, if used at all. After all, a friend you've known half your life will always give you a glowing recommendation, and employers know this. Instead, concentrate on references such as former and present supervisors and teachers; these references will lend more credibility than will personal references. Also, be sure that your references aren't all male or all female; balance is the key.

OTHER CATEGORIES

The wonderful thing about the résumé is its flexibility. There is no one format that you must use, and there are no set categories, other than education and work experience, that **must** appear on your résumé. You should gather your information, group it by subject, and then decide what categories would best describe your background.

Here is a list of suggested categories. Feel free to make up your own.

Computer Skills	Military Experience
Special Skills	Scholarships
Languages	Research
Travel	Community Service
Conferences	Volunteer Experience
Foreign Study	Personal
Affiliations	

PERSONAL

It has become passé to use the personal section to indicate marital status, height, weight, age, and health status. Again, you're providing information that interviewers cannot legally ask you about, so why include it? Instead, you might use a personal category to inform the reader that you're bonded, that you're a U.S. citizen if that may be a legitimate question, or that you're willing to relocate if the company is regional or national. You might also wish to include activities here if you haven't under an "Activities" category. If none of these suggestions applies to your particular situation, the experts suggest you simply leave it off your résumé.

FORMAT

The format of the résumé is very flexible. However, there are some guidelines to consider as you create a winning résumé.

Length
A one-page résumé is highly recommended for recent college graduates. Many recruiters won't even look at résumés from inexperienced applicants that are longer than a page. Think of the one-page length limitation as the first test you must pass to get to the interview.

After you've been in the work force for a few years, you may lengthen your résumé to two pages. However, unless you've been asked to submit a curriculum vitae, your résumé should never exceed two pages.

Layout

Use one-inch margins on all four sides of the résumé. At the top margin, center your name. If you use a nickname, you should include it either in parentheses or in quotation marks as in the following examples.

Patricia "Patty" McCormick

or

Bruce (Bruno) Hallman

Be sure that your name is in a larger font size than the rest of the résumé, but don't go overboard. A 14 to 16 size font is generally large enough.

If you have two addresses, such as a school address and a permanent address, include both on the résumé. Don't make interested readers search you out because they often won't. If you use two addresses, put one on either side of the résumé under your name. Otherwise, space under your name, and center your address line by line. See Figures 12.2 through 12.6 for examples.

You should choose how you want to space your résumé. Remember not to cram information together; use plenty of white space to aid in readability. However, it's possible to use too much white space, especially at the top, bottom, and sides of the résumé. If your résumé has large gaps or isn't evenly balanced on the page, you need to re-format it after you finish typing.

There are many different acceptable ways to lay out the résumé, but most readers and résumé experts agree that the column layout is the most readable. Align your category titles along the left margin, keeping the column no more than an inch to an inch-and-a-half across. The right-hand column will be wider and will contain the information falling under each category. Sometimes résumé writers will line up dates, such as for employment, underneath the category titles. This format scans very easily and seems to be the one most commonly used. Notice that Figure 12.2 shows the column format.

Another format has the category titles centered down the page with pertinent information listed across the page or in two columns. This is also a very popular format;

however, it is harder to scan. You might try both formats and then decide which best highlights your information. Figure 12.3 is an example of the across-the-page layout.

One important rule to remember is **be consistent!** In other words, if you triple space after one job listing, you must triple space after the next. If you indent two spaces on one line, you must do the same on the next item's line. Look at the résumés provided in this chapter for spacing and other formatting ideas.

Graphics

You **must** produce your résumé on a computer or word processor. A typewriter simply will not provide you with the graphical options that a computer will, and your résumé will reflect that. Use bolding, bullets, underlining, different font sizes, and other graphics to enhance your résumé. The key word here is *enhance*. You certainly don't want to confuse the reader with too much diversity. Any stylistic devices you use on your résumé should of course be aesthetically pleasing, but your top priority is to create a résumé that will scan quickly and clearly. Too many different types of graphics will slow down the reader and reduce your chances of a positive response. Keep to one font style, and make sure that what you choose is traditional. Font styles that are appropriate for business graduates are Times New Roman, Helvetica, Bookman, and New Century Schoolbook. Any font style similar to these would be appropriate.

Font size, with the exception of your name and perhaps category titles, should remain between 10 and 12 point. Smaller type is hard to read, and larger type looks as though the writer is trying to fill space.

If you choose to use bullets, do so sparingly. Again, the bullets are there primarily to aid the reader, not to add beauty. Bullet only the first line of an item, not every line, or confusion abounds. See Figure 12.2 for effective use of bullets.

Bold the information that you consider most important, such as company names, position titles, G.P.A., or school, but don't bold dates or entire job descriptions. The same holds true for underlining.

WORDING

One very important rule to keep in mind is that complete sentences are rarely used in résumés. Instead, you should use strong verb phrases. See Figure 12.1 for a list of useful verbs.

Try to choose verbs that best describe the action. Don't use the same two verbs over and over again, or the résumé will sound monotonous. Work to begin each sentence with a good, strong action verb; avoid helping and auxiliary verbs such as *be* and *have*.

Use past tense with all jobs except your current one; instead, use present tense. Remember that you are the subject of the résumé, so all sentences should be written as if the word *I* were attached to them.

RÉSUMÉ PAPER

Don't work for days and weeks on your résumé only to send it through the mail on ordinary printer paper and printed with a dot matrix printer! Have your résumé printed on top-quality résumé paper with a laser printer. Most copy shops will offer you résumé paper in a variety of colors. However, as business graduates, you should choose an off-white, cream, or light gray. Choose a paper that's fairly heavy; studies have shown that paper weight is directly linked to the reader's first impression of the résumé. Finally, be sure that the paper is the correct 8-1/2 × 11 inch size.

PROOFREADING

We include a section on proofreading because it's an essential part of the résumé-writing process that many people neglect. It won't matter how much effort went into writing your résumé if it has misspelled words and typographical errors. Your résumé must be perfect, or it runs the distinct risk of finding its way into the "round" file. One survey of college recruiters taken in 1991 indicated that 30 percent would stop reading the résumé after finding one typographical error, and the percentage went up to 60 percent after two errors. Would you want to cut off that many job opportunities because of an easily correctable problem?

When you finish typing your résumé, run a computer spell check to find misspelled words. However, that's not all you must do. You should then check to see that all your words are used correctly. A spell check will not catch words that are used incorrectly. For example, if you meant to write "plain" but instead wrote "plane," the computer won't know the difference, but a reader will.

Next, make sure all dates, addresses, phone numbers, and company names are correct. Check also for consistency in spacing, indentation, bolding, and other graphic devices. Readers also notice format.

After you've completed your proofreading, repeat the process. Have someone else look at your résumé. Sometimes a fresh eye will find mistakes that you have overlooked.

FUNCTIONAL RÉSUMÉS

In this chapter, we have been discussing the chronological résumé (see Figure 12.2–12.5), which is the one most acceptable for recent college graduates. However, there is another type of résumé currently in use that you need to be aware of, especially if you think of changing jobs a few years down the road.

The **functional** résumé focuses on accomplishments and results on the job rather than on a linear job description. In pure functional résumés, dates of employment are omitted entirely. Instead, the writer details his or her accomplishments. This type of résumé is most often used by people who wish to change jobs after several years in the job market. It's rarely used by recent college graduates. See Figure 12.7 for an example of a functional résumé.

Perhaps more acceptable than the functional résumé is the **combined** résumé. This résumé also focuses on accomplishments and results, but it provides a work history with employer information and pertinent dates. The combined résumé uses the best attributes of both the chronological and functional résumés to provide the reader with the best possible résumé. Refer to Figure 12.6 for an example of a combined résumé.

WILLIAM F. HUMPHREY, JR.

QUALIFICATIONS   Strong background in academic and applied **marketing.** Significant experience in **leadership** and **entrepreneurship.** Effective **oral presentation** and **seminar** skills.

EDUCATION

Master of International Management   **December 1994**
American Graduate School of International Management
Thunderbird Campus, Glendale, Arizona
• Focused on marketing and international studies.
• Studied the European Union and the Single Market.
• Developed written and conversational French skills.

Bachelor of Business Administration, Marketing   **December 1993**
Texas Tech University
Lubbock, Texas

EXPERIENCE

Business Administration (B.A.) Advisory Council   **1991-1993**
President, Texas Tech University
• Supervised all B.A. organization presidents.
• Presented leadership/community service seminars to student leaders.
• Guest lectured for B.A. at University Day for incoming students.

Business Administration Ambassadors   **1992-1993**
Founder, Texas Tech University
• Created the student organization to improve student recruiting.
• Served as a liaison between the faculty and student body.
• Held an advisory role after founding the organization.

College Relations/Recruiting   **1992-1993**
Graduate Assistant, Thunderbird
• Processed and responded to student inquiries.
• Performed graphic and text design projects.

Texas London Business Program   **1992**
Participant, London, England
• Studied international marketing, European Union, and British culture.
• Focused on the formation of the Single Market of the European Union.

Texas London Alumni/Recruitment Organization   **1993**
President, Texas Tech University
• Coordinated the recruitment of students for the London Program.
• Directed the marketing and promotion of the project.
• Presented information seminars to prospective students.

AWARDS

Presidential Endowed Scholarship, Texas Tech University.
International Scholarship, Thunderbird.
Academic Citizenship Award, Texas Tech University.

COMPUTER   Microsoft Word, Works, Excel, WordPerfect, Harvard Graphics, and Datatel.

15010 N. 59th Ave.   Undergraduate G.P.A.: 3.7
Glendale, Arizona 85306   Graduate G.P.A.: N/A
(513)547-1935   G.M.A.T. Score: 580

FIGURE 12.2 Sample Résumé

DON R. SALISBURY
1001 University Avenue, No. 15
Lubbock, Texas 79401
Phone: (806) 555-9315

SKILLS & KNOWLEDGE

Comprehensive experience with MS-DOS, Microsoft Windows, Apple Macintosh, and VAX/VMS environments. Additionally, have completed software development tasks on above platforms using languages such as C, FORTRAN, COBOL, Pascal, BASIC, Visual BASIC, and JCL. Proficient with Lotus 1-2-3, WordPerfect, Microsoft Excel and Word, and a perpetual amount of other software packages on the Apple Macintosh and PC environments. Have special knowledge of MS-DOS PC to Apple Macintosh communications, networking, and cross platform connectivity. Network skills include experience with Novell NetWare, AppleShare, and TOPS.

EDUCATION

B.B.A., Management Information Systems, December, 2000
Texas Tech University, Lubbock, Texas
MIS G.P.A.: 4.0

WORK EXPERIENCE

Precept Computer System Design & Consulting, Lubbock, TX, Founder/Senior 3/99-present. **Consultant**. Provide computer services for students, small/medium-sized businesses, and home computer buyers. Skills include software development, networking, system design and assessment, and training.

Texas A&M Research and Extension Center, Lubbock, TX, Research 5/98-present. **Assistant/Software Programmer**. Work 20-25 hours per week developing software and hardware for use in outdoor field experimentation, agricultural modeling, and data collection and manipulation.

Audio Synthesis DJ Service, Dallas/Lubbock, TX 9/95-5/98. **Founder/DJ/Equipment Technician**. During high school and college, worked mostly on weekends providing music DJ services for local schools and organizations. Designed and constructed stereo and lighting equipment used for DJ service.

ACTIVITIES & HONORS

DPMA, Dean's List, President's List, Clifford Jones Scholarship (three years).

PERSONAL

Enjoy programming, music, science, sports, and coaching youth soccer.

FIGURE 12.3 Sample Résumé

THOMAS DIXON
5301-A Louisville Avenue
Lubbock, TX 79413
(806) 555-9129

COMPUTER SKILLS	Fourteen years experience with personal computers. Familiar with and quick to learn operating systems, languages, system utilities, databases, word processors, spreadsheets, communication software. Experience installing software, peripherals, memory. Tutored COBOL to classmates.

EDUCATION

7/98 to Present	**Texas Tech University**, Lubbock, TX B.B.A., Management Information Systems, May 2001 Cumulative G.P.A.: 3.7 President's List: Fall 1999 Dean's List: Spring 1999 through Spring 2000
<u>Systems:</u> <u>Languages:</u>	DEC VAX (DCL), IBM PC (MS-DOS, Windows). C, COBOL, SQL, Quick BASIC, Assembly Language.

WORK EXPERIENCE

12/97 to 8/99	<u>Lockheed Support Systems</u>, Reese AFB, Lubbock, TX. <u>Position</u>: Aircraft Hydraulic Component Repairman. Troubleshot, inspected, repaired and tested brake, landing gear, and flight control hydraulic components before aircraft installation. Updated aircrafts' maintenance records in computer system.
9/92 to 12/97	<u>U.S. Air Force</u>, Reese AFB, Lubbock, TX. <u>Position</u>: Aircraft Pneudraulic Systems Mechanic. Troubleshot, removed, and installed aircraft hydraulic components. Troubleshot, repaired, and tested components in-shop. Honorable Discharge.
Prior to 9/92	Busboy, 9/90 to 12/92. Construction, 6/86 to 12/90. Paperboy, 1983 to 1986.

INTERESTS

<u>Financial:</u>	Own and manage residential rental property, invest in mutual funds, maintain personal tax plan.
<u>Athletic:</u>	Weightlifting, bicycling, swimming.

FIGURE 12.4 Sample Chronological Résumé

GREG W. KESTERSON

Permanent Address:
9406 Edgewood Drive
Spring, TX 77379
(713) 555-6941

School Address:
Texas Tech University
Murdough - Room 508
Lubbock, TX 79406
(806) 742-6833

OBJECTIVE

To obtain a summer internship position where I can develop the skills being learned in the MIS curriculum to the benefit of the employer and me.

AVAILABLE FOR EMPLOYMENT

May 16 - August 31, 2001

EDUCATION

Texas Tech University
Major: Management Information Systems
Junior - 73 Semester Hours
GPA: 3.5

Fall Semester '99:
Attended Foreign Study Program
University of London, England
"Study Abroad" Scholarship

RECOGNITION

President's List '99
Dean's List '97, '98
Member of ToastMasters
Vice President of London Alums

Alpha Lamba Delta Honor Fraternity
Phi Eta Sigma Honor Society
Golden Key Honor Society-Spring '99
Data Processing Management Assoc.

WORK EXPERIENCE

Summer, 1998
- **United Way of Texas Gulf Coast** - Headquarters office, Company Store. Supervisor of summer/temp. employees. Expanded use of software to increase office efficiency.

Summer, 1997
- **COMPAQ** - Houston, Texas. Assigned as Quality Control Inspector in the computer production area. Developed a database file update program.
- **United Way of Texas Gulf Coast** - Assignment in the Headquarters office, in the Company Store, using computerized order processing and inventory controls. Helped implement new inventory method that increased efficiency by **32%.**

FIGURE 12.5 Sample Chronological Résumé

this type of résumé focuses on both accomplishments and work history

EMILIO BASALDUA

School Address:
2102 40th Street
Lubbock, TX 79408
(806) 769-0013

Permanent Address:
1234 Swanson
Santa Fe, New Mexico
(505) 768-1235

SKILLS:

Extensive supervision training, including counseling, managing, and hiring personnel. Experienced in fields of accounting and drafting, as well as with computers. Willing to work long hours to benefit a growing company.

EDUCATION:

Enrolled in the 150 Program (Combined BBA and MS)
B.B.A., Accounting - Candidate
M.S., Accounting - Candidate
Texas Tech University, Lubbock, Texas
• Graduation Date: May 1995
• 3.6 G.P.A.

EMPLOYMENT EXPERIENCE:

James Teague & Co., C.P.A.s, P.C. Lubbock, Texas	July 1993 - present Junior Accountant
Builder's Square Lubbock, Texas	June 1993 - July 1993 Cashier
The Tax Stop Lubbock, Texas	January 1993-April 1993 Tax Preparer
Veterans Outpatient Clinic Lubbock, Texas	June 1992 - December 1993 File Clerk
H & R Block Clovis, New Mexico	January 1992 - April 1992 Tax Assistant
Military Service U.S. Air Force	October 1984 - April 1992 Mainframe Computer Operator
Pyramid Stone Co. San Antonio, Texas	May 1983 - October 1984 Draftsman

FIGURE 12.6 Sample Combined Résumé

EMILIO BASALDUA   Page 2
Résumé

MILITARY SERVICE:
U.S. Air Force   Staff Sergeant

Military Training
- Noncommissioned Officers Leadership School
- OJT Trainer/Supervisor course
- Mainframe Computer Data Base Management course
- Speery System 1100 Mainframe Computer course
- Supervisor Safety training course

Military Supervision
- Plan work assignments and priorities
- Plan and supervise on-the-job training
- Maintain training records
- Counsel personnel and resolve individual problems
- Assign personnel to work crews

Military Achievements
- Air Force Achievement Medal — April 1992, May 1987
- Noncommissioned Officer of the Month — October 1991, May 1991, October 1990, March 1990, September 1989
- Below-the-Zone (early promotion) — April 1987
- Airman of the Year nominee — 1986
- Airman of the Quarter — 3rd quarter 1986

ACTIVITIES AND HONORS:
- 1992 Scholarship Recipient, American Women's Society of Certified Public Accountants
- Golden Key National Honor Society, member
- Fall 1992, Dean's List
- 1992 Volunteer Income Tax Assistance, participant
- 1991 Special Olympics Program, hugger
- 1992 U.S. Air Force Squadron Income Tax Assistance, participant

PERSONAL:
- Born in Corpus Christi, Texas.
- Lived in Germany for two years.
- Interests include running, racquetball, golf, playing guitar.

FIGURE 12.6 *continued*

the main
focus here is
on job
accomplish-
ments

ELEANOR J. HITCHCOCK

8790 Destiny Road
Houston, TX 77042
(713)345-7897

SUMMARY

Licensed as an attorney in the state of Texas on November 2, 1993. More than seven years of corporate and law firm experience. Known for strong writing ability and thoroughness in handling work. Advised clients; maintained warm, cordial relationships with clients, even after the work was completed. Experienced in WordPerfect and Windows.

ACCOMPLISHMENTS

Real Estate and Oil & Gas

- Negotiated and drafted agreements and contracts, including but not limited to oil and gas leases, surface leases, powers of attorney, and Affidavits of Heirship.

- Handled numerous bank real estate loans and loan extensions, as well as real estate sales and mobile home sales.

- Handled the sales and acquisitions of oil and gas properties by negotiating and preparing the Purchase and Sale Agreements, Assignments and Bills of Sale, and any other necessary legal documents.

- Coordinated both within and without the corporation on these conveyances with such entities as the Tax Department, on tax-free exchanges; the Accounting Department, on the financial ramifications; the Environmental, Safety, & Health group, on the environmental state of the properties; and with such government agencies as the Texas Railroad Commission and the Bureau of Land Management.

- Supervised brokers in lease acquisitions.

- Corresponded with the oil and gas industry, landowners, and royalty owners.

Office Practice

- Drafted wills covering customary and unusual circumstances, meeting all client specifications.

- Probated estates, filed inventory with court, and advised clients of multi-state requirements.

FIGURE 12.7 Sample Functional Résumé

Eleanor J. Hitchcock   Page 2

- Resolved property damage claims with various landowners to mutual satisfaction of company and landowners.

- Reviewed land files and examined state regulations to ascertain corporation's interest, options, and obligations.

- Foreclosed on properties for bank.

- Researched and wrote legal briefs in such areas as commercial law, civil rights, workers' compensation, personal injury, and deceptive trade practices.

- Handled divorces and drafted division of property and child custody agreements.

- Dissolved corporations and incorporated corporations.

EDUCATION

- University of Texas at Austin School of Law
  J.D. Degree, May 1993

- Rice University, Houston, Texas
  B.A. Degree, May 1990
  Majors: Mathematical Science, English

PROFESSIONAL ASSOCIATIONS

- Member, State Bar of Texas, 1993-present
- Member, American Association of Petroleum Landmen, 1995-present
- Member, Houston Association of Petroleum Landmen, 1997-present

ACTIVITIES

Volunteer tutor at Landis Elementary School, Houston, Texas, 1995-1996
United Way Coordinator for Chevron's Central Land Division, 1995
U.S. Savings Bond Coordinator for Chevron's Central Land Division, 1995
Rice University President's Club Committee, 1994-1995

FIGURE 12.7 *continued*

ELECTRONIC RÉSUMÉS

Although hard-copy, or visual or presentation, résumés will likely never go out of style, the advent of computer technology and the Internet has dramatically changed the form and content of the résumé. Most large companies and many medium-sized organizations routinely search their own databases for scanned résumés and the Internet for online résumés. Not only do these résumés make the employee search much easier, but they also indicate potential employees' computer comfort level. As these résumé techniques become more commonplace, it becomes increasingly more important that job seekers possess the skills needed to create successful electronic résumés.

The online résumé has gained in popularity for the same reason that the Internet, in general, has become so popular: price, speed, and availability. Several new online résumé forms have sprung up within the recent past. However, two that seem destined to persevere are the scannable résumé and the e-mail résumé.

Scannable Résumés

The scannable résumé is a hard-copy version of your presentation résumé that's formatted to easily scan into a company's database. Even smaller companies that don't have their own scanning equipment use résumé services that do, so the importance of knowing how to create a scannable résumé shouldn't be underestimated.

Because the hard copy of your scannable résumé itself is sent to a potential employer, it's essential to follow a few guidelines to ensure that your résumé can scan easily and accurately.

- Send originals because copies or faxes may scan inaccurately.
- Don't fold or staple the résumé.
- Use a sans-serif font, such as Arial, so that letters don't touch each other.
- Avoid bolding, underlining, italics, bullets, shading, and graphics.
- Avoid horizontal and vertical lines.
- Use a laser printer, if possible.

By using these tips, you will ensure that your résumé will scan accurately.

In terms of content, traditional résumés rely on action verbs to convey skills and achievements. However, since the scannable résumé will be searched via a database, it's best to create what are called *keyword summaries* that utilize nouns and noun phrases to describe your skills. You should spend adequate time brainstorming your keyword summary so that your résumé will receive numerous "hits." Conversely, you don't want to include so many diverse keywords, or create so many different versions of your résumé, that your résumé "pops up" no matter what is input into the database. This will send the wrong message to a potential employer: either you've spent little time tailoring your résumé, or you're not very truthful.

Use your keyword summary to highlight areas of professional and technical expertise, jargon related to your industry, projects, and any other relevant background information.

William F. Humphrey, Jr.
15010 N. 59th Avenue
Glendale, Arizona 85306

KEYWORD SUMMARY
Marketing. Entrepreneurship. International Management. International Marketing. Leadership. Sales Representative. Knowledge of Single Market of the European Union. Seminar skills. Oral presentation skills. Conversational French.

EDUCATION
Master of International Management
American Graduate School of International Management
Thunderbird Campus, Glendale, AZ   December 2000

Bachelor Business Administration, Marketing   December 1999
Texas Tech University
Lubbock, TX
GPA 3.7

WORK EXPERIENCE
Business Administration Advisory Council   1997-1999
President, Texas Tech University
Supervised all B.A. organization presidents. Presented leadership and community service seminars to student leaders. Guest lecturer for B.A. at University Day for incoming students.

Business Administration Ambassadors   1998-1999
Founder, Texas Tech University
Created the student organization to improve student recruiting. Served as a liaison between the faculty and student body. Held an advisory role after founding the organization.

College Relations Recruiting   1998-1999
Graduate Assistant, Thunderbird
Processed and responded to student inquiries. Performed graphic and text design projects.

Texas London Business Program   1998
Participant, London, England
Studied international marketing, European Union, and British culture.
Focused on the formation of the Single Market of the European Union.

Texas London Alumni Recruitment Organization   1999
President, Texas Tech University
Coordinated the recruitment of students for the London Program. Directed the marketing and promotion of the project. Presented information seminars to prospective students.

Grade Appeals Committee, Business Administration   1997-1999
Voting Member, Texas Tech University
Served as a voting member of the judicial body for grade appeals.

FIGURE 12.8 Example of a Scannable Résumé

AWARDS
Presidential Endowed Scholarship, Texas Tech University
International Scholarship, Thunderbird
Academic Citizenship Award, Texas Tech University
Who's Who, Texas Tech University

COMPUTER
Microsoft Word, Works, Excel, WordPerfect, Harvard Graphics, Datatel.

FIGURE 12.8 *continued*

Here is a keyword summary example for a recent graduate in Management.

MANAGEMENT
Leadership. Management. Management Training. Human Relations Skills. Personnel Management. Budget Management. Hiring and Training. Written and Oral Communication Skills. Teamwork Skills. Retail. Supervision. Sales. Self-motivated.

You can tailor your keyword summary to a particular job, but keep your summary consistent. Figure 12.8 shows the résumé in Figure 12.2 written as a scannable résumé.

E-Mail Résumés

While scannable résumés are hard copies sent through the mail to be scanned into databases, e-mail résumés are sent online. Some companies give you the option of completing an e-form, or specified fields that you fill in, but most request an e-mail résumé. Although more expedient than scannable résumés, e-mail résumés do require some knowledge of computers to ensure that they can be searched by the largest number of companies.

E-mail résumés can be sent as an attachment or pasted directly into an e-mail message. However, with the recent rash of viruses infecting entire databases, more and more companies are rejecting e-mail that is accompanied by attachments, so it's best to send your résumé as text-only. In fact, many companies give explicit guidelines about how to submit online résumés; be sure to follow their directions carefully.

E-mail résumés can be sent in RTF (Rich Text Format) and ASCII (American Standard Code for Information Interchange). RTF will support graphics, tabs, special characters, and fonts, so if physical appearance is important, use RTF if no version is specified. However, a quick glance at just a few online company guidelines will show that ASCII is the preferred submission format. The drawback to ASCII is that it's a plain-text format, but the advantage is that it's universally recognized. Both RTF and ASCII can be found in word-processing programs in the "Save As" feature in the "File" menu.

In terms of content, e-mail résumés are much like scannable ones: they utilize a keyword summary consisting of easily retrievable words and phrases to describe your background.

SUMMARY

The résumé is vital in gaining the reader's attention and securing an interview. Some entries will especially interest the reader; "Education" and "Job Experience" are sections that most employers look for. You can personalize your résumé with entries that focus on additional skills, study and research, personal facts, and activities. Regardless of whether you use a chronological, functional, or combined format, include a variety of strong verbs and phrases (not complete sentences). For electronic résumés, use descriptive nouns and noun phrases to describe your skills.

In formatting your résumé, use spacing and graphics wisely. White space draws attention to key facts and helps your page look balanced. Graphics, when used sparingly, make the résumé easy to scan and help guide the reader to important points.

Finally, pay attention to "small" details. Light-colored, superior-quality paper is ideal for résumés. Most importantly, proofread the résumé. All the energy you spend on your résumé will be in vain if you don't catch (and correct) errors in spelling, spacing, content, and consistency. This is one document that must be perfect!

CHAPTER 13

Job Application Letters

In many cases, an employer forms an impression of you, for good or ill, based on your written correspondence. Therefore, application letters, which include cover letters, thank-you letters, and job-acceptance letters, should be crafted with care to reflect favorably upon you.

THE COVER LETTER

In an ideal situation, there would be one perfect job waiting for each job applicant. A job applicant would receive several offers, but that perfect job would be ripe for the picking when the job applicant took notice of it and asked for it. This applicant would be the only one applying for the job, of course.

As we are all aware, there can be hundreds or even thousands of applicants vying for a single job. Oftentimes, the first contact you make with a prospective employer will be the letter of application (also called a cover letter). This letter should prepare the employer to read your résumé and should make a good enough impression that he or she will want to consider you for the job. Because so much depends upon this letter, it can be the most important letter you will ever write.

The letter of application is a persuasive sales letter; you will be selling your qualifications and character. To be effective, this letter must set you apart from the competition. Most employers agree that "cutesy" or shock-effect letters are not impressive. Especially when you apply for jobs in the business market, a mature, well-thought-out letter that draws attention to your abilities and accomplishments will make a good impression. Remember: this letter represents YOU. Use the "you attitude;" that is, focus on how your abilities can benefit the company you are applying with. Your letter should also demonstrate the best of your writing skills. Employers will judge you based on this letter, so it must be excellent!

A letter of application's content interprets, and explains in detail, key items you have on your résumé. Most employers by-pass applicants who cannot express themselves succinctly; include details, but limit yourself to a single page.

Regardless of whether a position you are applying for has been advertised (solicited) or unadvertised (unsolicited), your letter of application should be tailor-made for that specific position. With word processors, personalizing letters is easy to do. One note, however: Make sure you proofread the entire letter carefully to eliminate wording that sounds too general. You never want the reader to think you are sending a form letter. Chances are that you will need to change more than just the inside address to tailor your letter effectively. Your goal is to make the employer think you want only this particular job. Try to send your letter to a specific person, and call the company to check the spelling of his or her name. Letters sent to individuals always get a better response than those sent to a department or group.

CONTENT

Your first paragraph in the letter of application is often the first contact you make with the recipient. Use a warm, confident tone. In a solicited letter, mention how you found

out about the job; in an unsolicited letter, you can make a sincere compliment about the company's reputation. Mention the specific job you wish to apply for. Rarely will applying for "any job that is available" impress the reader. Finally, make clear to the reader that you want to be considered immediately for the job. Don't lead the reader to believe that all you want is further information about the company or the job. You must clearly ask to be considered for the position.

The number of body paragraphs in a letter of application can vary. Most applicants discuss their main selling points in order from the most important to least important, and some applicants have more points they want to discuss than do other applicants. Typical main selling points include education, job experience, and professional activities and memberships. Don't try to cover all these points in a single paragraph. It says more for your powers of organization if you discuss each selling point in detail in its own paragraph. Avoid jumping from main selling point to main selling point and back again. Each paragraph should have one selling point as its topic; when you've finished a paragraph, consider that topic closed.

Some job applicants choose to take a different slant in their body paragraphs. They devote each body paragraph to the qualifications that the employer is looking for and point out that they have those qualifications. Of course, basing a letter of application on the desired qualifications requires research on the part of the applicant. You must use the you attitude and ask yourself, "If I were the employer, what qualifications would I be looking for?" For example, if the employer is looking for leadership qualities or computer expertise, you could include two body paragraphs that demonstrate your abilities and skills in these areas. Writing body paragraphs that focus on your desirable qualifications offers you the opportunity to sell the reader on your abilities.

In your body paragraphs, you should never make generalizations without support. For example, rather than saying that you have lots of experience in a field, say that you "had interned with Bobco, Inc. for two summers and have held a part-time auditing job with USA Bank since last May." Follow general statements with specific details.

One last note about organizing your body paragraphs: Because the letter of application is primarily a sales letter, you should "tie in" your qualifications (be they educational, work-related, or social) to the job you are applying for. In other words, tell the reader how you can benefit the company. The more closely linked your qualifications are to this job, the more perfect for the job you will seem. In a way, you are helping to draw the reader's conclusions for him or her. Doing this skillfully will result in strong persuasive paragraphs.

The logical place to "tie in" to the job is at the end of each body paragraph. In a paragraph discussing job experience, for instance, your tie-in could read like this: "I noticed that your ad states you would like someone with sales experience. My three years with Amico sharpened my customer-relations skills and netted over $300,000 in sales for Amico. My experience could prove an asset to your firm." Notice the use of active voice and specific details, as well as the reader-oriented focus.

Many writers are concerned that they will sound boastful and immodest as they discuss their accomplishments. However, the reader is expecting to see a letter from someone who is confident in his or her abilities and who will honestly recount details of the past. If your accomplishments are impressive in themselves, and if you describe them honestly, the reader's focus will be on your message instead of any boasting that you might be worried about.

A good tone to aim for would "sound" like this: "I proved myself capable in the marketing field when I worked for Resnow, Inc. While there, I devised a new sales strategy plan that netted the company $35,000 in additional sales over a three-year period." If the information is verifiable and if you view your accomplishments realistically, your tone will probably be fine.

Your concluding paragraph should prompt the reader to action. Your letter should have interested the reader enough so that he or she will look at your résumé and ask you for an interview. You could also mention (in a non-aggressive way) that you will be contacting the reader's office at some future point. The enclosed résumé should be mentioned in this paragraph or in the previous paragraph. Because the reading of the résumé is the next logical step, mention it toward the end of the letter. Be reader-oriented here, too: offer to meet at the reader's convenience.

Here is a quick checklist that summarizes the content of the letter of application:

FIRST PARAGRAPH

1. Tell how you found out about the job.

2. Mention the job specifically.

3. Request to be considered for the job.

BODY PARAGRAPHS

1. Include information from the résumé that you think is most important.

2. Give details about each of your main selling points (usually education, work experience, activities, or qualifications sought out by the employer); devote a single paragraph to each selling point.

3. End each body paragraph with a tie-in sentence.

CONCLUDING PARAGRAPH

1. Offer to meet for an interview at the reader's convenience.

2. Mention the résumé if you haven't already done so.

3. Express your hopes of meeting with the reader personally.

FORMAT

A traditional format and look will imply that you respect convention. In formatting your letter of application, use modified block with indented paragraphs and a heading. Don't use letterhead stationery from your current company if you are already employed because you are writing this letter on behalf of yourself, not your current company. Light-colored paper is traditional in business, with off-white and cream being the favorite colors. Use the same type of heavy, high-quality paper for both the letter and résumé.

The print should be 10 to 12 point font and dark enough to be easily read. Avoid printing on a dot matrix printer. Put the letter on top of the résumé, and clip them in the upper left corner.

Many applicants feel justified in sending the résumé and letter of application in a large brown envelope, which requires no folding. The résumé and letter of application will lie flatter and appear neater. The résumé will also be easier to scan into a database if it is free of creases from folding. Figures 13.1–13.3 illustrate several letters of application.

FOLLOW-UP LETTERS

After you have sent your letter of application, it's important to send one or both of the follow-up letters discussed here, depending on your circumstances. Thank-you letters can help clinch a job; acceptance letters confirm necessary specifics. Both types of letters help to create a feeling of goodwill.

Thank-you Letter

Let's say you sent out your cover letter and résumé with good results and have already been interviewed. You will make the best impact if you follow up with a well-worded, typed letter that expresses your gratitude for the interviewer's time and attention. Far too few prospective employees use thank-you letters, but those who do impress the employer with their persistence and good manners. Your thank-you letter might just be the deciding factor in your getting the job.

Mailing out a thank-you letter after an interview serves another purpose: It jogs the interviewer's memory so that you stand out in his or her mind. Chances are that the interviewer has visited with many job seekers, possibly in a matter of a few days. The thank-you letter, sent within a few days after the interview, will remind the interviewer of who you are.

Generally, this letter is short because you simply want to make your presence felt without being verbose and wasting the reader's time. Your first paragraph should thank the reader for taking the time to interview you; be sure to state when and where the interview took place. Your next paragraph or two should reiterate your interest in the job and state the highlights of your track record. Personalize the letter further by referring to something specific that you discussed with the interviewer. You could also use this opportunity to clarify or elaborate on an answer you gave in the interview. In the closing paragraph, be reader-oriented and offer your services to the company. If you have a specific start date when you would be available to work, mention it here. Sincerely thank the reader again, and close the letter. See Figure 13.4 for a sample thank-you letter.

Acceptance Letters

Your all-time favorite business letter to write will no doubt be the acceptance letter to your new employer.

An acceptance letter is especially vital if the job was offered to you over the phone; the letter provides you with a chance to confirm specifics in writing. Mention the date you will begin, to where and to whom you will report, and your starting salary. If your understanding differs from that of the employer's, you will be informed of the change before a critical mistake is made.

1001 Main Street
Lubbock, Texas 79401
September 1, 200-

Mr. Kraig Bryant
Director of Recruiting
Andersen Consulting
901 Main Street
Dallas, Texas 78202

Dear Mr. Bryant:

how you heard about the job

Through my membership in the Data Processing Management Association at Texas Tech University, I learned of the Assistant Director of Programming position open at Andersen Consulting. I would like you to consider me for that position. I have seen numerous presentations about your company, and I am very impressed by your integration of computers into the business world. I believe my background of management and management of information systems will further contribute to the vital link of business and computers.

ask directly to be considered

main selling point: education

In December of this year, I will receive a B.B.A. in Management and a B.B.A. in Management of Information Systems from Texas Tech University in Lubbock, Texas. My education has included programming courses in Pascal, COBOL, and C languages to solve business problems, database management, systems analysis, and information systems design. I have also received training in corporate administration, personnel management, and the business environment. I think you will find my diverse background a strong asset to your company because it involves the two areas of business you employ.

provide tie-in for this paragraph

second selling point: work experience

My work experience shows my ability to work effectively with co-workers from various backgrounds and my hard-worker mentality. This is evident from my summer employment of 1998 and 1999 where I worked two jobs and my continued employment throughout the school year. My strong personnel relation and management skills will be a valuable contribution to the Assistant Director of Programming position.

provide tie-in for this paragraph

mention résumé; request interview

Finally, I would enjoy working for a "leading edge" corporation like Andersen Consulting. Please consider my résumé; I would appreciate an interview with you at your convenience. I look forward to hearing from you.

Sincerely yours,

Shannon P. Webre

Shannon P. Webre

Enclosure: Résumé

FIGURE 13.1 Sample Letter of Application

2903 31st Street
Lubbock, TX 79410
August 2, 200-

Ms. Nancy S. Maurice
Recruiting Manager
Price Waterhouse
1700 Pacific Avenue
Suite 1400
Dallas, Texas 75201-4698

Dear Ms. Maurice:

mention the job you're applying for

how you heard about the job

ask directly to be considered

Thank you for your letter about a tax-accounting position at Price Waterhouse. My education and experience have prepared me to make a positive contribution to the company. Please consider me for the position.

main selling point: college (academics)

In May of 2001, I will receive a B.B.A. in Accounting from Texas Tech University. While in college, I have participated in numerous activities—including cheerleading, intramural basketball, and student government—that have enabled me to become a more complete individual. Although these activities are demanding, I have maintained a high grade point average.

further discussion about college (academic honors)

My academic progress while in school has earned me such honors as the President's Honor Roll and the Dean's List. In addition, I have been inducted into both Beta Gamma Sigma and the Golden Key National Honor Society. This combination of extracurricular activity and academic success has given me the tools to make a positive contribution to Price Waterhouse.

tie-in about academics and honors

second selling point: work experience

I have been fortunate enough while in college to gain a wide variety of work experience. For the past year, I have worked as both an accountant's assistant and tour guide at Llano Estacado Winery in Lubbock. In addition, I was also able to interact and communicate with diverse groups of people. I gained additional accounting experience while working as the accounts payable clerk at Ashland Chemicals, Inc. during the summer of 1999. My work and college experience have given me the skills to be a good accountant.

tie-in for this paragraph

mention résumé; request interview

I have enclosed with this letter a copy of my resume. If you are able, I would like to come in and visit with you the next time I am in Dallas.

Sincerely yours,

William R. Parks, Jr.

William R. Parks, Jr.

Enclosure: Résumé

FIGURE 13.2 Sample Letter of Application

8003 Prairie Lane
Lubbock, Texas 79424
April 30, 200-

Mr. David Martin
Recruiting Director
Ernst & Young
2001 Bryan Tower
Suite 2550
Dallas, Texas 75201

Dear Mr. Martin:

I enjoyed meeting you last week at the Jobs Fair during Accounting Emphasis Week at Texas Tech. I have read the information you gave me about the opportunities available at Ernst & Young for graduating accounting students. I cam confident that upon completion of my degree program I can be an asset to the Ernst & Young organization. Please consider me for an entry-level accounting position.

I will graduate in December of this year from Texas Tech University with a B.B.A. in Accounting. In addition to the required accounting courses, I will complete the following courses: Advanced Accounting Problems, Public Sector Accounting, and Advanced Income Tax. Currently, I have a 4.0 G.P.A. in accounting and a 3.95 cumulative G.P.A. The completion of my degree program will prepare me for an entry-level accounting position and enable me to be a productive, competent employee of your firm.

I am an active member of Beta Alpha Psi, the accounting honorary fraternity. Since 1998, I have also been involved as a volunteer for various activities at All Saints Episcopal School. I believe my involvement in these activities will help me to interact effectively with other members of the Ernst & Young team.

I will be in Dallas the last week in May, and I would like to contact you by phone to arrange a mutually convenient time to meet. My resume is enclosed for your review. I am looking forward to seeing you next month.

Sincerely,

Carol Norfleet

Carol Norfleet

Enclosure: Résumé

Annotations (left margin):

mention how you found out about the job

ask to be considered for a specific job

main selling point

tie-in sentence for this paragraph

second selling point; end with tie-in sentence

ask for an interview

mention enclosed résumé

FIGURE 13.3 Sample Letter of Application

3456 Blitz Avenue
Yonkers, New York 32190
September 1, 200-

Ms. Linda Moreau
Sales Manager
Burlison and Burlison, Inc.
8907 Burke Road
Harlingen, Texas 78550

express
sincere
thanks

Dear Ms. Moreau:

Thank you for meeting with me yesterday.

reminder of
interview;
mention your
interest in
the job and
selling points

I enjoyed our discussion about the role that sales plays in our society's views of "the norm." We share similar viewpoints about the responsibilities of marketing agencies toward the buying public.

what you'd
contribute to
the company;
provide
contact
information

I am convinced that I would fit in at Burlison and Burlison, Inc., and would like the opportunity to contribute to your marketing department. If I can provide any additional information, please call me at (674) 598-4706.

Yours truly,

Jack Glass

Jack Glass

FIGURE 13.4 Sample Thank You Letter

8745 98th Street
Cheyenne, Wyoming   79967
March 22, 200-

Mr. Joshua Adams
Vice-President
Royalty Suits
113 Blimey Road
Madison, Wisconsin   53534

Dear Mr. Adams:

provide a purpose— you accept the job!

I gladly accept your offer for the position of Sales Manager in the Customer Service/Sales Department.

specifics about starting date, salary, etc.

As we discussed on the phone this morning, I will report to you on May 15 at 9:00 A.M. I understand that my assignment within a month from that time will be in either London or Malta; the prospect of visiting with our foreign markets is especially appealing to me. Additionally, I accept your generous offer of $36,000 a year.

goodwill statement; offer for further communica-tion

I appreciate the part you have played in helping me join the Royalty Suits Company. If there is anything that I should do before June 1, please let me know.

Sincerely,

Larry Prescott

Larry Prescott

FIGURE 13.5 Sample Letter of Acceptance

Figure 13.5 is a good model of an acceptance letter. The letter is short and to the point. The tone is upbeat, sincere, and professional because that is how you want to begin your association with your new company.

SUMMARY

Among the most important letters you will write are those sent out in relation to your job search. In general, letters of application support the résumé and seek to win you an interview. Thank-you letters sent shortly after an interview spark the reader's memory of you and make a good impression. Acceptance letters clarify details about your new job and confirm those details in writing.

All job application letters should be written in a concise, well-detailed, and reader-oriented style. Because these letters are so important to your future, it makes sense to compose and format them with care.

CHAPTER 14

The Speaking Process

Many people mistakenly believe that effective speakers stand and speak effortlessly without any preparation. The truth is that good speakers put considerable time and energy into both developing speeches and their speaking ability. Many good speakers developed speaking skills by taking advantage of speaking opportunities in high school and college. Others have joined organizations such as Toastmasters or have participated in professional organizations that provide the opportunity to give presentations. Good speakers, even professional comedians, will tell you that a successful performance comes at a price.

The price is developing good speaking material and practicing delivery. Below, we provide guidelines for preparing and delivering a speech. First, we discuss guidelines for developing a speech. Then we provide suggestions for delivering a speech, including practicing the speech and handling nervousness.

DEVELOPING A PRESENTATION

One basic mistake made by many speakers is waiting until the last minute to prepare a speech. Often, the result is a very tense speaker giving an unimpressive presentation. Neither the speaker nor the audience is satisfied. Even if you're a novice speaker, when you start early, prepare, and practice, using the guidelines provided below, you and your audience will be pleased with the outcome.

Establish a Specific Objective

In training managers to speak, one of the authors asked managers to give presentations that they had given at work. After speaking, the presenters were asked to state the objective for their presentations. In most cases, the response was either, "The boss asked me to talk about this" or "I'm not sure." Again, these managers were asked what they wanted the audience to learn from the presentation. The managers replied that the question hadn't occurred to them. With some discussion, they were able to think of what the audience should gain from the speech. When they reorganized their presentations to accomplish a specific objective, their presentations were significantly improved.

The goal or objective for your presentation should guide all other preparation decisions. It clarifies what you expect of your audience. Your goal statement should have the following characteristics.

The objective should be specific and measurable. Define your objective, specifically indicating the number of things the audience will learn.

The objective should be audience-oriented. Indicate what the audience will gain from listening to you. For example, when you develop objectives, use the following as a model.

Don't say: I'm going to talk about technology.

Do say: You'll learn four ways that cell phones can improve productivity in your business.

Don't say: I'm going to discuss MBO—management by objectives.

Do say: At the conclusion of my presentation, you'll know the three principles necessary for management by objectives to succeed.

The poor objectives listed above are vague and speaker-oriented. They provide only the topic that the speaker will discuss. The good statements are specific and measurable; they address the *four ways* cell phones can help and the *three principles* necessary for MBO. They're also audience-oriented; they point out what the audience will gain rather than what the speaker will do.

Analyze Your Audience

We refer you to chapter 2 for in-depth guidelines about audience analysis. In addition, we suggest that you determine who'll attend your presentation, and adapt your presentation to that audience. One of the best ways to analyze an audience is to ask audience members about their interests and concerns. Don't assume you know what audience members are thinking. One of the authors of this text gave a presentation to other faculty members recommending changes in curriculum. He didn't ask for input and mistakenly assumed that he understood faculty concerns. At the end of the presentation, he found that he had not addressed most audience concerns. His proposal was rejected—a result he could've avoided by asking a few questions.

When you're well prepared and highly confident, you might try two other approaches for learning about audience concerns. First, when you can't speak to them prior to preparing the speech, arrive early and informally chat with selected audience members. Get a sense of their knowledge, interests, and questions. Then, during your presentation, you can acknowledge and even incorporate audience views and concerns.

Second, you might allot time in your introduction, as a part of your presentation, to take audience questions about your topic. List the questions on a flip chart, overhead transparency, or a computer connected to a projector. Then, answer questions using the material you've prepared for your presentation. Try to answer all questions. When providing answers, reorder the questions in a manner that makes the most sense to you and that's consistent with your preparations.

One type of audience adaptation should occur in every presentation. Your audience provides constant live feedback, which can be used to your advantage by adapting to your audience as you speak. If the audience members appear bored or tired, arouse their interest by taking a break, increasing your animation and enthusiasm, asking questions to stimulate discussion, or telling a vivid story. If the audience seems confused, you can stop and ask if your presentation is clear, or you can review relevant content. You'll find that when you respond to the nonverbal messages given by your audience, your audience will respond more favorably to you.

Organize the Body of the Presentation

Although some people start at the introduction and outline the entire presentation from beginning to end, it is more efficient to list, then organize, and then add support

material for your main points. Add the introduction and conclusion after you have the outline. Then you'll know what you're introducing and how to conclude.

Begin by listing the main points, then organize those points in a manner that's easy for your audience to follow. For example, two organizational patterns that are easy to follow are (1) discussing points sequentially from beginning to end, or (2) beginning with the simple and moving to the complex. Chapter 4 suggests other methods of organizing the speech. As you complete your written outline, use the general principles for outlining described below.

For business documents or presentations, keep your message brief and easy to understand. For example, for a five-minute presentation, we recommend you limit yourself to a maximum of four main points. We've found that it's often difficult to adequately discuss more than four points in five minutes. In addition, if you include subpoints, you should probably have no more than six points total in the speech. The following example of a speech outline has a total of five points (three main points and two subpoints under the third main point):

A. Make the First Statement Interesting.
B. Build Movement into Your Introduction.
C. Use Visuals to Focus Attention.

    1. An overhead transparency of a cartoon, quote, or joke gains interest.

    2. An object focuses everyone's attention.

People in business like to get to the point. Therefore, most business presentations should use a deductive organizational pattern, explaining what you want at the beginning of the presentation instead of at the end. Tell the audience up front what you expect it to do or know after listening to the speech. If you're seeking financing, selling a product or plan, or providing information, state your objective immediately.

Plan to use your main points as a guide or a road map. We've noticed that when the number and title for main points are introduced at the beginning of a speech, the audience is more likely to keep track of each successive point during the speech. Labels help those who keep notes to stay organized. Like signposts, labels guide the audience through your presentation.

Each point should be given a label and, in most cases, a number. Use these labels and numbers as road signs throughout your presentation (*My first point is, Be a good listener*). Use the labels in the preview of your speech. Then use labels to keep the audience on track during the presentation. Refer to them again at the end. Repeating your main points will give your presentation coherence and help the audience remember those points.

Provide Support for Each Point

The body of your presentation includes main points *and* support material. The primary mistake most speakers make is that they try to cover too many points and don't provide enough support material. Novice speakers tend to overestimate how many points they can adequately discuss. The result is that the audience is overwhelmed by lots of points that it doesn't understand.

Therefore, if you have a point in your speech, support it. Use the suggestions in chapter 3 as a guide in supporting points. Remember that for each point in your speech, you should (1) state the point, (2) explain the point, and (3) add support material for the point. Presentations enable you to use a variety of media to amplify support material and clarify your points. For example, you might use handouts for supporting detail, overhead projections of main points to keep the audience on track, pictures to help the audience visualize possibilities, videos to show processes, and objects or actual equipment for demonstrations. You can also use your own verbal and nonverbal behavior to illustrate or clarify. You might illustrate a friendly greeting by "meeting" and shaking hands with a member of the audience.

Use your creativity and take advantage of the broad range of media that is available. Choose the media that convey your point quickly and clearly. For example, a live demonstration of a safety procedure can convey a message much more quickly than a written or verbal description. As another example, a scale model of a new plant conveys a vision of the planned facility immediately and vividly.

Create the Introduction

After you've developed the body, create the introduction—the beginning for your presentation. A good introduction grabs an audience's attention and answers questions important to your audience: What is the topic? Why is this topic important to me? Why should I listen to this speaker—what credentials does he or she have? What kinds of things will be discussed? How does the speaker feel about me, and how do I feel about him or her? Answers to these questions determine whether the audience will respond positively. Do the following in your introduction to help the audience respond favorably.

Gain the Audience's Attention

You've probably heard the saying, "You never get a second chance to make a first impression." This statement applies to any social encounter and certainly to presentations. The beginning of any presentation is very important. As you plan your presentation, think about the kind of impression you want to make.

Design the opening of your presentation to gain attention. The opening statement in your introduction **should not** be your name and your topic: "Good morning, my name is Peter Johnson, and I am speaking about effective interviewing." This statement is boring and doesn't establish rapport. In most cases, someone will introduce you. In cases where you're not introduced, give your attention statement before introducing yourself.

Begin your speech with a startling statement, quotation, story, rhetorical question, visual aid, or some other interesting device designed to gain attention. We've seen all of these devices work effectively to gain attention. Because we've also seen some introductions fail, we suggest the following about using some attention-gaining devices in speeches.

Humor: Avoid telling jokes unless humor fits the situation and your personality. Get feedback about the joke from a member of the audience before you use it. Never use humor that would offend the audience. Use jokes that relate to your topic; then, if your audience doesn't laugh, you can still smoothly transition to the remainder of your speech.

Visuals: Visuals work when they relate to your speech, are in good taste, and are visible to the entire audience. There's no limit to the variety of visuals. For example, speakers have burned checks to symbolize that the company is throwing money away, and displayed models of clothing to visualize a particular style. **Actions: Actions gain attention, but try them out, and be sure they work.** One speaker at a regional Frito-Lay management meeting began the speech by taking off his coat, removing his tie, and then unbuttoning his shirt. He had the audience's attention! Underneath his shirt was a white t-shirt with the objective for his speech printed on the front. When he finished his speech, he turned around, and the conclusion was written on the back of his t-shirt. The audience loved it. However, before the management meeting, he practiced his presentation at a Toastmasters meeting and used feedback to improve his approach. **Cartoons: Read the caption for cartoons out loud for the audience.** Speakers frequently begin presentations by displaying a cartoon. A common error in displaying cartoons is that speakers don't leave them on the screen long enough for the audience to read the caption. Reading the caption for the audience eliminates this problem.

Perhaps the most important part of your opening is the way you deliver it. Your goal is to gain attention and build the desired relationship with your audience. Thus, you need to add a good delivery to any attention-gaining device. Even when you have an excellent attention-getter, if you deliver it in a quiet tone with little eye contact, the audience won't perk up and listen; such actions may actually convey that you don't want to be there and that you want nothing to do with the audience.

You're more likely to gain attention and establish rapport when your introduction is dynamic. You can be dynamic when your introduction includes the following elements:

Volume. Loud volume conveys confidence and gains attention. The audience should easily hear you. Don't shout, but practice speaking with volume that commands attention.

Gestures. Gestures add dynamism and attract visual attention. Make your gestures natural as you do in everyday conversation. But also make them large, and keep them high, above your waist, particularly if you're standing behind a lectern.

Movement. You attract attention when you move. Unless you're giving a very important statement of policy or a very formal presentation, you should arrange to have movement in your presentation. If the audience is large, arrange to use a traveling microphone. Come out from behind the lectern to begin the presentation, and move to both sides of the lectern.

Eye Contact. Look at your audience, or it may quickly lose interest in you. Eye contact suggests you're interested in the audience and conveys confidence. Know your opening well enough to minimize looking at notes.

Expression. A smile and animation generate interest and warmth. Because most audiences are large, you need to be more expressive than usual. In particular, you should practice smiling. A smile and a friendly tone are great ways to establish rapport.

State Your Objective

After your attention-gaining statement, clarify your objective; indicate what the audience will gain from the presentation. For example, you might say, "At the end of my presentation, you'll know four ways to present yourself most effectively in employment interviews." Audience members will not initially know how the presentation will be helpful to them. Help them to see potential gains, and make them want to listen to you.

Establish Your Credibility

Audiences are more likely to pay attention to you when you're viewed as a credible source of information. Credibility means you're worthy of belief or confidence. Often, students or new employees aren't viewed as experts. No matter who you are, the audience might wonder why you're qualified to deliver your presentation.

When you're not an expert, you can gain credibility by basing your speech on and citing other credible sources. Chapter 4 provides a list of those potential sources. Provide an overview of your expertise on the subject, if you have any, and the sources from which you've obtained support material. Indicate the extent of your sources' expertise. If you use yourself as a source for employment interviewing, for example, indicate the extent of your experience.

If you refer to another expert, tell the nature of his or her expertise—positions, degrees, or noted experience, etc. Don't make the description of expertise long. Simply give an idea of the extent of a source's knowledge. For example, you might say, "My comments about interviewing are based on a best-selling text by Charles J. Stewart and William B. Cash, Jr., both professors of communication, and from my three years experience as an employment interviewer for a major corporation."

Preview Your Main Points

A preview is a statement of your main points. Enumerate the points you'll cover, providing labels for each point. Then use these labels throughout your presentation. Take time to make the preview clear. Draw attention to your main points. Use visuals, vocal emphasis, or pauses to clarify each main point. For example, you might list the main points for your speech on an overhead transparency or PowerPoint slide. If you don't use a transparency, you could call attention to each point by indicating with raised fingers the number of each point while stating the label for the point.

Establish the Desired Relationship

Relationships are the emotional connections that are established among people. Your relationship to the audience is initialized in your introduction with your nonverbal behavior and visuals. Because they're unprepared or timid, some people inadvertently create a distant relationship by failing to maintain eye contact and by speaking too quietly.

You need to develop your presentation so that your nonverbal behavior signals the kind of relationship you want with your audience. If you want a warm, friendly relationship, plan to come out from the lectern, smile, and maintain eye contact. Include visuals that have vivid colors or interesting drawings. If you want to establish dominance and distance, plan to stay behind the lectern, emphasize your credentials, and speak forcefully.

Develop the Conclusion

The conclusion is the mirror of your introduction. It reminds your audience of your objective, summarizes what you've said, and concludes with an interesting statement that helps your audience remember your presentation. Include the following in your conclusion.

Restate Your Objective

Part of wrapping up a presentation is reminding your audience what you set out to accomplish: your objective. A straightforward way of doing this is to simply restate your objective statement and note that it's been accomplished. For example, you might say, "At the beginning of this presentation, I told you that you would know how to be a better listener. You've learned the two key elements of listening."

If you promised a specific action at the conclusion of your presentation, now is the time to act. For example, you might say, "My objective in the presentation was to persuade you to sign a contract for our services. Here is the contract."

Review Your Main Points

The conclusion provides you the opportunity to reinforce your main points. You should do two things in your review. First, to help your audience remember your main points, refer to your labels once more. They are the tags that your audience will use to recall the information you've given them.

Second, restate supporting information that you want the audience to remember. For example, you might say something like the following.

My first point was "maintain eye contact." Remember, as you listen, you show that the other person is important when you maintain eye contact. My second point was "paraphrase." When you paraphrase, you demonstrate that you understand the speaker.

State Your Expectations   Tell the audience members what you expect them to do with the information you've provided. The audience will be more likely to retain and use information if you provide guidelines. For example, you might say, "The next time you listen to a subordinate, please use the listening guidelines I've offered." Or, you might say, "I've given you many reasons to consider changes in our organizational structure; I strongly suggest that we put this on our agenda in the upcoming management retreat."

Provide a Concluding Statement   The concluding statement provides an opportunity for you to reinforce the principle idea in your presentation and to make a lasting impression. Think about what you want your audience to remember and find an interesting way to state it. Similar to your opening statement, you could use a startling statement, quotation, story, rhetorical question, visual aid, or humor.

For example, one simple way of concluding is to restate an opening quotation or startling statement. You could also use an extension or variation of the opening statement. One speaker started her presentation by holding a typewriter in front of her and letting it drop to the floor. Then, she discussed how it was the technology of the past. For her conclusion, she picked up the typewriter, dumped it into a garbage can, and said, "Remember, this is the technology of the past."

The major weakness we've seen in conclusions is that speakers don't give them enough emphasis. As with the introduction, practice a dynamic delivery of the conclusion. Include volume, movement, gestures, expression, and eye contact. Too frequently, speakers are eager to leave the lectern, and they don't present the conclusion with emphasis and expression. A good final statement, delivered effectively, makes your speech appear polished and professional.

Speaking Notes

If you're giving an extemporaneous speech, write the notes you'll use during the presentation on 3-inch by 5-inch cards, particularly if you plan to carry notes with you. Small pieces of paper are easier to manage and don't draw attention to the fact that you're carrying your notes.

Use the following guidelines for note cards.

- **Write on one side of the card using large print.** This will help you easily see the content.
- **Number your cards so that you can easily put them in the right order.** We've seen speakers drop cards just before or during their speech and panic when they can't quickly put them in order.
- **Limit notes to main points and brief reminders of support material.** Don't try to write out the entire speech. This strategy will help you avoid reading your speech; instead you'll talk directly to the audience.
- **Indicate when you plan to cite references.** Citing reputable references during your speech increases your credibility, so remind yourself to refer to them.

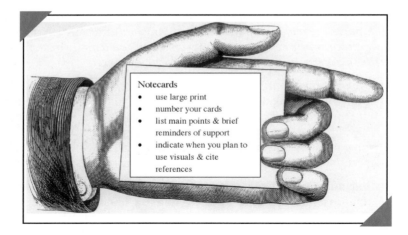

- **Include the transition sentences you'll use between points.** Often, speakers can't think of good transitions on the spot. Good transitions add professionalism to your speech.
- **Note when you plan to use visuals.** Some people get tense in front of an audience and forget to use their visuals.

DELIVERING A PRESENTATION

Watch friends in an animated conversation with one another. Their voice rate and volume vary, their faces convey emotion and meaning, they look directly at each other, and they use descriptive gestures and movements. This type of conversation is filled with rich information. It attracts attention and is enjoyable to watch.

Now observe someone reading a document. Compared to the animated conversation described above, vocal, facial, and hand expressions are likely to be reserved and limited. The reader limits eye contact. The delivery lacks animation and emotion. Less expressiveness leads to less actual communication. Listeners are less interested and easily distracted.

In a presentation, your goal is be an animated speaker, not a rigid reader. When you deliver the speech well, you're more likely to maintain audience attention, present your presentation clearly and effectively, and establish a desired relationship with the audience. Here is some specific advice to improve your delivery.

Conversation Skills

Speakers are usually at their best when they use conversation skills. Like an old pair of jeans, these skills feel comfortable, and they also improve presentations. All of us have had lots of practice expressing ourselves in conversation. We know how to be natural and spontaneous. Our faces and gestures animate our talk; our voices disclose our convictions and doubts. The key to speaking effectively in small or large groups is to use these well-practiced skills of conversation.

When speakers try to use skills other than conversational ones in presentations, they usually meet with little success. Speakers often become uncomfortable and rigid when they read or memorize presentations. Oral reading and recitation are seldom-practiced skills and much less natural than conversation. Few people can either read or memorize a presentation and inject the spontaneity of an animated conversation. Instead, most of us appear like bad actors struggling with a difficult and unpracticed part. Memorization is also so hard and so stressful that we may lose our place and freeze.

As you practice and deliver your speech, use your conversation skills, but amplify them to meet the needs of the size of the audience. You'll need to use larger gestures and movements, a louder voice, and more animated facial expressions than you would in a quiet conversation with a friend. Practice will make you feel comfortable with the exaggerated expression.

Voice

The primary responsibility of any speaker is to be **heard.** If you normally speak quietly, practice your speech much more loudly than you would in the actual speech. As you practice, have a friend sit at the back of a room about the size of the one in which you will speak and give you a signal when you're not loud enough. You could ask a colleague to do the same thing when you actually give your speech. Once you're sure that you can be heard, work on **varying your volume** using either extremely loud volume or softer volume for occasional emphasis.

When you're sure you can be heard, work on **rate** and **expressiveness** as well. Recording your speech can help you make judgments about your voice. You may want to speed up or slow down. The ideal rate is one that's easily understood but not so slow as to bore your audience. Once your rate is about right, work on varying it and pausing occasionally for emphasis.

Most people have expressive voices in everyday conversation. Your voice reflects how you feel. If you're bored, your voice is monotonous. If you're excited, your voice reflects enthusiasm. As you practice, if you think your voice isn't expressive enough, you might try two strategies to become more expressive. First, find parts of your presentation that are interesting to you or to which you have strong reactions. Often, a vivid example or a story will involve you emotionally. When you practice the presentation, simply **amplify your own emotion.**

Second, when you practice, be much more **expressive** than you would ever be when actually delivering the speech. This kind of practice allows you to expand your "comfort zone" of expressiveness. If you're highly animated when you practice, you can reduce the level of expressiveness when you speak and still maintain more intensity than normal, while staying within your own comfort zone.

Finally, if you tape yourself, when you play back the recording, note how often you have unnecessary **pauses** or add **fillers** such as *you know, uhm,* and *like.* These non-fluencies are very distracting and leave the impression that you're unprepared and disorganized. There are two ways to overcome these problems. The first is to be well prepared. People pause and use fillers more when they're unprepared because they're trying to think of what to say next.

The second strategy is to become highly aware of nonfluencies in everyday conversation. If you break the habit in conversations, you'll use them less frequently in presentations. Try wearing a rubber band on your wrist and snapping yourself when you use an *uhm*. Or pay a friend a quarter each time she catches you saying *like* or *you know.*

Eye Contact

Eye contact is crucial in presentations. Maintaining visual contact with the audience signals that you're interested and helps to establish a positive relationship. Sustaining eye contact also suggests that you're confident, prepared, and sincere. Audience members are more likely to pay attention when they see the speaker looking at them.

Eye contact also allows you to **monitor the audience** to check for reactions such as understanding, boredom, and fatigue. You can then adapt your presentation to meet the audience's needs, as you would in a one-on-one conversation. In a conversation, if you see that someone is confused, you add more explanation or ask questions about the confusion. If you see that someone is bored, you move to more interesting topics or enliven your comments. You can do the same kinds of things in a presentation if you observe the audience's reactions.

The **more eye contact, the better.** If you're well prepared, you should be able to get through a speech by briefly glancing at your notes as you move from one main point to the next. Writing notes that are very brief and easy to read will encourage you to use them infrequently.

If you have a large audience or an audience that's spread out in a room, **include everyone,** or every section of the audience, in your gaze for several seconds sometime during the presentation. Look at one person for a few seconds as you speak, and then shift to another person in another part of the audience for a few seconds and so on. Avoid turning your head but not your body when making eye contact. Be sure to **address the audience with your entire body** as well as your eyes.

At first, you may feel uncomfortable looking into the eyes of the audience as you speak. To gradually develop ease with eye contact, you can first look at foreheads, noses, or earlobes, and later into eyes. The audience members will still have the impression that you're looking into their eyes.

Facial Expression

Facial expression is one of the primary ways to reveal emotions. Facial expressions indicate how you feel about your words and about the audience. It's hard to imagine someone giving a speech without any facial expression. It would be almost like seeing a flat printed page without any breaks or pictures. Smiling, grimacing, clenching teeth, winking, looking puzzled, showing anger, demonstrating delight, and showing anxiety are examples of facial expressions that add dimension to your words.

Facial expressions help **build rapport** with audiences. A look of pleasure or delight on your face at the beginning of a presentation invites the audience members to reciprocate through their warmth. On the other hand, if you look bored, you're not likely to stimulate much audience enthusiasm.

Facial expressions can **reflect hidden feelings** as well. High speech anxiety may result in a stiff face and no demonstration of feelings. Good speakers learn to control anxiety. Later, we'll discuss ways to manage your anxiety. Once you have anxiety controlled, you can increase your positive expressiveness.

If you can **pick out friendly faces in the audience and direct your comments to those individuals,** you'll be more expressive. Talking to one individual at a time is like

being in a conversation. But don't make the mistake of singling out only one person for the entire speech. Try to be conversational with many individuals in different parts of your audience.

Your face also reflects feelings about your ideas. Your face is more expressive when you're presenting ideas you believe in and thoughts that are easily visualized, such as a story. It's hard to be expressive when you're listing cold facts and figures, but much easier when you discuss what those facts and figures mean to you or how they'll specifically affect the audience.

Gestures

Although you probably use very creative and meaningful gestures in daily conversation, when you're in front of an audience, the naturalness may disappear. We suggest three basic guidelines for gestures. **First, gesture naturally.** We tend to use descriptive gestures in everyday conversation when we tell specific stories and when we're emotionally involved in talk. If you find your speech lacks gestures, your subject matter may be too abstract and non-emotional.

Second, make your gestures visible to the audience. To make gestures visible, you may need to practice making gestures large and high. **Third, avoid irritating gestures** that may detract from your speech. Audiences quickly become impatient with bothersome gestures. For example, avoid doing the following:

- Leaning on or gripping the lectern
- Locking your hands in front of or behind your body
- Scratching yourself
- Rubbing hands and twisting rings or other jewelry
- Playing with your hair or clicking a pen
- Covering your mouth

- Sticking your hands in your pockets
- Jingling change in your pockets
- Gesturing at the audience with a pen, marker, or pointer

A videotape of your presentation can provide the best feedback about your gestures. You may find that they're not very expressive. One way to improve the expressiveness is to **exaggerate when you practice.** In addition, if you're speaking behind a lectern, avoid leaving your hands on the lectern throughout your presentation. Instead, take one short step back and **hold your hands above your waist** and off the lectern so when you want to gesture, your hands will be free and high enough to be seen.

You may wonder what to do with notes during your presentation. The easiest strategy is leaving them on the lectern. However, if you move away from the lectern while you speak, feel free to carry your notes with you. While you're holding them, avoid gesturing with the hand holding the notes. Some people also wonder what to do with their hands when not they're gesturing. Just let them hang at your side.

Movement

A lectern can be useful because it conveys a sense of authority and provides a place to lay your notes. However, when you have the opportunity to move from behind the lectern in a presentation, do it. Movement attracts attention and creates dynamism. Some speakers remove lecterns from a podium because they hinder movement and block contact with the audience. For example, most entertainers work without lecterns.

Plan and practice your movement before you give your speech. Avoid constant movement or pacing. **Walk** to one side of the podium, **stay put** for several seconds, and direct your comments to that part of the audience. **Then move** to the other side of the podium, and repeat the process. Even a small amount of movement around the lectern adds dynamism to your presentation. If your notes are in large print, you can leave them on the lectern and still refer to them when you're one or two feet away.

Speakers have reported that movement helps to reduce anxiety. For example, one speaker used two flipcharts as visuals and placed them on both sides, about six feet from the lectern. She said movement to and from the flipcharts helped her relax.

Practice

Successful delivery depends on practice, not luck. Practice your entire presentation at least three times before you give it in front of an audience. If you haven't previously given a speech, you may need to rehearse 10 or 12 times before it flows naturally. Be sure to practice it **all the way through.** Sometimes speakers practice the introduction many times but never make it completely through the presentation until they're in front of the audience. They do well at the beginning but not at the end.

DELIVERY CHECKLIST
- Project your voice, and vary intensity and rates.
- Avoid fillers and long pauses.
- Make eye contact with each part of the audience, and sustain it for a few seconds.
- Let your face show your emotional involvement and feelings.
- Gesture naturally and high enough to be seen.
- Move from behind the lectern, addressing all parts of the audience.

Practice the presentation as you'll actually give it. **Use your visuals** as you practice; otherwise, you'll find visuals awkward to handle during the presentation. If you plan to use an overhead projector but don't have access to one, put a briefcase on a table next to you, and lay transparencies on the briefcase as if it were a projector. Place the transparency so that you can read it—that's the correct position for it to be seen on the screen. If you plan to use a computer, place it where you'll likely use it during the presentation. If you plan to use a chart or an object, include it in your rehearsal.

Practice the movements you plan to use. Avoid pacing as you go over the speech. Many who pace when they practice will pace in front of the audience. Practice as if the audience were actually in front of you. Maintain eye contact with every part of the room. Move to different parts of the podium as you will in the presentation.

Also **practice gesturing.** Make gestures larger than normal. **Practice your vocal delivery.** If you normally speak quietly, practice speaking very loudly to accustom yourself to a louder volume. Or if you believe you have little vocal variety, practice with extreme variety. When you use exaggerated volume or vocal variety in practice, during the speech, you can speak more loudly and expressively than normal and still feel comfortable.

Videotape or record your presentation. Ask a friend to watch and give you feedback, for extra polish. If you expect questions during or after presentations, have someone ask questions, and practice your answers.

Nervousness

The primary obstacle to effective delivery is **speech anxiety** or nervousness. If you feel anxious about giving presentations, you have a lot of company. Almost everyone does. Even some well-known people in show business say that they have stage fright.

An important thing to remember is that **anxiety is your body's way of giving you energy to perform well in situations that matter.** In fact, you may not perform

extremely well if you *don't* experience some anxiety. Professional athletes, actors, cheerleaders, and other performers experience the anxiety that gives the body adrenaline to perform effectively. No one should expect anxiety to be completely eliminated. Instead, work on channeling it so that it enhances rather than hinders performance.

Take comfort in the fact that the audience **doesn't actually see all the anxiety** you feel. You may be in turmoil inside, but the audience members see you only from the outside. They probably notice only about 10 percent of the nervousness you feel.

The key to overcoming nervousness before the presentation is to **be well prepared** and to **practice.** Much nervousness is the result of uncertainty about whether the presentation will go well. Preparation and practice may remove much of the uncertainty or doubt. For example, consider how the following concerns about a presentation are resolved through preparation and practice.

Question: What will I say in the presentation?
Answer: Prepare an outline, and get your support material together.

Question: Will the audience like my presentation?
Answer: Analyze the audience, and use sure crowd-pleasers like stories and close-to-home examples.

Question: Will my visuals work in my presentation?
Answer: Practice using the visuals with an audience of friends.

Question: How do I look when I give my presentation?
Answer: Use videotape, or ask friends for feedback.

Once you've prepared and practiced, you probably have the situation under control, but you may still feel some nervousness. Here are some things you might do to control nervousness while you speak:

1. **Get started on the right foot.** Take ample time getting set up, and make sure everything is ready and in place before you begin speaking. The audience is willing to give you the time to get settled. Also, be very familiar with the opening of your presentation. This may be the only part of the presentation that you should memorize. Some people don't recover from a poor beginning. Thus, make sure you do well in the opening. Doing well here will help ensure that the rest of the speech will also go well.

2. **Find friendly faces** in the audience and talk to these people. A friendly response will make you feel the presentation is going well. In contrast, don't focus on faces that are tired or bored, and don't assume that you're causing these reactions. Often, an apparently negative reaction may be the result of some unrelated cause such as a long night or personal problems, not your presentation. Find the friendly, responsive faces, and you'll feel better about your presentation.

3. **Use deep, slow breathing** to control your anxiety. When people are anxious, they tend to take shallow, short breaths. You can reverse this physiological reaction by taking deep breaths and exhaling slowly. Deep breathing as you're waiting to speak is an excellent way to control nervousness.

4. **Use movement and action** to help you get rid of anxiety. Build movement into your presentation by planning where and when to move during your presenta-

tion. Physical activity before and during your presentation can help you reduce anxiety.

5. **Plan an opening that involves the audience** in a task related to your topic. Ask a question and seek actual responses. Or ask people to list their concerns about your topic. Such activities remove you from the audience's attention. Instead, the audience focuses on the topic.

SUMMARY

Effective delivery means that you be yourself—your best self. You express yourself best when you're natural and conversational, and you can be most naturally conversational when you're highly familiar with the content of the presentation. So either choose familiar material, or spend time getting to know it. Prepare thoroughly, and practice the entire speech, just as you plan to present it, several times. Work on dynamic movement, gestures, voice, and expression. Go prepared to manage nervousness by using deep breathing and other techniques. Using these suggestions and tips can go a long way toward making your speech a success.

CHAPTER 15

Types of Presentations

A udiences will expect different kinds of presentations depending on the purpose of the meeting. For many meetings, such as formal quarterly reviews, you have time to prepare and organize presentations. For others, such as decision-making meetings, you're asked to speak without preparation. Sometimes, you may be expected to inform, as you would in a quarterly report. Other times, the situation may require persuasion, as in a sales presentation. In many business presentations, you'll be asked questions either during or after the presentation.

Effective speakers must know strategies for handling a variety of situations. In this chapter, we provide guidelines for mastering four different types of speaking. For two types—speaking from notes and manuscripts—you have time to prepare and organize. For the other two types—impromptu presentations and answering questions—you have little or no time to prepare. We also provide suggestions for handling the two primary purposes for speaking: informing and persuading. When you're able to use the guidelines described in this chapter, you'll be prepared for most business-speaking situations.

EXTEMPORANEOUS PRESENTATIONS

Most presentations given in business are given from notes or outlines. Speaking with notes is also called extemporaneous speaking. Speaking room arrangements usually

allow for eye contact between the speaker and listener. In addition, you generally have time to prepare and practice the presentation. Such speeches don't require precise wording or a printed text that will be distributed. Although you're expected to be accurate, you have the flexibility of using your own speaking style and wording.

As a speaker, you have a great advantage when you can speak from notes instead of a manuscript. Reading or memorizing a speech reduces your ability to interact with your audience. Reading cuts off eye contact, and memorizing preplans how you will respond to the audience, which limits your ability to interact with the audience. Speaking from notes enables you to maintain eye contact, respond to the nonverbal behavior of the audience, and communicate spontaneously as you would in conversation. Therefore, you're better able to make your speech interesting and to maintain attention.

Some speakers don't take advantage of the opportunities available in an extemporaneous speech. They speak in a monotone voice and eliminate any emotion, eye contact, and expression. Unfortunately, you have undoubtedly suffered through dry lectures or business meetings that could've been much more interesting if the speakers would've seized the opportunity to express themselves. Ironically, if you could talk with these speakers outside the presentation, you would probably find them to be animated and expressive.

Speaking from notes enables you to be yourself—your expressive self. It enables you to use all the skills you've learned from years of conversation. You can use the facial expression, gestures, and movements that vividly depict thoughts and feelings. To enhance the likelihood that you'll be expressive in this kind of presentation, use the guidelines for delivery recommended in chapter 14, "The Speaking Process."

In addition, we recommend you do the following to enhance the likelihood that you use your conversation skills.

- Use a minimum of notes.
- Personalize the presentation.
- Use vivid examples or stories.

Use a minimum of notes in extemporaneous presentations. Some speakers use notes as a kind of crutch or safety net. They tend to add more notes until they almost have a manuscript presentation. Reliance on these notes often saps expression out of the presentation. One of the authors tried to limit notes by allowing students only two 3×5 note cards for a five-minute presentation. Some students, feeling a lack of confidence, wrote extensive notes in tiny, almost microscopic print. You must resist the urge to add more notes.

We recommend that you limit notes to short phrases, words, or abbreviations. You might even try limiting your notes to an outline listed on your overhead transparencies or on a computer in a multi-media presentation. Using limited notes forces you to avoid reading and to use the natural expressiveness of conversation. When you combine limited notes with a personalized presentation and vivid examples or stories, you'll remember your presentation and deliver it in a conversational manner.

Our second recommendation is to personalize the speech; make it your own. We've found it very difficult for a speaker to be expressive when delivering a speech that comes from someone else. If you must rely extensively on someone else's material, take the time to make that material meaningful in your own life.

For example, suppose you were speaking about conducting an employment interview and found an article that provided excellent guidelines. Think about how those guidelines would apply to you in your job. How would you implement them? Think of supporting examples from your experience. Use those examples in your speech. As you develop thoughts and examples, you'll also develop attitudes and feelings about the topic. This thought process makes it easier to remember your speech. In addition, the thoughts, attitudes, and feelings you've developed will be communicated nonverbally and will enrich your presentation.

Third, we recommend that you use vivid examples and stories as support material. The use of vivid examples or stories creates images in your mind. You'll find those images easy to remember. You'll also find that as you try to communicate a clear mental image, your whole body will get involved—facial expression, gestures, and movements. When you memorize or read a lot of words, you have much more detail to remember, and you lose the vivid visualization that drives expression. You may have noticed that when people describe scenes from a movie or tell stories, they easily recall their story and are animated and involved when they tell it.

MANUSCRIPT PRESENTATIONS

Manuscript presentations are frequently long speeches, delivered from written documents. Occasionally, they're short, official declarations that become a part of public record. Examples of the longer speeches are papers delivered at professional meetings that are often read and then published in proceedings. Audiences generally expect authors to read at least parts of such papers. They may be less critical of delivery than audiences of extemporaneous presentations.

However, even the most tolerant audience may tire of a flat delivery. There are several things you can do to spice up your presentation. We suggest four things to make your delivery more **dynamic** or forceful.

1. **Write your speech using conversational wording.** Create an outline, speak from the outline into a tape recorder, and write your manuscript from the recording. This strategy helps you retain the natural wording of your speaking style.
2. **When you can, speak directly to the audience.** Find places within the manuscript where you can afford to be less precise and more extemporaneous. Mark these sections to remind you to look up from your manuscript to speak directly to the audience.
3. **Practice reading the presentation as dynamically as possible.** Exaggerate your vocal expression during practice, and practice a lot. Professional speechwriters recommend that you divide the manuscript page into two columns: one for the manuscript and one for your notes. They also suggest double-spacing within and triple-spacing between paragraphs. This extra space can be used to underline or mark text that you want to emphasize by speaking more loudly, quickly, or expressively to add variety to your delivery.
4. **Know your manuscript well.** Become so familiar with the manuscript that you can look at the audience frequently while reading.

IMPROMPTU PRESENTATIONS

Impromptu presentations occur when you're asked to give remarks without preparation, notes, or notice. In many business meetings, you'll be called upon to make impromptu comments. Most frequently, you'll be asked because of your position or expertise. Sometimes you might want to offer your comments when a subject interests you.

Whatever the reason for the impromptu remarks, the challenge is to find something appropriate to say. When you're asked to make comments without preparation, and you need time to think before you take a position, you might try one of the following strategies.

1. **Clarify the question.** Restate the question in your own words, and ask if you understand. Or ask the speaker to repeat or paraphrase the question.
2. **Preface your remarks.** You could begin with cordial statements like *I'm glad you asked that question . . . , I'm happy that I can join you today. . . ,* or *Let me preface my remarks with a brief background . . .*
3. **Respond with a story or an example before drawing a conclusion.** Use examples from the questioner's, or your, background that might relate to the question and provide an answer. It's easier to tell a story or give an example than to jump into vague generalities.
4. **Create a hypothetical situation that relates to the question.** For instance, say, *Well, let's imagine what our company would be like if the conditions you suggest existed.*

Once you've given yourself time to think of something to say, take this general approach in an impromptu presentation:

1.   **Assert a point of view, make a point, or take a stand.**
2.   **Explain your perspective.**
3.   **Give examples or other support material.**
4.   **Summarize what you've said.**

ANSWERS TO QUESTIONS

Questions and answers often play a major role in business presentations. Occasionally, speakers address an audience for the primary purpose of answering questions. For example, a company president may call a news conference to make a brief announcement and answer questions regarding a new product or a plant opening. In many business presentations, you're expected to answer questions during or after the presentation.

Your goal is to answer these questions *and* to maintain control of the question–answer period, while retaining a professional image. Your success will depend on how you handle both the audience and the questions. Maintaining control may not be easy, especially when key decision-makers, detractors, or others want to shift the focus from your topic and ask difficult questions. Entering the presentation with a strategy for handling questions will help to make the questions work for you.

Your primary job is to **maintain control.** Questions asked during your presentation can force you into topics you're not prepared to discuss. One way to maintain control is to take questions only at the end of the presentation. At the beginning of your presentation, announce that you'll take questions at the end or, as an alternative, that you will pause for questions at specified points—for example, after each major portion of your speech.

Even though you announce when you'll take questions, listeners may attempt to ask questions in the middle of an important point. Instead of allowing them the floor in mid-sentence, acknowledge their requests, and indicate that you will get back to them. Finish your point, and then take the question.

Occasionally, an insistent person will interrupt you to ask a question. At that point, your best strategy may be to give a short answer and go on. If there is a longer answer to the question, still give a brief reply, and promise the complete answer at the end of the presentation. Try to avoid being pulled into a lengthy discussion that's irrelevant to the prepared presentation.

Sometimes questions from the audience become impromptu speaking situations. In those cases, refer to the guidelines given earlier about impromptu speeches for buying time to think and responding to questions. Here are some general guidelines that should help you when you're on the firing line.

- **Before answering, repeat major points and relevant material from your speech.** Use the answer as an opportunity to reinforce your presentation.
- **Rephrase the question** into an acceptable form that fits your presentation.
- **Ask for more explanation, information, or clarification,** putting the burden on the questioner.
- **Don't get bogged down in answering a specific question.** Provide a reasonable answer, and move on with your presentation or with other questions. The audience has assembled to hear you, not a member of the audience.

What happens if you just don't know the answer to a question? Should you admit you don't know? You certainly shouldn't lie and try to make up an answer. On the other hand, you want to present yourself in the best possible light. You might try saying, *I have that information in my office, and I can send it to you.* Another response might be, *I don't have that information with me, but I'll get back to you with an answer,* or, *here's where you can find it.* Then, get back to the listener with the answer, or give the listener possible sources. In other words, be **helpful.**

Although sometimes it's difficult, be as **friendly and interactive** as possible with those who ask questions.

- Come out from behind the lectern to ask for questions.
- Thank those who offer questions.
- When you've completed your answer, ask if you've answered the question.
- Restate the question so the entire audience can hear before giving an answer.
- Avoid letting one person dominate the question–answer period by indicating that you want everyone to have an opportunity to ask questions.

Enter every presentation with a plan to handle audience questions. You might think of questions that will arise and prepare yourself to answer them. If important questions aren't asked, you may choose to bring them up yourself during the question–answer period.

You may be surprised at how well you answer questions. Questions sometimes shock us into becoming direct and natural, and they impose a conversational structure into our responses. For some people, responses to questions can be the best part of their presentations because when they get away from their prepared remarks, they act more natural and actually improve their delivery.

INSTRUCTIONAL PRESENTATIONS

The introduction, body, and conclusion for an instructional presentation is provided in chapter 14, "The Speaking Process." Chapter 4 suggests a number of different organizational formats for instructing. Combined, these two chapters will help you organize most instructional presentations.

As discussed in chapter 4, there are two types of instructional presentations: "How To" and "What" presentations. "How To" presentations describe steps and processes. The following are examples of "How To" presentations.

- Teach a new employee how to handle customer complaints.
- "Show and tell" how to use the company's e-mail system.
- Describe the typical agenda of your team's meetings.

"What" presentations provide and explain new knowledge, usually of a more general nature. The following are examples of "What" presentations.

- Explain the roles played by each team member and the manager.
- Describe the rationale behind adopting a new accounting system.
- Outline the general responsibilities of management.

The purpose of instruction is to increase audience understanding. Three important principles that should be used in instructional presentations to help an audience understand are as follows: be direct, be simple, and be repetitive.

Be Direct

For most instructional presentations, get directly to the point. Make your point immediately, and then support it. Occasionally, for "What" presentations, you may use a less direct approach. However, most of the time, you'll have more impact with a direct approach.

Provide an objective and a preview. Your audience members will learn fastest when they know what you want them to know or do at the conclusion of the presentation and the steps you'll take to get them there. State the objective and preview at the beginning.

Tell the audience exactly what you expect. Tell audience members exactly what you want them to do with the information you provide. Explain the consequences of following or failing to follow instructions.

Be Simple

Instructional presentations should be simple, easy to understand, and "user friendly." You can simplify your presentation by doing the following.

Eliminate unnecessary information. Eliminate unimportant information, and keep what the audience needs to know. Avoid overwhelming with information or too many visuals.

Use titles and labels. Give titles or labels to your main points, to the steps or parts of the process, and to content you will refer to frequently. The labels help the audience simplify, categorize, and remember information.

Present the information in steps or parts. Dividing the information you present into "four easy steps" or the "five key elements" will help the audience understand and stay on track. For example, an instructional presentation about conducting team meetings might present the following steps:

1. Introduce the agenda.

2. Ask for reports.

3. Make assignments.

4. Share information and answer questions.

5. Summarize agreements and schedule the next meeting.

Be Repetitive

Audiences often have difficulty remembering instructional presentations. You enhance the likelihood that your audience will understand and remember your instructional presentation when you repeat information. The following guidelines provide means for using repetition during presentations.

Preview, present, and summarize. The optimum number of times to repeat a message is three times. When you "tell 'em what you are going to talk about," "tell 'em," and then "tell 'em what you told 'em," you've repeated the message three times.

Use visuals. Visuals of important points dramatically increase the likelihood that the audience will remember. Visual combined with oral presentation is one of the best ways to help an audience remember a message.

Provide hard copy. If the audience can take the message with them in hard-copy form, they will have a visual reminder and reference. Be careful about providing detailed copy during your presentation. Audience members will have a tendency to read the handout instead of listening to you. Either hand out the detail when you use it in the speech, or hand it out at the end of the presentation. You might, however, provide an outline for the audience to refer to during the presentation.

Use vivid illustrations, examples, and analogies. This method of amplifying and repeating points gets the audience's attention and helps them remember your points.

When possible, get the audience involved. After you've instructed, have the audience immediately apply information.

PERSUASIVE PRESENTATIONS

A successful instructional presentation changes the audience's level of knowledge about a topic. Persuasive presentations influence the audience to change their minds or to act. To do so, **persuasive speakers must go beyond straightforward explanations and convincing arguments to motivate the audience to action.**

For example, you may successfully inform a friend that smoking cigarettes is bad for her health. But this information will probably not keep her from smoking. She has other reasons that support her cigarette smoking. The opinions of experts are not enough. To persuade your friend to stop smoking, you must (1) show her that she has a need to stop, (2) overcome her objections to stopping smoking, and (3) help her reduce her uncertainty about how she can stop.

A business communication scholar and trainer, Eric Skopec (1983), notes that these three goals—establishing a need, overcoming objections, and reducing uncertainty—may not be accomplished in *one* speech. Rather, you may have to discuss the issue three or more times, presenting your arguments and overcoming objections. In other words, you would need to conduct a **persuasive campaign.** In cases where you're requesting changes, don't become discouraged if your proposal isn't accepted with one presentation. Plan on a series of persuasive messages. To convince your audience, you may need a series of private discussions, presentations, memos, and reports. Some of these efforts may focus only on the need for change or overcoming objections. Once your audience is sympathetic, you may then reduce the uncertainty about your plan by showing how it would work.

One of the key elements of a persuasive campaign is a persuasive speech. Understanding the elements of a persuasive speech will help you understand the bases for persuasion in most situations. The following provides guidelines for designing a persuasive speech. To these guidelines, you should add the strategies for persuasion outlined in chapter 4.

The first step in preparing any persuasive speech is **determining your purpose.** Specifically, what do you want the audience to do after your presentation? Do you want them to sign a contract, vote in favor of a proposal, or change the way they talk with subordinates? As suggested in chapter 2, your purpose should guide every decision made about the presentation.

The second step in preparing your presentation is **audience analysis.** Successful persuasion requires that you understand your audience's concerns. People tend to be **self-centered;** they evaluate any message based on how it will affect them. When you present your persuasive speech, they'll ask themselves "What's in this for me?" Thus, if you want to be successful, you need to know what the audience members desire and how your proposal can help them achieve those desires.

In addition, people are **problem-solvers,** and they tend to approach solving problems differently. When you convince audience members that there's a problem, they'll begin considering alternatives. As they analyze the situation and their alternatives, each person will use a different kind of logic. As chapter 4 points out, some will use analytical logic and will be convinced by hard data and statistics. Others will be guided by personal preferences and emotion and will be convinced by the speaker's opinions and stories or examples.

Thus, you need to understand members of the audience to be a successful persuader. You'll need to address their issues and goals, their objections, and their preferences for making decisions. Once you've established a specific purpose and examined your audience, you're ready to organize your speech. The elements of a persuasive presentation are (1) gain attention, (2) establish a need, (3) provide a solution, (4) visualize results, and (5) secure commitment.

Gain Attention

The **attention step** is the entire introduction to your speech. As is suggested in chapter 14, the opening of your presentation should (1) gain the audience's attention, (2) state your purpose, (3) establish your credibility, and (4) preview your main points. **Gaining attention** is the most important element of the introduction. If you don't gain the attention of your audience members, you can't persuade them. Notice commercials on TV and radio, and how they often go to great lengths to attract attention by presenting unique or entertaining anecdotes. These commercials work; they gain your attention.

The following, for instance, is what a consultant might say to gain the attention of a group of executives from a small manufacturing firm:

We offer our congratulations! Your annual report shows an 8.5 percent increase in earnings last year. We also offer condolences! Your federal taxes increased 13.5 percent. Let me repeat that . . . a 13.5 percent increase in federal taxes! The bad news is that your present accounting method is costing you and your stockholders income: it generates inflated values for your products that are then subject to high rates of taxation. The good news is you can do something about this lost income.

Second, your statement of **purpose** should directly tell your audience members what action you wish them to take. To illustrate, the speaker might state,

At the end of my presentation, I'll ask for your approval to implement a LIFO (last-in/first-out) accounting method for the next fiscal year.

Be as specific and precise as possible when stating your purpose.

Third, establish your **credibility** in at least one of three ways. First, highlight aspects of your background or your current work that indicate your success and expertise. Second, refer to credible sources you've used for research. Third, indicate the strength, success, or competence of your company. Continuing our example, the consultant recognizes that her audience is highly educated and has heard many other consultants on the topic she'll be addressing. She reasons that the executives will be as interested in what she knows about their firm as in her academic and business credentials.

> *The information I'll share with you today is based on interviews with the directors of your accounting and finance departments and my examination of your tax and income records for the last five years. The picture of your firm's financial health is similar to that of other firms with whom I've consulted during the last three years as a senior accountant for Arthur Andersen. As one of my graduate professors told me while I was pursuing my MBA, "Lots of companies make money, but not many are able to retain it."*

The last part of the attention step is the **preview** of the presentation. The preview of a persuasive presentation indicates that you'll be discussing (1) the need, (2) a proposal, (3) a visualization of proposal results, and (4) a request for commitment. You don't need to use the wording we've used to describe each part of the speech. For example, you might call the need a problem or refer to the proposal as a plan. Remember, the preview gives an indication of how you will proceed through the presentation. To continue the previous example, the consultant believes that the audience will accept the need for change, but she is uncertain about the value of different accounting methods.

> *First, I'll show you the need to change by illustrating how the LIFO method saves money compared to your current accounting method. Second, I'll show you how the LIFO system works. Third, I'll help you visualize what it will be like when you adopt the LIFO method. Finally, I'll ask for your approval to implement the system.*

Need

Successfully executed, the **need step** will make audience members recognize that there is a problem with some aspect of their business. Moreover, they will feel that the problem is urgent enough to require their immediate attention. If the audience is already convinced of the seriousness of the problem, you can make the need step brief. However, if the audience is satisfied with the way the business is performing, the need step will be your most elaborate and crucial step in the presentation. Unless the audience members are convinced that they face an urgent problem, they won't be willing to hear your proposal.

To develop this step, break the need into four phases: statement, illustration, ramification, and pointing. During the **statement** phase, plainly announce the audience's need. To **illustrate** this need, provide examples so the audience can easily recognize the problem. Make the examples vivid using statistics or concrete descriptions. In the **ramification** phase, show the audience why this need is urgent by explaining the extent of the problem or the implications for the organization. Use statistics and hypothetical or real examples to discuss implications. Finally, use **pointing** to show that the problem affects each individual in the audience.

The key in the need step is to show the audience that it has a demonstrated problem. Such a problem may have both factual and perceptual bases. Our consultant might say something like the following in the need step.

> **Statement.** *Your accounting system cost you a lot of money last year in taxes.*
> **Illustration.** *Here's your federal tax statement using your accounting method* (show overhead of federal tax statement). *I calculated what your taxes would have been had you used LIFO* (show overhead of federal tax statement based on LIFO). *You can see you would've saved $54,220 last year using LIFO* (show overhead of figures).
> **Ramifications.** *If you continue your current rate of growth and retain the same accounting system, I've calculated it will cost your company $211,000* (show overhead of figures).
> **Pointing.** *Assuming that you distribute profits equally to owners, these figures suggest that each of the owners lost $18,073.33 last year. Jack, you could've paid for a new car with that amount of money. Over the next three years, each owner stands to lose $70, 333.33, the cost of a new luxury car.*

Proposal

The **proposal step** provides the solution to the problem, satisfying the need you've demonstrated. On one hand, if the audience wasn't aware of the problem and hasn't considered various solutions, you can shorten this step by simply stating and explaining your proposal. On the other hand, if the audience was previously convinced of the problem but has been uncertain about how it can be solved, this step will be the most important part of your presentation. When you need to fully explain the proposal, use three phases: (1) statement, (2) explanation, and (3) theoretical demonstration or practical experience.

During the **statement** phase, concisely note the solution or plan that the audience needs to adopt. As you **explain** or describe the proposal, be sure to use visual aids to help the audience understand. Then use a **theoretical demonstration** to show that your proposal solves the problem described in the need step. Or, if possible, show by **practical experience** how another company or individual has successfully implemented the solution. Provide examples, statistics, and other support. Be convincing by citing the sources for any statistics and examples that you mention.

The consultant might say something like the following in presenting the plan.

> **Statement:** *My proposal is that you adopt the LIFO accounting system.*
> **Explanation:** *The LIFO system works by changing the method of costing inventory so that the most recent costs incurred should be charged against revenue.*
> **Theoretical Demonstration and Practical Experience:** *Here's how the system would work in your organization* (explain the plan using a specific example of an inventoried item, using overheads to show figures). *This is how another company implemented LIFO* (use overheads and statistics to show how the company implemented the system and how much money was saved).

Visualization

The visualization step projects the audience members into the future, illustrating how they or their business will fare under one of three different conditions: (1) if they

adopt your proposal, (2) if they fail to adopt your proposal and address the problem, or (3) if they adopt some other plan—including not doing anything—versus if they adopt your proposal. In other words, portray one of three types of images: a positive image, a negative image, or a contrasting image. Visualization is particularly valuable because it allows you to answer any objections that you anticipate your audience might raise. For example, the contrasting image method will allow you to compare the costs of your proposal against the costs of alternative plans.

Using **positive images** simply means that you should help the audience visualize the benefits they would receive if the plan you've proposed were enacted. Use concrete and vivid images that appeal to the audience, and picture conditions likely to arise in the future. These one-sided messages are most effective with an audience that already believes in you and recognizes a problem but is uncertain about how your proposal will help.

As its name implies, using **negative images** takes the opposite perspective. Here you indicate what will happen to the audience members if they don't adopt your proposal. Again, use both graphic and plausible images to make audience members feel the dangers inherent in an unchanged future. The warning in this one-sided message is most effective with an audience that isn't convinced that the problem is serious.

The method of using **contrasting images** combines positive and negative aspects of the future. This two-sided message is particularly effective when your audience is leaning toward your proposal but still has some objections. However, you must decide which image should be presented first. Generally speaking, you should present the positive image first. However, if your audience is bored or unfamiliar with the subject, begin with the negative.

Our consultant might use the positive image in the following way.

Consider the results of implementing the LIFO system. If business continues as it has done for the past year, each of you could have an additional $20,000 in profits next year—enough to buy that new car. You may not buy the car. But think of what an additional $60,000 would mean to you and your business.

Action

The **action step** is your conclusion, and in it, you present a recap of (1) *why* the audience needs to do something, and (2) specifically *what* they need to do. In addition, you should (3) *seek commitment* for action, and (4) provide a *memorable conclusion.* Make special effort to provide specific instructions, give dates and names, or distribute contracts or sign-up sheets—*make it easy for the audience members to act.*

For example, the consultant addressing the executives from the small manufacturing firm might close by stating the following:

> **Why and What.** *In summary, I've shown you that your current accounting method is costing you money by increasing your taxable income and decreasing your retained earnings. To solve this problem, I've suggested that you implement a LIFO accounting method for the current fiscal year. The advantages of this method over others include its ease of implementation and an immediate impact on your firm's taxable income.*
>
> **Seek Commitment.** *But the opportunity to change your accounting method is quickly slipping away. To take advantage of the LIFO method for the current fiscal year, you must file your quarterly tax statements using this method within the next three weeks. I encourage you to enlist my services within the next five days so that you can reap the rewards that your firm deserves.*
>
> **Memorable Statement.** *Why not become one of those few businesses that not only makes money but also keeps it?*

SUMMARY

You'll be asked to give a variety of different kinds of presentations in organizations. Some will allow for preparation, and some will not. You'll use notes or manuscripts for many presentations, but you'll also be asked to make impromptu comments and answer questions. Become familiar with the guidelines offered in this chapter to handle these speaking situations.

Most business presentations are informative or persuasive. They get to the point quickly and are results-oriented. Instructional presentations focus on what something is and how to do it. Use the organizational pattern that best matches the content of the speech. As you design either kind of presentation, adapt the speech to meet your goals and the needs of the audience.

Persuasion also requires that you understand audience concerns and interests. To change attitudes or to generate action, you need to adapt your arguments to members of the audience. Show how your solutions can help the audience achieve its needs. Help the audience see the benefits of adopting your solutions. Your presentation will be most persuasive when you understand and adapt to your audience.

CHAPTER 16

Team Writing and Speaking

During the course of your career, you will undoubtedly be a member of many teams that produce reports and presentations. You may find team participation frustrating. When required to do a team project, you may grudgingly do the bare minimum. The result of this approach may be resentful team members and an unsatisfactory project.

Because working in teams seems to be the way many tasks get done in organizations, we suggest you will gain the most from teams by taking a proactive approach. Join with team members and cooperate in accomplishing the common goal. Provide input, express your concerns, and let the team know about your limitations. Share your expertise and energy. Develop interpersonal skills that promote teamwork. You'll find that when teams work together effectively, they can produce a superior product.

Below, we provide guidelines for managing teams to create documents and presentations. First, we discuss guidelines for managing team interaction. Then, we provide guidelines for team writing and speaking.

TEAM MANAGEMENT

Writing and speaking as part of a group are becoming increasingly common in the workplace and for good reason. If successful, a group can produce outstanding work. We discuss the advantages and disadvantages of team writing and give pointers in how to manage the process.

Advantages

Long business documents and presentations, such as business reports or proposals, are often superior when written by a team instead of a single person. Different group members can take the formidable task of developing the document or speech and divide it up into separate, more manageable jobs. For many documents and presentations—like an audit report—that will have a wide audience or represent different fields of expertise, the varied perspectives of a team can provide a more complete final product.

Finally, the process of forming a consensus may produce the best thoughts and decisions for an organization. Many team members not only strengthen the document or presentation, but more completely represent the thinking of the organization. In addition, the team process causes individuals to challenge and influence one another as the product is developed and will, therefore, make it more thorough, accurate, and logical. The team process encourages the development of quality because it reflects both on the team and the business.

Disadvantages

Of course, the team process can have problems. Group members need to deal with the potential disadvantages of teams to avoid problems that could result in poor documents or presentations. Meeting times must be found. Differing personalities must find accord. Varying perspectives must be accommodated. Individual preferences for document content, format, and style must be resolved.

To be successful, a team must manage team interaction and the writing and speaking process. The first concern is managing team interaction.

MANAGING TEAM INTERACTION

Although most teams want to immediately dive into the task of writing or speaking, attention should first be given to managing team interaction to prevent many problems. The following provides suggestions to guide team efforts.

First, **get to know one another.** Developing rapport among group members will provide a positive reservoir of feelings to call upon when disagreements arise. Developing the ability to talk casually will help individuals express honest opinions and resolve differences. Find out about team members' backgrounds, personal interests, and schedules. You might want to discuss when future meetings will take place. If possible, address concerns about working together as a team.

Sometimes **a leader will be useful** in overseeing a large project, particularly in a workplace setting. If all team members agree that team leadership is needed, discuss which group member or members will have this responsibility. Leaders often remind members about meeting times and can conduct the meetings. Leaders can also come up with an agenda, which should be distributed to all group members before the meeting.

All team members, whether working on a project for class or for work, should **attend meetings regularly.** Missing meetings and failing to honor one's commitment create resentment, anger, distrust, and discouragement among team members. Only emergencies should keep group members from attending all meetings or completing assignments. Even then, as soon as problems arise, the team's leader should be notified so that members can adjust work assignments and schedules.

> **Important Steps in Team Management**
> - Get to know one another
> - Assign a leader, if necessary
> - Attend meetings regularly
> - Encourage input from all team members
> - Record and share group progress
> - Allow ample time to complete the project
> - Support group decisions

FIGURE 16.1 Steps for Managing Teams

To help ensure that all group members contribute their good ideas, members should **encourage input** among other members, particularly introverts who might hesitate to speak up. Encourage everyone to participate by asking such questions as *"What are your thoughts?"* or *"Does everyone agree?"*

To help everyone focus on the same issues, **record and share group progress.** Sometimes writing a document can best be accomplished by gathering around a computer, or interconnected computers, so that all can see and work on the same screen. Hard-copy printouts for all group members can be brought to team meetings for revisions. Teams might write outlines on white or black boards or on overhead slides. If all else fails, a team member might make a record and read it back to the group members for approval.

Keep in mind that groups can take longer than an individual to complete a task. Getting started early helps groups forecast the efforts required. Take into account that good writing and speaking require revisions. **Give yourselves plenty of time** to produce a high-quality finished product.

Finally, remember that group members are individuals with unique opinions. The best groups are those that have disagreement but find ways to manage differences. Once ideas are heard and group decisions are made, group members should **be supportive** and go along with the group's decisions. Because all team members are unique, you will disagree. The aforementioned rules will make conflicts constructive and keep the group on task.

Figure 16.1 summarizes guidelines for successful team writing.

MANAGING THE WRITING PROCESS

For best results, all the elements described in chapter 6, "The Writing Process," must be present for teams to write effectively. In addition, teams must coordinate varied perspectives to create a unified product. The following provides a process for teams to coordinate their efforts. The process includes establishing objectives, agreeing on a framework, writing the document, revising the document, and editing and proofreading. Figure 16.2 summarizes the process.

Once you've developed rapport with your team, you're ready to begin the team writing process. We recommend that you meet to establish personal objectives, to define your target audience, to share and develop ideas, and to agree on the purpose of the document. This part of the process may occur in one meeting or in several meetings.

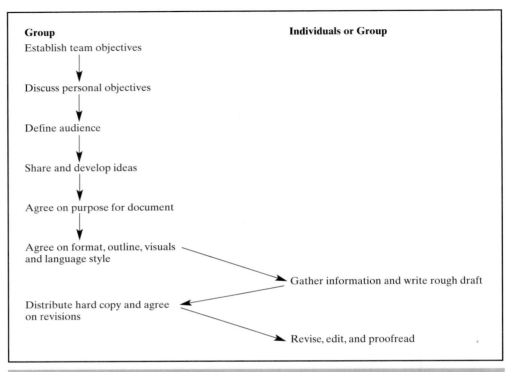

FIGURE 16.2 Team Writing Process

Establish Personal Objectives

Before you write, discuss the personal objectives of each team member because they will influence how individuals participate. For example, although the team may be assigned to write a quarterly report under a standard process, a team member may want to upgrade the way quarterly reports are done to make them more professional. An individual may be up for a promotion and want to do an exceptionally good job on the report. Or a team member may want to finish the report early because of other commitments. Getting personal objectives out on the table early will help team members understand one another, accommodate various goals, and prevent conflicts.

Define the Audience

Your team should also spend time discussing the audience: Will the document be written for a few people inside the organization or for the general public? Will you want to influence many people or just one key decision-maker? What are the expectations of the audience? What are its knowledge levels and interests? What kind of document would be acceptable to the audience?

Share and Develop Ideas

Before forming specific objectives, explore whether team members have different ideas about the project. Discussing these ideas as a team will stimulate thought and discussion. You may want to gather ideas from additional sources before establishing specific team objectives. For example, you might want to research how other companies do their quarterly reports or read experts' opinions on a problem you must address. Consider meeting more than once as you develop your ideas.

Agree on the Purpose of the Document

After settling on ideas for the writing project, decide on the specific purpose of the document. What do you want the audience to know or to be able to do after reading the document? Be specific. For example, you might want to outline the content that you want your audience to know. Or you could specify the principal parts of a proposal you want the audience to accept. These objectives should be accepted by team members and written down for all to see.

Meet to Agree on the Framework

To save time and frustration, the team should agree on the framework of the document, which includes the format, outline, visuals, and language style.

Format

The format is the basic structure for the document, including the use of spacing and headings. For some documents, the format may be specified by guidelines or by normal practice in the organization. If a format is available, use it. In certain organizations, documents aren't accepted unless the proper format is used. For some reports—a problem-solving report, for example—the format may not be specified. Thus, the team may need to borrow or create a format.

Outline

The outline is a list of basic points, and support material for points, that will be included in the document. The outline should be sufficiently detailed so that team members have a clear idea of the major content of the document. A shared organizational scheme for the writing task is also critical for dividing up the writing and getting the most synergy from a team.

Visuals

Figures, tables, charts, graphs, and other illustrations are crucial to many business reports. Such visuals portray vital information that can be difficult for your readers to grasp as a whole when only written. Special care should be given to preparing clear and useful visuals. Team members should not only agree on the kinds of visuals, but should see the visuals and agree on their format, content, and placement.

Style

Team members should agree upon the approach, tone, and desired impact of the document on the audience. Style includes such issues as whether the document should be perceived as friendly or distant, informal or formal, conversational or legal, black-and-white or colorful, and basic or professional. Usually, team members have to see examples of documents—either samples of finished documents or rough drafts—to agree on a style.

Write a Rough Draft

The goal when writing a draft is not to provide a finished product, but to write down the content. One or more team members may participate in fleshing out the outline. If the

team consists of four or more, it may be easiest to divide the task. Alternatively, one individual may wish to draft the document based on the notes and research provided by all the other members.

Some people prefer to write alone. Others like to sit at the keyboard with one or two other people providing input as they compose. Some companies experiment with small groups composing on networked computers. One popular method is to have each member work with a partner, sharing notes and ideas while composing both as a sub-group and as individuals. Team writing can be quick, efficient, and effective with the use of computers.

Meet to Agree on Revisions

The most efficient way to revise is to provide a hard copy of the rough draft to all team members and suggest revisions during a team meeting. This method allows all team members to hear one anothers' comments. Individuals can agree to changes quickly. The goal of this meeting is not to agree on each word, but to agree on general content. Teams can get bogged down and frustrated when they nit-pick over specific wording, especially when arguments are based on stylistic preferences. To avoid such pitfalls, try to divide responsibilities for detailed editing and proofing.

Edit and Proofread the Document

To keep the style, content, and word choice consistent, you may want to assign one person to do the final proofing. Select a team member who writes well and has a good sense of the team's preferred style to edit and proofread the document.

Also, give the edited document to someone besides the editor (or editorial group) to proof because the editor may miss some of his or her own errors. Examine the overall format, including page numbers, headings, and visuals. Check the document for mechanical errors, such as punctuation, spelling, sentence structure, and number usage. Plan on editing and proofreading several times.

MANAGING THE SPEAKING PROCESS

The challenge in a team presentation is to provide a consistent and coherent message that achieves a common purpose. To accomplish this outcome, plan and develop the presentation as a team. Don't yield to the temptation of immediately breaking the presentation into parts, working separately, and bringing the parts together the day of the presentation. Such an approach rarely produces parts that fit together well. In the fol-

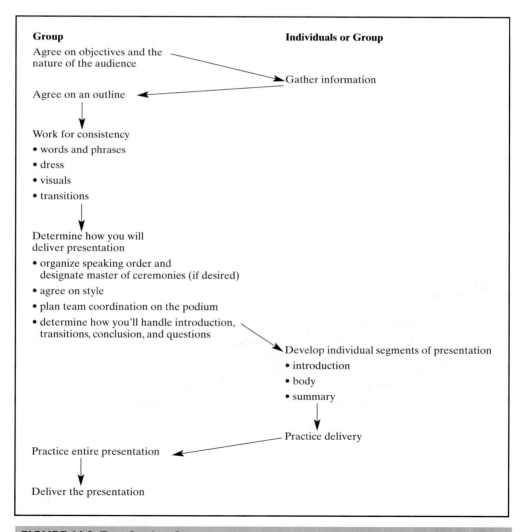

FIGURE 16.3 Team Speaking Process

lowing, we suggest how you might work together to develop a coherent presentation. Figure 16.3 summarizes the team speaking process.

Agree on Objectives and the Nature of the Audience

As a team, agree upon a purpose statement. Complete a statement similar to the following: "At the conclusion of our presentation, the audience will know or will do. . . ." When everyone on the team agrees on the ultimate objective, it will make the rest of the presentation easier to organize.

Gather Relevant Information and Agree on an Outline

After you've defined your purpose, gather information and agree on an outline. Use the suggestions provided about team writing to gain agreement on the outline. We strongly recommend that you outline the main points of the entire presentation on a white or blackboard so the entire team can see, discuss, and agree. If you can agree on the overall outline, it will help each team member prepare individual parts of the presentation and make it consistent with the rest of the presentation.

If you're delivering an instructional presentation, consider using one of the instructional formats suggested in chapter 4 as an organizational guide. If you're preparing a persuasive presentation, use the format for persuasion provided in chapter 15.

Work for Consistency and Coherence

Unless the team takes steps to prevent it, a team presentation can appear like a bunch of disconnected individual presentations. To give your presentation the sense that it's a *team* effort, you need to create consistency and coherence.

1. **Use the Same Words and Phrases for Important Concepts.** The team should agree on key terms and phrases. For example, if you're giving a persuasive presentation and want to make the point that the current approach for handling

customer complaints has deficiencies, all the speakers should use the word "deficiencies" frequently and consistently throughout. If you give your plan a label such as "the customer-first plan," use that term throughout.

2. **Dress Like a Team.** Unless you have a specific reason for doing so, all members of the team should dress about the same, either informally or formally. In most cases, dress will be business formal. Like a sports team, consistent appearance will help the audience perceive that you're engaged in a united effort.

3. **Maintain Visual Consistency.** There are several methods for creating visual consistency. "The look" should be the same throughout the presentation.

   - **Use the same type of visual.** If one person uses a flipchart, everyone should use a flipchart. If one person uses a projected outline, all team members should do the same.

   - **Use a common template.** If you use PowerPoint or a similar graphics program, use the same template for all slides. The goal is to have exactly the same background, colors, font, and font size throughout. If you use flipcharts, use the same colors and print on each chart.

   - **Use the same terms and symbols.** Each time a term is used on a visual, the exact same wording should be used. If you use company logos, use them on all the visuals.

   - **Refer to a master outline.** Introduce an overall outline of your presentation, and refer back to the outline as you progress through each segment of the presentation.

   - **Use running headers.** A running header reminds the audience of the topic or purpose of the presentation or portion of the presentation. It often appears at the top, in the upper left-hand corner, or the lower right-hand corner of the presentation.

   - **Use an "add-on" aid.** As each person speaks, add points or conclusions to a master visual that progressively summarizes the overall presentation.

4. **Use a Consistent Format for Transitions, Introductions, and Conclusions.** Introductions of speakers should include similar kinds of information. Transitions between speakers should have similar content. For example, you might consistently summarize one speaker's portion of the presentation before introducing the next speaker. Each speaker should use a similar pattern for previewing, emphasizing main points, and concluding his or her portion of the presentation.

Determine How You Will Deliver the Presentation

Before you give the presentation, make decisions ahead of time about how you will deliver the presentation so that your team acts as a coordinated unit.

1. **Organize how you will speak.** We've seen two general organizational patterns. Some teams use a master of ceremonies who introduces the presentation, provides transitions between speakers, summarizes, and conducts the question–answer period. We prefer this approach because it clearly identifies a leader, and the approach adds coherence to the presentation.

Other teams have different team members handle each part of the presentation. Each team member provides a transition to the next speaker at the conclusion of his or her remarks. If you choose this pattern, clearly indicate who is the leader for each part of the presentation by providing a clear preview that indicates who will speak and what each person will cover.

2. **Determine the overall style—formal or friendly.** One of the things you don't have to worry about when speaking by yourself is style consistency. With different personalities on your team, style becomes an issue. Do you want your presentation to create a formal relationship with your audience? If so, plan to use a more reserved style and speak primarily from behind the lectern.

    If you want to create a friendly, informal relationship, plan to have more gestures, movement, and upbeat interaction with the audience. Consider the personalities of team members, and choose a team member who can set the tone you desire, either formal or friendly, to speak at the beginning of the presentation.

3. **Plan team management on the podium.** The team should sit together. You might sit together behind or to the side of the lectern to show support. Or, you might sit with the audience facing the lectern to be supportive of each team speaker. To show who "has the floor," only the current speaker should stand.

    When the audience can easily see you, we suggest you sit together as a team facing the audience to take questions. The team member answering the question might choose to stand or sit. If the audience can't easily see you, you might stand together facing the audience. The person answering a question might take a step forward when answering and step back when finished.

4. **Determine how you will handle questions.** Decide whether you'll be willing to take questions during your presentation. At the beginning of the presentation, announce whether you plan to take questions anytime, at the conclusion of each team member's part of the presentation, or at the end of the entire presentation. If questions are taken during the presentation, you may decide to have the person speaking at the time the question is asked to be the moderator.

    Decide who'll be the moderator for the question–answer period. When the presentation has concluded, the moderator should ask for questions and use the question-handling techniques described in chapter 15 such as thanking questioners and making sure that everyone in the audience understands the questions. Also, decide who should handle different types of questions.

    When a question is asked, the moderator "gives the floor" to a team member to provide an answer. Each team member should use the guidelines for answering questions in chapter 15. The moderator might take a step back or physically turn toward the team member to indicate that the team member has the floor, and then step forward to moderate when the answer is concluded.

    The moderator should also watch the time and, when appropriate, ask for a final question. The moderator might conclude by thanking the audience for its questions and the team for its answers. When appropriate, the moderator might add a brief summary or reminder of the conclusions of the presentation.

Structure the Presentation

We suggest the following adaptations to the speech structure presented in chapter 14.

INTRODUCTION

- **Make a statement to gain the audience's attention.**

- **State the purpose for the presentation.**

- **Provide a preview of the presentation.** At this time, introduce the team members who will provide each part of the presentation, and give relevant background that establishes credibility, such as professional position or special preparations for the presentation. To reinforce team members' expertise, display names and qualifications on a visual. In this preview, also indicate when you'll answer questions.

TRANSITIONS

You might handle transitions in one of the following ways.

- **A team member acts as a presentation moderator.** The moderator provides the introduction, conclusion, and transitions between speakers. The moderator might provide a transition by saying, "Connie has outlined problems with our current accounting system. Richard will now present our solution."

- **Team members provide transitions at the conclusion of their presentations.** For example, to provide a transition to the next presentation, a team member might say, "I've outlined our transportation system in the East. Now, Alex will discuss transportation in the West."

BODY

Each speaker should

- Provide a brief preview of the main points that he or she will cover.

- Present the points along with support material.

- Provide a brief summary.

CONCLUSION

- Restate the purpose.

- Provide the overall summary point you want the audience to remember.

- Present a concluding statement.

- Ask for questions when appropriate.

Practice the Presentation Together

The advantage of a team presentation is that you can give one another feedback to improve the presentation. You need to practice the presentation all the way through at least twice as a group. Deliver the presentation exactly as you plan to present it including dress, visuals, transitions, movement, and gestures. Even though you may plan to sit on the podium during the presentation, when you practice, sit so you can get the same view the audience will have. Take notes on what you like about each speaker and what you would suggest to improve. Look for ways to make style and presentation consistent among speakers. Use the guidelines provided in the appendix for evaluating presentations. At the end of the presentation, discuss what you liked about each speaker and recommend what you would change.

Deliver the Presentation

Arrive early on the day you give the presentation to set up team seating and visuals. Remember that you're "on stage" on the podium even when you aren't speaking. So avoid whispering to team members during the presentation, and pay attention to the speaker.

SUMMARY

Teams can produce excellent documents and speeches. A team effort can also result in disjointed, uneven documents and presentations that poorly reflect the individuals' efforts. To be successful, teams must manage group processes as well as writing and speaking processes. Teams that do both usually produce the best documents and presentations.

CHAPTER 17

Communication Strategies for Seeking Employment

Finding employment requires that you use several communication skills. The first four chapters in this text provide guidelines for developing communication strategies. The remaining chapters help you develop writing and presentation skills. This chapter helps you apply the communication strategies and skills in a coordinated campaign to find employment.

WHO GETS THE JOBS?

Before you begin your campaign for employment, you might step back and ask how you can gain the advantage. What do you need to do in your campaign to sell yourself? What can you do to make your campaign a success? Who is successful in getting job offers? We've found that those who are most successful develop contact credibility, show they're qualified, and present themselves well in interviews.

Develop Contact Credibility

When someone who has credibility with the employer refers you, you have contact credibility. You stand out from other applicants because you were referred by a trusted source.

From the employer's perspective, even when applicants are thoroughly screened, hiring employees is risky. The applicant might appear to be qualified on paper, but will he or she make a good employee? Will the person work hard and be a team player? Or will the person be dishonest, lazy, or disruptive?

If a trusted source refers the individual, much of the uncertainty is reduced. Although letters of recommendation help, they don't give you contact credibility unless the persons writing the letters know the employer. Often, employers don't place a lot of confidence in letters of recommendation because of their tendency toward a positive bias. However, much of the skepticism is removed when the employer knows the recommending individual.

You can gain contact credibility by asking the contact to do one or more of the following.

1. Introduce you to the employer or make an appointment for you with the employer.
2. Write a letter of recommendation for you.
3. Allow you to use his or her name when contacting the employer.

If the person doesn't introduce you or make the initial appointment, always use the contact's name when you seek an appointment.

You can gain contacts in at least three ways. *First, seek to have acquaintances who know the employer act as your contact.* You may need to do a bit of investigating among family, friends, and acquaintances to find someone who knows the employer. If you ask around, you'll find acquaintances who know the employer. When you identify persons who know the employer, approach them, and describe your employment goal. Show them your résumé, and tell them of your qualifications. They may need to be convinced that you're qualified before agreeing to be a contact. Then, ask the persons if they would introduce you or make an appointment for you, write a letter of recommendation, or allow you to use their names when you contact the employer.

For example, upon completing her MBA, Linda wanted a job in banking. Although her father didn't work in the city where she sought employment, he knew some members of the banking community. With a few telephone calls, he was able to set up luncheon interviews for Linda that opened doors to employment.

Second, develop acquaintances that might act as your contact. For example, Stan knew no one in Seattle, but he wanted to live there. So he developed a résumé, drove to Seattle, and found organizations in the phone book that he thought he would enjoy working for. Stan chose a company and went to visit with the head of personnel. He explained his desire for a position, showed his résumé, and described his qualifications. The personnel director said she had no positions open. Stan asked her to keep his résumé on file.

Then Stan asked the personnel director if she knew of organizations that were hiring. She gave him the names of two organizations and persons to contact in those organizations. When he asked, she consented to allow Stan to refer to her name when he approached those other organizations. Thus, Stan had developed contact credibility. He continued to network in a similar manner until he found employment.

Third, develop contacts by conducting information interviews. The purpose of an information interview is to gather information about a desired position. Typically, you would conduct this interview several months before you apply for employment. You contact a manager who has a job you want in an organization in which you would like employment. You explain that you would like a short interview to learn about the desired position and ask what you must do to qualify. Managers are usually very willing to schedule such an interview. During the interview, do the following:

1. Ask the manager to describe the position and required qualifications.
2. Show the manager your résumé, and ask how you can strengthen your qualifications.
3. Ask the manager if you might contact him or her again when you're ready to apply for a position or for permission to refer to his or her name when you apply.

For example, Kelli conducted an information interview with a vice-president in a large hospital in Lincoln, Nebraska. The vice-president was so impressed with her qualifications that she hired her for a part-time position during the interview. Later, when Kelli was ready to start graduate school in another city, the vice-president arranged for Kelli to interview for a part-time position at a hospital in that community.

Show You Are Qualified

Of course, no matter how good your contact credibility, you must also be qualified. If you are to be hired, the employer must *know* that you're qualified. Unfortunately, some qualified individuals aren't hired because they don't clearly demonstrate their qualifications.

To demonstrate that you are qualified, you must (1) know the qualifications the employer wants, and (2) demonstrate that you have them.

Identify Qualifications

If you really want a position with a specific company, we suggest you do some "audience analysis" before applying. You can identify specific qualifications in the following ways.

1. **Make a list of the qualifications identified in the listing.** For example, the following qualifications were listed in a description for a market researcher in commercial real estate:

   Job requirements include a bachelor's degree from a major four-year institution (preferably in business or economics), excellent computer and writing skills, and the willingness to meet with people from other companies including cold calling.

   The qualifications listed in this position statement are

   - Bachelor's degree from a major four-year college or university

   - Computer skills

   - Writing skills

2. **From the duties listed, infer qualifications and add them to your list of qualifications.** The statement, "willingness to meet with people from other companies including cold calling," doesn't clearly identify the desired qualifications. You have two ways to identify the qualifications from listed duties. You can infer the qualifications, or you can gather more information. We discuss gathering information below. You might reasonably infer the following qualifications from the previous statement.

   - Interpersonal communication skills

   - Sales skills and abilities

3. **Gather information about the position and the company from someone who works for the company, and use the information to update qualifications.** The best source of information would be the manager responsible for the position. A personnel officer might also provide good answers to questions about qualifications. When you conduct what would likely be a telephone interview, *first, ask the person to clarify required qualifications.* For example for the above example, you might ask whether your inferences were accurate that interpersonal and sales skills are important qualifications. You might also ask about the kinds of computer skills needed and for any other information that might help you clarify the nature of the position.

   Second, ask about the cultural norms in the company. Is the culture laid back and easy going, or is it driven and hard working? Understanding norms will help you identify how your characteristics may fit with the company culture. For example, if the culture is highly competitive, you might describe your abilities to compete in letters of application and interviews.

Based on all the information you've gathered, make a final updated list of qualifications. The finished list should include all major qualifications and a statement that describes culture or norms. For example, the following is a final list of qualifications for the job described above.

- Bachelor's degree from a major four-year college or university
- Computer skills—Microsoft Office Suite
- Writing skills—advertising brochures and in-house reports
- Interpersonal and communication skills—especially for social events
- Sales skills and abilities—low key, one-on-one persuasion
- Company norms and culture—do whatever it takes to please customers

Show How Your Background Meets Qualifications

When you know the desired qualifications, you're prepared to show how you meet those qualifications in your letter of application, résumé, and interview.

In your *letter of application,* you may want to write a paragraph for each qualification. For example, the following paragraph was written to show that the applicant has writing skills. Notice how the italicized parts of the paragraph mention the various elements from the final list of qualifications described above.

> I am an *excellent writer.* I received As in all my writing classes and for almost all written work in college, including lengthy *reports.* Using *Microsoft Word,* I produced several *brochures* for my fraternity. Given my writing skills and experience, I could produce professional-quality *advertising brochures* and *reports* for your organization.

Your résumé can also be designed to specifically address each qualification. The functional and combined résumés described in chapter 12 enable you to organize your résumé around specific qualifications. The following is an example of how qualifications might be presented in a functional résumé. Notice how easily the employer can identify relevant qualifications.

COMPUTER SKILLS

- Expertise in Microsoft Word, Excel, Access, FrontPage, and PowerPoint
- Develop and maintain Web Pages
- University computer courses in business programs and applications

WRITING SKILLS

- High grades in writing classes and assignments
- Report writing and technical writing courses
- Developed brochures for fraternity

COMMUNICATION SKILLS

- University courses in public speaking, small groups, and negotiation
- Social officer and activities chairperson for fraternity, conducted numerous meetings

- Team leader for three term projects
- Captain for university soccer team

SALES SKILLS
- Server at The Olive Garden
- Clothing sales at The Men's Shop
- Sales and merchandising course

Finally, prepare to *present your qualifications in the employment interview.* You have the opportunity to present detailed information about qualifications in interviews. However, we've found that most people can't think of good examples to support qualifications *during* interviews. Therefore, we suggest that you prepare good examples and support for qualifications before interviewing. Put them together in the form of a speech that presents the following elements for each qualification.

1. State your qualification.
2. Provide specific, concrete support.
3. Indicate how your qualification can help the employer.

When you develop the speech, make the support specific and concrete; tell stories, provide anecdotes, and cite statistics. The following are examples of support that could be developed for the communication and sales skills for the job described above.

COMMUNICATION SKILLS

State your qualification. *One of my strengths is my ability to communicate and get along with people. Let me illustrate with three examples.*
Provide support. *First, I was elected the social officer and activities chairperson in my fraternity. Every year, we had a kick-off "smoker" barbecue. I always took the lead in getting people acquainted. I introduced them and found topics to get them involved in conversation. For example, I noticed one new member, Pete, was by himself. I talked to him and found he was a chess wizard. I introduced him to guys who play chess, and he quickly felt at home.*

Second, I often emerge as the team leader or captain of sport teams because I know how to bring people together. I recall that once at a practice, Pedro missed the ball and kicked Jim in the stomach. When Jim recovered, he got in Pedro's face and threatened him. I stepped between them and got them to talk. It wasn't long before I had them laughing about "the gut kick."

Third, as you can see on my résumé, I have taken several communication classes. I have straight As in those classes. I developed a persuasive speech designed to persuade an accounting firm to adopt a CPA training program. The professor was so impressed with my speech that he videotaped it and still uses it as a positive example in class. In my negotiation class, I established a reputation for getting a good deal, but also maintaining good relationships. I got the best deal in the class in a simulated home purchase negotiation.
Indicate how your qualifications can help the employer. *My communication skills will enable me to build good relationships and negotiate favorable contracts for your business.*

SALES SKILLS

State your qualification. *I'm a very good salesperson. Two experiences show my sales ability.*

Provide Support. *First, at The Olive Garden, I was chosen as the server of the month for three of the six months that I worked there. I got good feedback from customers and was very good at selling wine and desserts. The way I approached sales was to sell what the customers wanted. I would ask what their favorite wine or dessert was. Then, if we didn't have quite what they wanted, I convinced them that the substitute was very good.*

Second, at The Men's Shop, I was the top salesperson over 50% of the time that I worked there, about two years. I was able to develop customers who came back because I knew how to give them what they wanted. There was one rich, but ornery, old guy that no one wanted to deal with because he said things like, "No! You can't help me. You're too young and too stupid!" I took him on as a challenge and built a good relationship with him. I found what he was interested in and met his needs. He always asked for me when he came to the store.

Indicate how your qualifications can help the employer. *I'm confident that my sales skills and ability to persuade difficult clients will help your real estate sales.*

Although in the previous examples, we provide a script of what you might say, don't create a script and memorize it. You won't communicate as fluently and expressively when you memorize a script. Instead, speak from a memorized outline similar to the following.

COMMUNICATIONS SKILLS

One of my strengths is my ability to communicate and get along with people. Let me illustrate with three examples.

1. Fraternity social officer and activity chairman.

2. Team leader on sports and project teams.

3. Communication course, speaking, and negotiation success.

My communication skills will enable me to build good relationships and negotiate favorable contracts for your business.

SALES SKILLS

I'm a very good salesperson. Two experiences show my sales ability.

1. The Olive Garden

2. The Men's Shop

I'm confident that my sales skills and ability to persuade difficult clients will help your real estate sales.

One of our students, Cathy, had an interview to become a management trainee at Kmart. She asked how she could present herself well. We helped her develop a list of qualifications and a speech to demonstrate she had the qualifications. When she arrived, she found that five managers would conduct a group interview. She was intimidated until she was asked the first question, "Why do you think you are qualified to be a manager?" Cathy replied, "As I understand the position, you're looking for the following qualifications." She then listed six qualifications and presented the speech she had prepared. She felt prepared and confident. She performed well and was offered the position.

Like Cathy, you should go prepared to sell your qualifications. You may not be able to present the whole speech at one time, as she did. However, when you're asked relevant questions, you'll be prepared.

Present Yourself Well in the Interview

Your goal for the interview is to demonstrate that you're qualified for the job. The previous section shows you how to *prepare and organize* information so that it might be persuasive. This section shows you how to *present* the information persuasively. Your interview will be a success when you come across as being competent, confident, enthusiastic, similar to your employers, and friendly.

Show That You Are Competent

You demonstrate competence by the way you handle yourself in the interview. Present yourself as being knowledgeable, organized, and responsive. You demonstrate that you have *knowledge* when you *provide good information quickly* when answering questions. If you've prepared a speech about your qualifications, you'll have much information to draw upon when answering questions. In addition, you can present yourself as being knowledgeable by doing the following.

Demonstrate knowledge of the employer. Nothing turns off employers more than an applicant who knows nothing about their companies; it suggests you really aren't interested. On the other hand, you can impress the employer by knowing the employer's product or service, history, and activities. You can readily get information about employers from the Internet and from libraries and placement centers. You can also call the employer's personnel director and request that the employer send you information and answer questions over the phone.

Demonstrate knowledge of business. Get in the habit of reading about the business world. Regularly read publications like *Business Week, The Wall Street Journal, Forbes,* or similar business or professional publications. When appropriate, integrate your knowledge into the interview.

Use the language of the profession. Whatever your profession, you should understand and use its language. Match your use of the language to that of the interviewer. If he or she uses a lot of professional language, you should also.

Try to *organize* your answers. You are perceived as being more competent when you're organized. When you have several points you want to make, say "First, I have . . . Second, I have . . ." When possible indicate the number of things you'll present: "I have two primary leadership strengths."

Finally, *respond* to questions asked. You demonstrate *interpersonal competence* by being responsive to the interviewer. Listen carefully, and provide the information requested. When you've provided an answer, you might occasionally ask, "Have I answered your question?" If you want to provide information not asked for, provide a transition to that information similar to, "Related to that question, I have considerable communication experience . . ."

Show That You Are Confident

Confidence means that you're self-assured; you know what you're doing. It's the opposite of being anxious and uncertain. You can do three things to increase your confidence.

Prepare. If you've prepared to present your qualifications, researched the employer, and developed a good general knowledge of business, you'll feel more confident in the interview.

Practice. You can practice two ways. First, participate in simulated interviews, and have a friend or family member act as the interviewer. You might videotape the interview and see how you can improve your presentation of answers. Second, interview with companies that are of secondary interest before you interview with companies of primary interest. This will allow you to "break the ice" in a relatively low-stress setting and help you build confidence.

Manage anxiety. Use the suggestions in chapter 15 for managing anxiety. In particular, take a deep breath and exhale slowly before going into the interview. Arrive early so that you have time to get settled and organized.

Be Enthusiastic

Enthusiasm conveys happiness or excitement about being in the interview. When you exhibit warmth and excitement, you're likely to generate similar feelings in the interviewer. You can do several things to exhibit enthusiasm.

Generate a positive attitude. You know what puts you in a positive frame of mind. It may be music, friends, food, or thoughts. Before you go to the interview, arrange to listen to that music, talk to your friends on a cell phone, eat your favorite breakfast, or focus on pleasant thoughts.

Be expressive. Enthusiastic people use lots of facial expression and gestures. When you practice your interview, practice being more expressive than you would be in the actual interview. Then you'll feel relatively comfortable being expressive during the interview.

Talk about subjects you feel positively about. When you talk about qualifications, include vivid stories that are fun and interesting. You're naturally enthusiastic when you enjoy what you talk about.

Emphasize Similarities

Like you, employers prefer to be with people they feel comfortable around, people who can "talk their talk" because they have similar attitudes, interests, and values. Interviewers will evaluate you more positively when you're similar to them than when you're different. Here are some things you can do to highlight similarities.

Before the interview, identify attitudes, interests, and values that you have in common with the employer. When given the opportunity, bring those similarities up during the interview. You can identify company culture, norms, and values from company literature or from interviews with employees. You can identify individual interests and values by networking to find people who know individuals who work for the employer.

We're not suggesting that you misrepresent your interests or values, but that you find genuine similarities and bring them up in interviews. If you find that your interests and values aren't the same as those in your target company, we suggest you find another company that has orientations similar to yours. You'll be happier working there.

A colleague of ours, Jim, is a good example of networking to identify similarities. He was ranked 7th in terms of qualifications to be a dean at a major university. However, he did his homework, presented himself well in interviews, and was offered the job.

At professional meetings and over the phone, Jim asked colleagues about the university and about potential interviewers. Jim identified issues and interests he shared with the university and with interviewers. When he interviewed, he emphasized how his university experience and expertise was a good match for the university.

In private conversations, Jim discussed common interests. He found that one interviewer liked running, so Jim, an avid runner, brought up his interest in running. Another interviewer was a Presbyterian, so Jim, also a Presbyterian, asked about local congregations. A third interviewer had children, so Jim brought up the issues about moving his children to the community.

During the interview, focus on common attitudes, interests, and values. This is a common way of building relationships in social settings. People typically find common interests to discuss. For example, people share attitudes about the weather: "It is so good to have some rain." They also sometimes share interest in sports: "I have really enjoyed the NCAA playoffs." Look for and discuss common interests.

As another example, the interviewer may mention he plays golf. If you don't play golf, you might indicate that your father plays golf and really enjoys it, mention that you intend to play in the future, and ask the interviewer the best way to get started.

Communicate in a manner similar to the interviewer. The interview is like a dance, with the interviewer taking the lead. Your interviewer will communicate nonverbally the preferred tone and style of the interview; adapt your behavior to the interviewer's behavior. If the interviewer prefers to use technical, professional language, use that kind of language. If the interviewer prefers to be casual and informal, relax and be casual. However, you should probably be a bit more formal than the interviewer. If the interviewer is formal and focuses on getting to the point, be formal and quickly make your point. However, you should also try to inject some friendliness and enthusiasm into the interview.

Dress for the company. Start with the norm of a conservative business suit and then adapt to the company culture. Every culture has its own expectations for dress. In large financial firms that deal with wealthy clients, employees are expected to have the "right" clothing, including style and brand name. In a very casual company, employees may never wear suits. If you're not sure, ask about

dress norms. When interviewers see you for the first time, your dress should suggest that you "belong" in the company.

Be Friendly

We find that in simulated employment interviews, students rarely smile. They miss an opportunity to build rapport and a positive relationship with the interviewer. This is unfortunate because interviewers rate friendly applicants more positively than neutral or unfriendly applicants. Therefore, even though you might be nervous, find a reason to smile and be friendly. Here are some ways to generate some smiles and a friendly attitude.

Express your happiness to meet the interviewer and participate in the interview. If you're genuinely interested in working for your target company, you should be excited to talk with the interviewer. Smile and tell the interviewer you're happy to meet a representative from the company and to participate in the interview.

Talk about subjects you enjoy. Plan to include enjoyable stories, anecdotes, or experiences in your answers. Talking about subjects you enjoy will make it easy for you to smile and be friendly.

Be helpful and genuinely interested in the interviewer. Interviewing is a difficult task. Some interviewers are novices and may be more nervous than you are. Others are worn from numerous interviews. Be helpful and cooperative during the interview. Offer information when the interviewer doesn't seem to know what to ask. If the interviewer is visiting your city, offer suggestions about places to visit and to eat. And finally, thank the interviewer.

SUMMARY

You'll use many of the communication strategies and skills taught in this text in your employment campaign. You analyze your audience (the employer), select appropriate communication channels, develop relationships, write, and speak. If you develop the skills taught throughout the book, you'll find it relatively easy to develop and implement them into your communication campaign.

APPENDIX A

Grammar

SENTENCE FRAGMENTS

A sentence fragment is an incomplete sentence. There are two ways to correct this problem.

Join the fragment to the sentence that immediately follows or precedes.

No: He is an understanding person. Like my father. [*Like my father* is a fragment.]
Yes: He is an understanding person like my father.

No: Because eating always puts me in a good mood. She suggested eating a bowl of mango ice cream. [*Because eating always puts me in a good mood* is a fragment.]
Yes: Because eating always puts me in a good mood, she suggested eating a bowl of mango ice cream.

Rewrite the sentence so that it expresses a complete thought.

No: Having jogged through the park during my lunch hour.
Yes: Having jogged through the park during my lunch hour, I missed my surprise birthday party.

RUN-ON SENTENCES AND COMMA SPLICES

A run-on sentence is two or more sentences joined without punctuation.

No: The staff marched in the Fourth of July parade the company president rode in the red convertible.

A comma splice is two or more sentences joined by a comma.

No: The staff marched in the Fourth of July parade, the company president rode in the red convertible.

There are three ways to correct these errors.

1. Insert a period to separate the two sentences.

   Yes: The staff marched in the Fourth of July parade. The company president rode in the red convertible.

2. Use a semi-colon to join two closely related sentences.

   Yes: The staff marched in the Fourth of July parade; the company president rode in the red convertible.

3. Use a conjunction to join the two sentences.

Yes: The staff marched in the Fourth of July parade, but the company president rode in the red convertible.

Yes: While the staff marched in the Fourth of July parade, the company president rode in the red convertible.

SUBJECT/VERB DISAGREEMENT

A subject/verb disagreement occurs when the verb does not agree in number (singular or plural) with the subject. Remember the rules of subject/verb agreement.

A singular subject takes a singular verb.

No: Everyone in the offices are going to "The Big Camp Out" this weekend. [*Everyone* is singular; *are* is plural.]
Yes: Everyone in the offices is going to "The Big Camp Out" this weekend.

A plural subject must have a plural verb.

No: The names for each position has been announced. [Don't be misled by the words between the subject and the verb, *for each position*. *Names* is plural and *has* is singular.]
Yes: The names for each position have been announced.
Yes: Nicholas and Kimberly are going to represent the company.

In "either/or" and "neither/nor" constructions, the verb should agree with the subject closer to it.

No: Either the secretary or the engineer are mistaken about when the report was completed.
Yes: Either the secretary or the engineer is mistaken about when the report was completed.
Yes: Either the secretary or the engineers are mistaken about when the report was completed.
Yes: Are either the secretaries or the engineer mistaken about when the report was completed?

UNCLEAR OR SHIFTING PRONOUN REFERENCE

A pronoun reference shift occurs when the writer uses pronouns inconsistently. There are two rules for correcting such shifts.

1. The pronoun should agree in number (either singular or plural) with the noun or pronoun to which it refers (the antecedent).

No: Each of them said they were going to spend the weekend fishing in the mountains. [*Each* is singular; *they* is plural.]
Yes: Each of them said he [if all men] was going to spend the weekend fishing in the mountains.

Yes: Each of them said she [if all women] was going to spend the weekend fishing in the mountains.
Yes: All of them said they were going to spend the weekend fishing in the mountains.

No: When you sign all three copies of the contract, please return it to my office.
Yes: When you sign all three copies of the contract, please return them to my office.

No: The group of students were dismayed at the low test scores.
Yes: The group of students was dismayed at the low test scores.

2.   Consistently use the same pronoun to agree with the noun to which it refers.

No: In completing these personnel forms, one should follow the directions carefully. Otherwise, you may have to wait an extra month for your paycheck.
Yes: In completing these forms, follow the directions carefully. [The subject you is implied.] Otherwise, you may have to wait an extra month for your paycheck.

FAULTY PARALLELISM

Faulty parallelism occurs when the writer uses different grammatical forms for ideas in a list or for two items connected by a conjunction.
Begin each item on the list using the same grammatical form.

No: All employees will receive lifetime memberships at Disco Dynasty, weekend passes to the movies, and spend $50.00 gift certificates at their favorite fast-food place.
Yes: All employees will receive lifetime memberships to Disco Dynasty, weekend passes to the movies, and $50.00 gift certificates for their favorite fast-food place.

No: A recent survey of employees indicates that they like working for Arc Electronics because it provides generous benefits, job security is offered, and professional growth. [None of the items in the list is in the same grammatical form.]
Yes: A recent survey of employees indicates that they like working for Arc Electronics because it provides generous benefits, offers job security, and encourages professional growth.

No: We have to decide between inputting the highly sensitive raw data ourselves or hire an outside firm to do it.
Yes: We have to decide between inputting the highly sensitive raw data ourselves or hiring an outside firm to do it.

DANGLING OR MISPLACED MODIFIERS

Dangling or misplaced modifiers are words that are separated from the idea they describe. There are two ways to correct dangling or misplaced modifiers.

1. Move the misplaced part of the sentence next to the word it modifies.

    No: She sold posture chairs to the secretaries with built-in padding. [In this sentence, the secretaries have built-in padding.]
    Yes: She sold posture chairs with built-in padding to the secretaries.

2. Rewrite the sentence to make the reference clear.

    No: Being lost and confused, the police officer helped the little boy. [Here, the police officer is lost and confused.]
    Yes: Because the boy was lost and confused, the police officer helped him find his way.

APPENDIX B

Punctuation

Correct punctuation can make your writing easier to read. Though some people suggest that the best rule for punctuation is "when in doubt, leave it out," the careful writer follows a wiser rule: "When in doubt, look it up." The following guidelines give you a brief and useful reference when you must look up a particular punctuation mark.

THE COMMA (,)

Use commas between items in a series.

Yes: He brought a calculator, a lap-top computer, and a cellular telephone to the office party.

While some grammarians and journalists say that the comma before the *and* is unnecessary, you should use a comma there to keep the items clearly separate and improve readability.

Use a comma after an introductory expression.
An introductory expression is a word, phrase, or clause that comes before the first subject of the sentence.

Yes: Moreover [a word], we feel confident that our staff meetings would not exceed one hour.
Yes: After discussing the problem with our manager [a phrase], we felt confident that our staff meetings would not exceed one hour.
Yes: After we discussed the problem with our manager [a clause], we felt confident that our staff meetings would not exceed one hour.

Use a comma before *and, but, for, nor, or, so,* and *yet,* when they connect two complete sentences.

No: Both sides found the negotiations difficult, but were able to compromise. [*Were able to compromise* is not a complete sentence.]
Yes: Both sides found the negotiations difficult but were able to compromise.
Yes: Both sides found the negotiations difficult, but they were able to compromise.

Place commas around expressions that interrupt the flow of the sentence.

Yes: Apparently, despite what we have heard, he is going to be promoted to supervisor.

Yes: We met on April 17, 2000, to discuss access rights to beaches. [The year is considered an interrupter and is set off by commas when it follows the month and day.]

Yes: Please send this to Jan Doty, Personnel Director, Humungous Oil, P.O. Box 751, Midway, ND 85731.

THE SEMICOLON (;)

Use the semicolon between two closely related complete sentences.

No: A woman swam across the Molokai Channel yesterday; there is life on Mars. [The ideas are not closely related.]

Yes: A woman swam across the Molokai Channel yesterday; she set a new record.

Use a semicolon with conjunctive adverbs such as *therefore* and *however* when used between two complete sentences.

No: The chair was too low for the workstation, therefore, she experienced lower back pain.

Yes: The chair was too low for the workstation; therefore, she experienced lower back pain.

SOME CONJUNCTIVE ADVERBS

also	moreover
consequently	next
finally	still
furthermore	then
however	therefore
meanwhile	thus

Yes: The river rose quickly as a result of flooding; consequently, hundreds of people were evacuated from their homes.

Use a semicolon with items in a series when the items have commas within them.

Yes: Attending the meeting were Gloria Cook, a member of the review board; Jonathan Chew, the Division Manager; and Lori Esteban, the employee representative.

THE COLON (:)

Use a colon after a complete statement to introduce a list, quotation, or title.

No: In the back of the van were: a dozen beach mats, two surfboards, and a cooler of passion-fruit juice. [*In the back of the van were* is not a complete sentence.]

Yes: In the back of the van were a dozen beach mats, two surfboards, and a cooler of passion-fruit juice.

Yes: The following items were in the back of the van: a dozen beach mats, two surfboards, and a cooler of passion-fruit juice.

No: Section 15 of Contract No. 12345, "Agreement for Professional Services," states: Confidentiality. All information given to the CONTRACTOR under this agreement shall be confidential and not made available to any person or organization by the CONTRACTOR without prior written approval of the COMPANY.
Yes: Section 15 of Contract No. 12345, "Agreement for Professional Services," states the following: All information given to the CONTRACTOR under this agreement shall be confidential and not made available to any person or organization by the CONTRACTOR without prior written approval of the COMPANY.

Use a colon after a heading.
To: James Smithson
Land and Natural Resources Department [*To* is the heading.]

THE PERIOD (.)

Place a period at the end of a sentence and after most abbreviations. Use only one period when an abbreviation comes at the end of the sentence.
Yes: Please tell Ms. Rodriguez that the consultants are from Island Construction, Inc.

THE APOSTROPHE (')

To show possession of a singular noun, use the apostrophe and s.
Yes: He appreciated the attorney's free advice.
Yes: The Governor encouraged the child's questions.

To show possession of a singular noun ending in s, add the apostrophe and s or only the apostrophe.
Yes: I gave **James's** (or **James'**) report to the committee.

To show possession of a plural noun ending in s, add only the apostrophe.
Yes: He appreciated the three attorneys' free advice.

For plural words not ending in s, use the apostrophe and s.
Yes: The Governor encouraged the children's questions.

To form plurals, use either the apostrophe and s or just s.
the 1900's or the 1900s
their BMW's or their BMWs
all B's or all Bs

When combining words, use an apostrophe where letters have been omitted.

are not = aren't	I would = I'd
cannot = can't	it is = it's
could have = could've	she will = she'll
have not = haven't	they have = they've
he is = he's	were not = weren't
I am = I'm	you are = you're

Avoid contractions in formal writing. In less formal writing, negative contractions such as *don't* and *isn't* are often used because the negative is much clearer to the reader.

THE QUOTATION MARK (" ")

Use quotation marks around a direct quotation, the title of a short work or report, and words used in a special sense, such as puns or slang.

Yes: "Tom," she said, "let's go body surfing at North Beach."
Yes: To understand the situation, read the Department of Health and Human Services' report, "The Changing Needs of the Nation's Aging Citizens."
Yes: The angry hospital cook did a "slow burn."

Periods and commas are always placed inside the quotation marks as in the preceding examples. Colons and semicolons are always placed outside the quotation marks.

Yes: The manager asked about "down time"; the supervisor told the manager more than she wanted to hear.

Question marks and exclamation points are placed inside the quotation marks when the quotation marks apply to the entire quotation.

Yes: The Marketing Manager asked, "What is truth?"

Question marks and exclamation points appear outside the final quotation marks when they apply to the entire sentence.

Yes: What is "truth"? [*Truth* is only part of the sentence; therefore, the question mark is placed after the quotation mark.]

THE PARENTHESES (( ))

Use parentheses to insert extra information that your reader might want to know.

Yes: He was a social services investigator for 30 years (1950–1980) and never missed a day of work.
Yes: Plea bargaining (see page 67) was developed to speed the judicial process.

No terminal punctuation or capitalization is needed for a complete sentence within parentheses.

Yes: You are a careful writer (we know this because you bought the book, and you are reading the preface).

THE DASH (—)

Use a dash to indicate an abrupt change of thought or to clarify what follows. In most writing (there are exceptions in journalistic writing), there are no spaces between the dash and the words which immediately precede and succeed it.

Yes: We hope he goes far—very far.
Yes: It isn't often—maybe twice a year—that I'm asked to speak before a large audience.

THE HYPHEN (-)

Use a hyphen to express the idea of a unit and to avoid ambiguity.

Yes: She took the Dallas–Fort Worth shuttle every morning, sipping her heavily sugared coffee on the flight. [Adverbs, like *heavily* in this sentence, are rarely followed by a hyphen.]
Yes: We are experiencing a small-shipment problem. [The *small-shipment* is a type of shipment problem.]
Yes: We are experiencing a small shipment problem. [The *shipment problem* is small.]

APPENDIX C

Mechanics

When do you capitalize *president*? Do you write out *21*? Are titles of reports underlined? Is it *commitment* or *committment*? The answers to these questions come under the general heading of mechanics—the "humbug" of writing. These guidelines will help you with common problems.

CAPITALIZATION

First Letter of a Sentence
Capitalize the first letter of a sentence.
All administrative assistants were asked to develop contingency plans.

First Letter of a Quoted Sentence
Capitalize the first letter of a quoted sentence unless the quotation blends into the rest of the sentence.

The President said, "This is an idea for tomorrow that we must start planning for today."

The Governor spoke of "an idea for tomorrow that we must start planning for today."

Proper Nouns
Capitalize proper (specific) nouns but not common (nonspecific) nouns.

PROPER NOUN	COMMON NOUN
God	a god
Business Studies Center	a study center
University of Nebraska	a state university
Department of Corrections	a state department
The State Capitol	a state building

Titles as Part of a Proper Name
Capitalize titles of persons when used as part of a proper name.

King George
Representative Ramirez
Captain Horner
Judge Ikeda

Titles of Public Officials

Capitalize titles of public officials when the titles are used alone to refer to the specific person.

> The President stopped at Andrews Air Force Base on his way to Brazil.
> We asked the Governor to speak at the awards banquet. He was among seven state governors who had been given special recognition this year.

Job Titles for High Rank

Job titles indicating high rank or distinction may be capitalized when they refer to a specific person.

> The Adjutant General was happy to hear that a judge, a state representative, the President of Browning Corp., and the Board Chairperson of Walston Company would also be serving on the board.

ABBREVIATIONS

Titles Before or After Names

Abbreviate titles immediately before or after proper names.

Lt. Gov. Samuelson	or	John Samuelson, **Jr.**
Dr. Louise Wilson	or	Louise Wilson, **M.D.**
Rep. Gayle Kennedy	or	Gayle Kennedy, **J.D.**
Mr. Mark Ward	or	Mark Ward, **Lt. Col.**

Names of Organizations, Programs, and Materials.

Abbreviate names of organizations, programs, and materials after they're first spelled out.

> Personnel officers from the Department of Human Services (**DHS**) and the Department of Personnel Services (**DPS**) met to discuss their administrative needs.

> The Board of Directors (**the Board)** met to discuss the effects on sales of the North American Free Trade Agreement (**NAFTA**) and the General Agreement on Tariffs and Trade (**GATT).**

NUMBERS

Less than 10

Spell out all numbers less than 10.

> Jack carried **two** trays of sushi to the manager's office.

Ten and Above

Use the numeral for numbers above nine.

> Suddenly, 75 excited school children descended on our office.

Beginning Sentences

Spell out all numbers that begin sentences.

Ninety-six of the employees wanted to enroll in the new pension plan.

If a large number such as 1,156 begins the sentence, rewrite the sentence so that the number is not the first word.

Two or More in a List

When two or more numbers are used together in a list and one of the numbers is above nine, use numerals for all the numbers.

The list included **5** from Maui, **6** from Kauai, and **21** from Oahu.

Dates, Addresses, Percentages, Fractions, Decimals, Statistics, Money, Time, and ID Numbers

Use numerals for dates, addresses, percentages, fractions, decimals, statistics, exact amounts of money, time, and identification numbers.

Date:	August 21, 1999
Address:	830 Locust Street
Percentage:	60 percent
Fraction:	1/2
Decimal:	.075
Statistic:	6 out of 100
Exact amount of money:	$275.22
Time:	5:00 P.M.
Identification number:	575–75–7575

ITALICS (OR UNDERLINING)

Titles

Italicize or underline the titles of books, plays, films, long poems, musical compositions, magazines, newspapers, pamphlets, and long reports.

To ensure that we accurately apply the restrictions, please read Sections 8 and 52 of *Internal Revenue Service: Taxing Your Almighty Dollar.*

Ships, Trains, Planes, and Spacecraft

Italicize or underline the names of ships, trains, planes, and spacecraft.

The student applied to NASA to ride *Adventurer III* to the moon.

Emphasis

Italics or underlining may be used to emphasize ideas.

It was not the third but the *fourth* time this week that he came in early to work.

SPELLING

Committment or Commitment?

Spelling errors reduce your credibility as a writer. Even if your computer has "spell-check," keep a dictionary handy, or find a coworker to proofread your writing. Whatever technique you choose, don't use the excuse, "Well, it looks okay—" Look it up!

APPENDIX D

Style

The following conventions are intended to help you determine what writing style to use according to your particular audience. Know these conventions so you can make more intelligent choices about reader expectations.

Tell the Reader What Can Be Done, Not What Cannot.
Your reader will appreciate your message when you focus on the positive.

> **No:** People who have not been employees for at least six months may not participate in the "Employee of the Year" program.
> **Yes:** Anyone who has been employed for at least six months is eligible for the "Employee of the Year" program.

> **No:** You are reminded that the law prohibits the construction of access roads without a permit granted by this department.
> **Yes:** To construct the access road, you will need a permit from this department.

Help Your Reader.
Show readers that you care by taking an extra step to help them.

> **No:** We are not responsible for mosquito eradication. We suggest you try the Department of Health to see if someone there will help you.
> **Yes:** I have contacted Bill Thompson at the Department of Health, Vector Control, who can help you. Please call him at 765–1234 to give him more specific information about the drainage in your area.

WRITE IN A NATURAL STYLE

Don't create a "paper monster" that makes you sound bureaucratic or legalistic. Make your writing readable by using a natural-sounding style.

Avoid pompous words and phrases (unless your reader expects them).

> **No:** Pursuant to the above referenced matter, a re-analysis of your expense report reflects a discrepancy in the manner in which it was computed.

We may think our letters sound more "businesslike" when we sprinkle them with inflated words and phrases as in the previous example. More often, these words and phrases do not make us look more important or "legal"; they only make us sound pompous.

> **Yes:** You are right. You did make only six trips out of town last month.

If you find a phrase leaps onto the paper too quickly, check to see if it is one of those pompous clichès that sometimes litter business writing. Then use a more natural-sounding phrase.

POMPOUS	NATURAL
Aforementioned	Previous
Ascertain	Determine
Assistance	Help
Attached herewith	Enclosed
Enclosed herewith	Enclosed
Facilitate	Help
Finalize	Complete; finish
Forthwith	At once
Hereafter; heretofore; hereby	(Eliminate)
Humbly request	Ask
I am cognizant of	I know

JARGON

When writing to people outside your area of expertise, don't use jargon or occupational "lingo."

> **No:** Our department's multidimensional, multiethnic, and multifaceted program is designed to facilitate the individual's performance capability in interfacing with the community-at-large.
>
> **Yes:** Our department's new training program will make it easier for you to work with our clients.

JARGON	NATURAL
I am in receipt of	I have
Kindly advise	Let us know
Optimal	Best
Pending your reply	Until I hear from you
Per our conversation	When we spoke
Please be advised	(Eliminate)
Pursuant to	Concerning
Take under advisement	Consider
The undersigned/the writer	I
Utilize; usage	Use
With reference to	Regarding; about
Your communication	Your call, your letter

Use the Active Voice.

Conversational writing is usually "active" writing. Being "active" means that there is a "doer" who "does" something. The pattern for active sentences is the subject plus an action verb.

> **Active:** The consultant said we should install more accurate time clocks in our factories.

Passive sentences are usually longer than active sentences, adding words that do not contribute meaning. The pattern for passive sentences is the subject, plus a "be" verb, plus the past participle of an action verb. In passive sentences, the subject is not "doing" the verb; rather, it is being "done to." Use passive voice when the doer of the sentence is either unknown or unimportant.

> **Passive:** It is felt that more accurate employee time clocks are needed in the factory environment.

> **Active:** Please call Sherrie Singleton to let her know that you have received this letter. [The "doer" here is the understood "you."]
> **Passive:** Your acknowledgment of this letter by phone to Sherrie Singleton is required.

REDUCE WORDINESS

Make reading easy for the reader: use few words. A good guideline to remember is an average sentence length of 17 to 22 words, or two typed lines. If most of your sentences are exceeding the 22-word limit, you are probably being wordy. Break up your longer sentences or cut unnecessary words.

Remember, however, that good writing uses sentences of varying length.

Eliminate Unnecessary Words from Each Sentence.

Take time after you write the first draft to get rid of empty words and phrases.

> **Wordy:** As you know, we all have the problem of not having enough funds to do all of the things that we want to do or need to be done and must allot the limited funds to areas that we feel will bring the best results. (45 words)

> **Concise:** We must work together to spend our limited funds wisely. (10 words)

Cut Clichés and Empty Phrases.

Many of the wordy and empty phrases that clutter your messages are holdovers from outdated writing. These clichés are passed from generation to generation, resulting in "gobbledygook." Because these phrases cloud your message, ruthlessly cut them from your writing.

AVOID THIS	**USE THIS**
arrived at the conclusion	concluded
at this point in time	now
because of the fact that	because
come to terms with	agree; accept
connect together	connect
during the month of May	during May
during the same time that	while
eight in number	eight
for the purpose of providing	to provide
has the capability of working	works
held a meeting	met
important essentials	essentials
in a great many instances	often
in an effort to	to
in order to	to
in the development of	in developing
in the event that	if
involving a great deal of expense	costly; expensive
long period of time	long time
make an investigation	investigate
on account of the fact that	because
prior to that time	before
put in an appearance	came
remember the fact that	remember
return back	return
shows a tendency to	tends
similar in character to	similar to; like
situated in the vicinity of	near
until such time as you can	until you can
was of the opinion that	believed

APPENDIX E

APA Documentation

Conscientious business writers take care to give credit to their outside sources when writing any kind of report. Business journals apply documentation guidelines set forth by the American Psychological Association (APA). As shown in this chapter, APA has extensive rules for documenting within the text and in the reference list.

Why is giving credit to your sources so important? The most obvious reason, of course, is to avoid plagiarism. By giving credit to sources, writers can avoid serious legal and ethical complications that could arise. Also, giving credit to outside sources can lend credibility to an author's opinion. Providing experts' opinions that coincide with yours is a powerful tool in helping to convince the reader.

IN-TEXT DOCUMENTATION GUIDELINES

By briefly citing the author and date of publication within the text, you enable the reader to find complete background information about that source on your Reference List. The following guidelines apply for in-text citations in the APA style and are based on the *Publication Manual for the American Psychological Association* (4th edition). Generally, include author and the year of publication; page numbers are included for direct quotations as shown.

1. A work with one or two authors, and with the author(s) not mentioned outside of the parentheses: list name(s) of author(s) and the year of publication within parentheses.

   - A recent article (Jones & Ruiz, 1994) gives support for tax increases.

   - An article in *Time* (Munroe, 1993, p. 7) notes "similar trends occurred in the Stock Market."

2. A work with author(s) mentioned outside of the parentheses: put only the year of the publication inside the parentheses.

   - Warren (1995) indicates that authorities were not convinced.

3. A work with three to five authors: mention all authors' names the first time you cite the source. Subsequently, mention only the first author followed by *et al.* and the year of publication.

   - Henderson, Quintero, Watson, Todd, and Kimond (1996) found support for the Harvard study. *First citation.*

   - Henderson et al. (1996) theorized that the findings were based on the most up-to-date data available. *Subsequent citation; if you mention the same source again in a paragraph in which this source is already cited, omit the date after the first citation in that paragraph.*

4. Sources that have authors with the same surname: include the authors' initials in the text citations. Follow with the year of publication.

   - T. L. Granger (1974) and Q. O. Granger (1978) demonstrated similar findings in their studies.

5. A work that has a corporate author: put the corporate author's name where the author's name would normally go. You may put the name inside or outside of the parentheses. Follow with the year of publication. Corporate authors can include associations, businesses, and government agencies.

   - Deadlines for filing a claim are May 1 and November 1 (Prudential, 1995).

   - Frito-Lay (1996, p. 56) asserts that "good salespeople display enthusiasm."

   If a corporate author's name is long or unfamiliar to the reader, the first time that you cite the source follow the full name with the abbreviation in brackets. Thereafter, simply use the abbreviation.

   - Caution is advised to Type A personalities (The American Heart Association [AHA], 1995). *First citation.*

   - Corporate climbers tend to have Type A personalities (AHA, 1995). *Subsequent citation.*

6. Same specific information that has come from several different sources: list all sources alphabetically and the years of publication. Separate entries with semicolons, and put everything in a single set of parentheses.

   - Several authorities have concluded that . . .(Andrews, 1993; Finnegan & Barr, 1987; Wong, 1995).

7. Reference within a source: list the person who is mentioned in the work outside of the parentheses; include the author's name and date of publication inside the parentheses. Or, list both names outside of the parentheses, making sure your wording is easy to understand.

   - According to Lee Iaccoca, "real leaders don't whine" (Spann, 1996, p. 821).

   - Spann (1996, p. 821) quotes Lee Iaccoca as saying, "real leaders don't whine."

8. Tagging: within a paraphrased paragraph, clearly refer back to the previously mentioned source. Include parenthetical information only the first time within that paragraph.

   - Ellis (1992) indicates that . . . She adds that . . .

REFERENCE LIST GUIDELINES

The specific information required in the reference list helps the reader retrieve each source if desired. Only articles that are actually used as sources in the text should be listed here. Generally, information that is found in the reference list includes the author, date of publication, title, and some background about the publisher. The rules that follow show exactly what information is required for different circumstances; these rules are also based on the *Publication Manual of the American Psychological Association* (4th edition).

1. List as references only the sources you cite within the text.
2. Indent the first line of each entry five spaces. The reference list should be double spaced. Or if you prefer, do not indent the first line of an entry, but indent subsequent lines.
3. List entries alphabetically.
   - Alphabetize by the last name of the first author or by the first significant word in the name of a corporate author. Ex.: The Crump Corporation.
   - If a work has no author given, alphabetize by the first significant word in the title of the book or article.
   - If there are several works by the same author, do the following: one-author entries by the same author should be ordered chronologically; references with the same first author and different second authors should be alphabetized according to the second author's surname.
4. Use first and middle initials of the given names of the author(s): Collingsworth, E. O.
5. Include the date of publication after the author's name or, if no author is given, after the article title.
   - monthly periodical: 1995, April
   - weekly and daily periodicals: 1996, March 11
   - books—use copyright date
   - republished works: 1941/1958
6. Capitalize the first word of the title and subtitle of articles and books: *Advanced marketing: An expert's guide.*
7. Capitalize all primary words of the name of a periodical: *The Journal of Accountancy.*
8. Underline or italicize titles of books and periodicals.
9. Omit quotation marks around the titles of articles in the reference list.
10. Underline or italicize the volume number if there is one. If there is also an issue number, put it in parentheses after the volume number: *10* (5).
11. Use inclusive page numbers for articles.
    - For periodicals whose pages are numbered consecutively over a year's time, do not include the abbreviation "pp."
    - For periodicals whose pages are numbered by issue, include the abbreviation "pp."
12. For books, put the place of publication and then the name of the publisher. Include the state as well as the city for places that might be unfamiliar to the reader.

13. On-line sources: the rules for referencing this material are still being established. However, the following guidelines apply.

- If print material of the same source is available, follow the rules for that particular type of print material.

- If print material of the same source is not available, list the author, date, and title, as well as an availability statement; omit mention of the name and location of the publisher. The availability statement indicates how you found the material and should include the protocol (Internet, Telnet, etc.), the directory, and the file name.

The Sample Reference list that follows shows accepted ways of listing on-line material within the reference list.

SAMPLE REFERENCE LIST

Note: the parenthetical information, which follows and explains each entry, should NOT be included as part of an actual reference list.

Ankara, B. V. (1994). Sources of secondary data. *Journal of Current Business, 11,* 321–243. (Journal article, one author.)

Baines, R. L., Letner, R.M., and Grouse, H. I. (1987). Internal records. *Monthly Business Review,* 15, 39–53. (Journal article, three to five authors.)

Breckler, S. J., and Pratkanis, A. R. (1985). Experiment Command Interpreter for the IBM personal computer [Computer programming language]. Baltimore: Authors. (Computer programming language. Instead of listing the authors' names again, indicate with the word "Authors" that the publisher is the authors.)

Clarke-American, Inc. (1990). *How to Order the Right Type of Banking Forms (2nd ed.)* [Brochure]. (Brochure with a corporate author. Brochures are formatted in the same way as books, but also indicate within brackets that this source is a brochure.)

Desired new product diffusion. (1996, January 28). *The New York Times*, p. B12. (Daily newspaper article, no author given; precede page numbers of newspapers with "p." or "pp.")

Foster, J. (1994, May 5). Innovation, diffusion, and the adoption process. *The Times Picayune*, pp. C3, C5. (Daily newspaper on discontinuous pages.)

Gallegos, D. G. (1993). Family buying behavior. *Annual Review of Sales*, 30, 93–112. (Periodical published annually; volume number but no issue number given.)

Jenkins, I. O., and Keene, C. (Eds.). (1995). *Overt purchasing patterns: Marketing significance.* New York: Holt Rinehart Winston. (Edited book.)

Little, M. V. (Ed.). (1984). *Business dictionary of consumer behavior* (3rd ed., Vols. 1–6). Austin, TX: Rand McNally & Company. (Encyclopedia or dictionary with author or editor given.)

Mead Data. (1995, July 19). Business law and statutes. [543 paragraphs]. *Internet* [on-line serial]. Available: Doc.; No. 89. on-line. (Journal article, subscriber based; indicate length of article and document number for retrieval.)

Merriam-Webster's collegiate dictionary (10th ed.). (1993). Springfield, MA: Merriam-Webster. (Book, no author or editor given.)

New marketing principles. (1993, May). *Business Digest,* 7, pp. 35–56. (Monthly periodical, no author given for the article.)

Namkin, J. (1990). *Fabricating material and parts.* (Report No. NCRMM-SV-90–5). Center for International Marketing. (ERIC Document Reproduction Service No. ED 123 340). (Report from the Educational Resources Information Center, or ERIC; provide the ERIC number at the end within parentheses.)

National Committee for Marketing and Management—Management of Sales Activities: 1990— Studies of Promotions (Version 2) [Electronic data tape]. (1991). El Paso, TX: National Center for Business Statistics [Producer and Distributor]. (Electronic data file or database. List as authors the primary contributors; give the date of publication or the year copies were made generally available; provide the title, then the type of source [data file or database] in brackets. Finally, give the locations and names for the producer [the person or group that encoded the data] and the distributor [from whom copies can be obtained].)

Promotions report (Version 3.0) [Computer software]. (1995). Cheyenne, WY: Advertising Management Software. (Computer software. Inside brackets, identify this source as software.)

APPENDIX F

Critiquing Presentations

One of the most successful ways of improving presentations is to observe yourself on videotape. Many students make marked progress in their delivery after seeing themselves as others see them. They also evaluate and revise the content of the presentation to more effectively get their message across on the next occasion. Here, we provide guidelines for analyzing presentations on content and delivery. These guidelines also provide a summary of advice about preparing and delivering presentations.

Some speakers are overwhelmed the first time they see themselves on videotape. At first, they are overly critical. *Do I really sound like that? I look overweight. I didn't know I paced that much. I wasn't aware I looked at the screen instead of the audience.* Others see only those parts they performed well. *Gosh, I really nailed the audience with my opener.* Effective evaluation requires becoming a more objective observer.

Begin self-analysis by looking at the tape once, for the **initial impact.** Then review it again using evaluation forms, and attempt to be more objective. Discussing the taped presentation with a friend might help.

As you view the tape, look for **strengths** and ways to **improve.** Check for both **content** and **delivery.** You may have had interesting content but did not deliver it with impact. If so, think of how you might become more dynamic by increasing volume, movement, gestures, eye contact, or vocal variety. On the other hand, your delivery may have been dynamic, but you had poor content. If so, think about gathering more information, using a greater variety of support material, or adding real or hypothetical examples in place of abstract statements. Here are some things to think about during your analysis.

Introduction
The introduction is vital to the speech's success. You should gain the audience's attention, indicate your purpose, establish your credibility, preview the speech, and create the desired relationship with your audience.

Did the Opening Gain Attention?
As you watch the tape, ask yourself if your opening statement gained the audience's interest. If not, there are two potential causes. The first is that the statement itself was not interesting. You need a good quote, question, story, or humorous statement. The second problem is delivery. Even the best introduction can flop when poorly delivered. Were you emphatic? If you asked a rhetorical question, did you pause to allow the audience to think about the question? Did you speak loudly and look directly at the audience? Did you include movement, visuals, or gestures that would attract attention?

Was the Purpose Statement Effective?

Did your purpose statement indicate what the audience would gain from the presentation? The audience members wonder, *What's in it for me?* Did you tell them what they will know or could do after listening to you? If you expect them to do something like sign a contract or vote for a proposal, did you clarify your expectations?

Did You Establish Your Credibility?

The audience is wondering, *Why should I listen to you?* If you cited textbooks or articles, did you explain why the authors were credible sources? For example, did you explain that they were professors or experts? If you cited your own experience, did you tell what kind of experience you have had? If you referred to your own research, did you indicate the extent of your research? If you were representing a company, did you say why the company was reputable?

Did You Preview Your Speech?

The audience is curious about what you are going to discuss. Did you use vocal emphasis and pauses, numbers and labels, or visuals to make the main points obvious?

What Kind of Relationship Did You Establish?

What kind of relationship did you desire with the audience? Did you communicate in such a way as to achieve that relationship? Did you suggest you were intimidated or unprepared by staring at your notes and speaking quietly? Or did you convey confidence and warmth by smiling, maintaining eye contact, and moving toward your audience? Did you convey a formal relationship by standing stiffly behind the lectern, or did you suggest an informal relationship by cordially greeting the audience and moving out from behind the lectern?

How Did You Organize Your Speech?

The organization keeps the audience members on track. To help them follow you, did you use effective transitions? When you came to each point, did you announce the number and label, or use a visual to clearly indicate the transition? Were transitions well-worded? Did you avoid repetitively using transitions such as *and, next,* or *also*? Could a member of the audience easily follow your presentation?

Was the Pattern Appropriate?

Was the structure of your presentation appropriate for your topic? Did you make the mistake of combining different organizational patterns? Did you choose an organizational pattern inappropriate for your audience? What points did you emphasize? Were they the ones most important for your purpose?

How Many Points Were Discussed?

Many speakers attempt to cover too many points in the time allotted. The result is that the speaker ends up simply listing the main points without support material. Count the number of main points and subpoints you presented. You may have attempted to discuss too much. The only remedy is to cut the number of points.

Support Material

Your speech should have sufficient support so the audience can visualize and define each point. At minimum, for each point, you should (1) state the point, (2) explain the point, and (3) provide additional support for the point in the form of an example, statistics, testimony, and so on. In a persuasive speech, support material is crucial for establishing both the need and proposal steps. Was your support material clear and vivid? Did it relate directly to your subject? Ask a friend to view the video and tell you if you provided enough support to clarify each point. If you stated the point and added only a sentence of explanation, you probably did not provide enough support.

Examine Your Speech Critically

If you made a claim, did you provide enough support and logic to substantiate it? For example, if you claimed that your organization has 10 percent turnover, did you support your claim with reputable studies and realistic figures? Or could the information be interpreted as hearsay? Much of your credibility comes from the way you support your main points.

Check for Variety of Support Material

Too many speakers bore audiences by relying only on explanations. Stories, examples, and illustrations add variety and keep the audience interested. If you are too abstract, try substituting more concrete support. For example, instead of simply describing the guidelines for conducting meetings, tell about a specific meeting which was conducted effectively or poorly. Use descriptions of real people and their actions. This helps you to be more animated and the audience to visualize your points.

You may also see that although you have vivid support material, it is without effect because the audience doesn't understand that it comes from a credible source. If you provided quotes, figures, studies, or guidelines, did you cite the source of these materials? Remember to provide enough background about your sources to establish their credentials.

Conclusion

The last thing you say to an audience often sticks. A conclusion should reinforce your message, focus on the main purpose, and be interesting. If your presentation was persuasive, it should also have requested some form of action from your audience. The summary should not restate only the main points but also the vital information within those points. For example, suppose you had cited a death toll statistic about industry-caused cancer central to your speech; you should refer to it in your summary. Did you restate the purpose for your speech? Did you provide a complete summary of the most important information?

Audience members wonder what they can do with their new knowledge. Did you answer the question and provide direction? If your speech was persuasive, did you appeal for an action, a vote, or commitment?

The last statement should indicate that the speech has ended, recall the purpose in a meaningful way, and be dramatic enough to be memorable. Was it interesting? Did it focus on the purpose? Did you hurry through the last statement or deliver it meaningfully?

Delivery

As we have noted, the way you present yourself is as important as what you say. As you observe your video, think of ways you can improve your presentation to more effectively project a dynamic and professional image. Listen to your voice. Could the audience hear you? Would more volume give your message more impact? If more volume is needed, practice much louder than you ever would actually speak in public. Do you need more vocal variety? If so, practice with extreme vocal variety. Do you have too many pauses, *uhms,* or *you knows?* These are best reduced by thorough preparation and by eliminating them in everyday speech. Were you too fast or too slow? Practice at the rate you plan to speak. Were you conversational? If not, avoid memorizing or reading the speech, and add more examples or stories that you feel confident presenting in your own words. When you attempted to persuade, did you speak with conviction? If not, practice with greater volume and more energy. If your voice broke or quivered, bring a glass of water with you. Sipping it will slow you down and help you avoid a dry mouth.

Consider Eye Contact

Were your eyes glued to your notes? You can cut down dependence on your notes by practicing the speech and reducing notes to brief phrases. Did you focus on only one part of the audience? If so, address each part of the room as you practice. Be sure to sustain eye contact with each section of the room for at least three to five seconds.

Observe Your Movement

If you constantly paced, practice standing still. When you move, move with a purpose. If you didn't move at all, give yourself a reason to move, such as walking toward the audience to ask a question or moving to a visual. Did you sway side to side or rock on your heels? Purposeful movements can eliminate nervous habits.

Note Your Gestures

Were your hands glued to the lectern? Solve this problem by taking one step back and holding your hands above your waist. If you had small gestures, practice with expansive ones. Also, you might add support material which lends itself to gestures. Often people gesture naturally when they tell a story, demonstrate a process, or illustrate an idea.

Observe Your Posture

Did you convey a professional image by standing on both feet, buttoning your coat, keeping your hand out of your pocket, and maintaining erect posture?

Visual Aids

Visuals are a very important way to reinforce or illustrate your points. They should be prepared with care to get the message across and convey a professional image. Did you use enough visuals? Ask yourself what you want the audience to remember most and what would be the best way to present material. Visuals gain attention and increase retention.

Were the Visuals Easy to See?

Did you use large print for overheads and charts? Did you hold objects where every-one could see? Could you have enlarged a visual or held it closer for more impact?

Did You Explain the Visual?

Speakers often forget that the audience has not seen a visual before and needs time to understand it. If you presented a chart, did you describe its layout and read through the important figures with the audience? Did the audience absorb the information? Did you refer to the visual as you used it?

How Well Did You Present the Visual?

Did you face the audience as you discussed it? Referring to a hard copy of an overhead transparency will help you avoid looking at the screen. Did you show the aid only when it was relevant to keep it from diverting attention? Did you use progressive revelation?

INDEX

A

abbreviations, using, 273
abstract of proposal, 162
acceptance letter, 202, 207, 208
actions that gain attention, 214
action verbs, 59, 178, 183
active voice, 45–47, 278
activities section of résumé, 179–180
adapting to audience, 60–61, 210–211
"add-on" aid, 69
analogy, using, 37, 52
analytical report, 147, 163–164, 172
analyzing target audience
overview of, 16–21
for presentation, 210–211, 234
for written communication, 72
anecdotal evidence, using, 52, 57
annual report, 163
answering questions, 230–231, 248
anxiety when speaking, 223–225
apostrophe, using, 269–270
appeal
to emotion, 55–56, 148
to logic, 56–59, 172
ASCII format, 196
attachment to e-mail, 196
attention
diverting, 59
gaining, 51–53, 213–216, 234–235, 285
attention line, 81, 82
attitude of audience
adapting message to, 60–61
toward speaker, 17–18
toward topic, 19
audience. *See also* attitude of
audience; target audience
adapting message to, 60–61, 210–211
attention, gaining, 51–53, 213–216, 234–235, 285
defining, 242
developing relationship with, 18–19
expectations of, 20–21
initial vs. ultimate, 16
maintaining control of, 230
rapport, building with, 53–54, 213, 214, 220, 261

report type and, 160
written communication and, 72
authority, communicating, 7

B

bad news letter
negative adjustment, 105, 107
overview of, 102
refusal-to-inquiry, 102, 105, 106
bad news memo, 131, 132
bandwagon, 59
"be" sentence, 45–47
big point first organization, 50
brainstorming, 73–74
breathing during speech, 224
buffer, 102, 105, 131
building rapport, 53–54, 213, 214, 220, 261
bullets, résumé and, 183, 185
business letter. *See* letter

C

capitalization, 272–273
cartoons, using, 214
categorical organization, 50–51
causal reasoning, 57
cause-effect organization, 51
channels of communication
characteristics of, 22
general objectives and, 23–24
specific objectives and, 24–26
types of, 21–23
chronological organization, 50
chronological résumé, 174–181, 187–188
clarity of message, 38–40
closing of message
action-oriented, 134
complimentary, 81–82, 85, 91
e-mail, 135
collecting data for report, 163–164
colon, using, 268–269
color, adding to visual aids, 64–65
column format of résumé, 182, 185
combined résumé, 184, 189–190
comma, using, 267–268
comma splice, 263–264
commitment, securing, 238
communication campaign, 15–16
communication process

establishing relationship, 6–10
overview of, 2
receiving message, 4–6
sending message, 2–4
comparison/contrast organization, 51
competence, demonstrating, 258–259
complimentary close to letter, 81–82, 85, 91
computer formats, 196
conclusion
to presentation, 216–217, 287
to proposal, 150, 156
concreteness, 38–39, 59
concrete symbol, 4
conference, electronic, strengths of, 23
confidence, increasing, 259
congratulations, letter of, 108, 111
conjunctive adverbs, 268
consistency in team presentation, 246–247
contact credibility, 252–253
content of written communication
job application letter, 199–201
report, 160
revision and, 75
contrasting images, 237
control, maintaining with audience, 230
controlling
information flow, 7
as management function, 24
conventions
for presentation, 20–21
for written communication, 20
conversational language, 42, 76, 218–219, 227–228
coordinating, communication channels for, 24–25
copy acknowledgment, 83
cover letter for résumé, 198–199
credibility
contact type, 252–253
establishing, 18, 54–55, 148, 215, 235
critiquing presentation, 285–289
culture of organization, 15, 18, 254, 260–261